William James Tilley

**Masters of the Situation**

Some Secrets of Success and Power

William James Tilley

**Masters of the Situation**
*Some Secrets of Success and Power*

ISBN/EAN: 9783337025083

Printed in Europe, USA, Canada, Australia, Japan

Cover: Foto ©Lupo / pixelio.de

More available books at **www.hansebooks.com**

# MASTERS
# OF THE SITUATION

OR,

*Some Secrets of Success and Power.*

BY

## William James Tilley, B.D.

---

"*NOTHING SUCCEEDS LIKE SUCCESS.*"

"When I asked an iron-master," says Emerson, "concerning the slag and cinder in railroad iron, his answer was : 'There is always good iron to be had. If there was cinder in the iron, it was because there was cinder in the pay.'"

"A little of *the inevitable* is worth more than much power merely to push and pull."

---

London:

T. NELSON AND SONS, PATERNOSTER ROW.
EDINBURGH; AND NEW YORK.

1888.

# Preface.

———•◦•———

TRUTH is as old as the world. As no two, however, see
exactly the same rainbow, so no truth presents itself to all
alike. So much has been written, we are told, that it is no
longer possible even to appear original. Yet all will agree
that the manner of presenting old truths is of the first importance. "The difference in men consists not so much in
mere knowledge, after all, as in the ability to reproduce
knowledge—that power of the mind which assimilates, tests,
and pronounces its own verdict on all the waifs of idea which
are borne to it from the minds of others."

Many of us can understand the feeling which prompted
him who, failing to find in his library the book he wanted,
went to work and *made* one. On the other hand, at rare
intervals we have *found* the book we wanted as well, only to
rise from its perusal with a keener appetite for others like
it. One can hardly read certain books without instinctively
wishing for more like them. Such books are "never crowded,
and never crowd." Of such there cannot be too many. Men
love Raphael none the less because they admire Correggio.

No one can contemplate youth, with its beauty and power,
its infinite hope and aspiration, without being touched to the
heart. While from one standpoint life seems "a joy for
ever," from another it impresses one as inexpressibly sad and
full of pathos. As one gets on in life, and realizes more and

more fully the lost opportunities of the irreparable past, and
scans the horizon, limited and narrowing at best, between
youth and old age, he longs to reach out a hand, to send out
a voice that perchance may be heard.

With all its buoyancy and hope and seeming assurance,
youth has its hours of discouragement and despondency, and
young men are often faint-hearted. They believe in all things
else save in themselves. Too often they lack the courage
to go out in pursuit of life's prizes and rewards. For such
this volume has been written. At the same time, it is
hoped it may not be found wholly wanting in hints and incentives of value to those farther on.

"My son," remarked the good old Quaker, "thee thinks
thee has a call to preach. Has thee also considered well
whether the people have *a call to hear thee ?*"

If those for whom this book has been written shall be
found to have "a call to hear," I shall not have laboured
in vain.

WILLIAM JAMES TILLEY.

St. Thomas's Rectory.
*December 1886.*

# Contents.

# MASTERS OF THE SITUATION.

## I.

## Promptness.

It is no use running; to set out betimes is the main point.—LA FONTAINE.

Never forget that others will depend upon you, and that you cannot depend upon them.—DUMAS, *Fils*.

Whilst we are considering when we are to begin, it is often too late to act.—QUINTILIAN.

Delays have dangerous ends.—SHAKESPEARE.

WE are all familiar with the trite old aphorism, "Procrastination is the thief of time;" but there is in it, doubtless, a far deeper significance than some of us realize. Not alone of time does it rob us; it filches away our possibilities even. Human life is like a kaleidoscope,—its scenes for ever shifting, and never twice the same. We imagine we can do, or leave undone—can seize to-day, or postpone till to-morrow, the circumstance which invites and is full of promise. The morrow comes, but not the same. The variation is slight, but permanent,—like the bauble which we have tossed upon the receding tide, thinking we can recover it at will: we can almost reach it; the next surge surely will bring it in. Vain delusion! We do not take into account the fact that, obedient to an occult, mysterious law, that which we would regain is already within the resistless grasp of an alien power, and momently receding, drawn farther and farther from us into the insatiate maw of the all-devouring sea.

So with our projects in life. We hesitate to-day. All is not just as we would have it. To-morrow will surely bring our object nearer. But to-morrow it is farther away than ever. Yesterday it was easily within our grasp. Now it is virtually within the realm of the impossible.

It seems almost incredible that so many should allow themselves to be cajoled and deceived by that phantom, that will-o'-the-wisp, *to-morrow.* How true to life is that picture, in Mr. Charles Reade's story, of Noah Skinner, the fraudulent banker's clerk! "A sleepy languor now came over him;...... but his resolution remained unshaken; by-and-by, waking up from a sort of heavy doze, he took, as it were, a last look at the receipts, and murmured, 'My head, how heavy it feels!' But presently he roused himself, full of his penitent resolution, and murmured again, brokenly, 'I'll—take it to—Pembroke —Street to—morrow; to—mor—row.' The to-morrow found him, and so did the detectives, dead." " I have spent all my life in pursuit of it," declares one of Hawthorne's venerable characters, "being assured that to-morrow has some vast benefit or other in store for me. But I am now getting a little in years, and must make haste; for unless I overtake to-morrow soon, I begin to be afraid it will finally escape me."

Doubtless one cause of the inertia so prevalent among young men, this lack of promptness, is the undefined feeling that one has infinite possessions in that commodity which men call time. To youth the vista is boundless, the horizon infinite. The thought, even if it find not expression in so many words, seems to be like this: "Soul, thou hast much goods laid up for many years." What need of haste? It will be time enough to grapple with life's problems by-and-by. The days glide noiselessly and imperceptibly on. Happy in an undefined hope, the present engrosses all the thought. The hands are empty, but the stream still hurries on. "We may be shipwrecked, but we cannot be delayed." And thus it happens that one is often well advanced upon the journey before he awakes to the consciousness that the horizon is narrowing, and that if he is to do anything in this world worth doing before he leaves it, it must be promptly done. He must bestir himself, and at once. Some fine morning he awakes to this fact. It occurs to him how short the distance is between him and "the night that cometh." How fast the days and months have been speeding on !

> " Remorseless Time !
> Fierce spirit of the glass and scythe !—what power
> Can stay him in his silent course, or melt
> His iron heart to pity ? "

Now it is doubtful if a young man does anything really worthy of himself before he has had impressed upon him an adequate conviction of this value of time, and hence of promptness in meeting each duty as it comes. In those famous " Rules " of Copperfield, where Dickens takes us so charmingly into his confidence, he makes this confession : " I have been very fortunate in worldly matters,—many men have worked much harder and not succeeded half so well,—but I never could have done what I have done without the habits of punctuality, order, and diligence, without the determination to concentrate myself on one object at a time, no matter how quickly its successor should come upon its heels, which I then formed. Heaven knows," he continues, " I write this in no spirit of self-laudation." Manhood is disgraced, says Blair, by the consequences of neglected youth. "Old age, oppressed by cares that belonged to a former period, labours under a burden not his own." One thing at least is certain, and that is, that nowhere is neglect or delay more annoying than in its influence upon a man's daily tasks. The manner

in which these crowd and jostle each other, if allowed the
advantage, is only too well known to us all.   On the other
hand, what so refreshing as the prompt and ready despatch
of a duty before another comes?   It is said that in his later
years, Mr. Drew, "Uncle Dan'l," as he was familiarly known
in Wall Street, used to delight in nothing more than to visit
the office of James Fisk, junior, and would sit by the hour,
watching with eager interest the promptness and despatch
with which that indomitable and in many ways remarkable
man disposed of the business which accumulated on his desk
from day to day.   Webster when at Marshfield, during the
intervals of the congressional sessions, was accustomed to rise
at daybreak, and before the family assembled at the breakfast-
table, had usually written twenty or thirty letters, and would
come in saying, "Well, my day's work is done.   Now I am
ready for fishing, hunting, or anything that may come to
hand."   The same habit of "breaking the neck of the day"
by taking Time "by the forelock" was true of Scott.

How striking the contrast between men of this stamp and
those who are for ever behindhand with their work ; who
allow one thing after another to accumulate on their hands
until a perfect chaos is the result !   Gibbon, we are told, was
in his study every morning, summer and winter, at six o'clock.
"Before nine o'clock in the morning," says Bowditch, "I
learned all my mathematics."   Bishops Burnet and Jewell
commenced their studies every morning at four o'clock.
"Whatever I have accomplished in the way of Commentary
on the Scriptures," says Doddridge, "is to be traced to the
fact of rising at four in the morning."   Hamilton has hit off
certain delinquents in a decidedly happy vein.   "A singular
mischance has occurred to some of our friends," he says.
"At the instant when he ushered them into existence, God
gave them a work to do, and he also gave them a competency
of time ; so much time that, if they began at the right moment
and wrought with sufficient vigour, their time and their work

would end together. But a good many years ago a strange misfortune befell them. A fragment of their allotted time was lost. They cannot tell what became of it, but sure enough it has dropped out of existence; for just like two measuring lines laid alongside, the one an inch shorter than the other, their work and their time run parallel, but the work is always ten minutes in advance of the time. They are not irregular. They are never too soon. Their letters are posted the very minute after the mail is closed. They arrive at the wharf just in time to see the steamboat off; they come in sight of the terminus precisely as the station gates are closing. They do not break any engagement nor neglect any duty; but they systematically go about it too late, and usually too late by about the same fatal interval." And some of these same individuals, let us add, are very good people indeed. Their intentions are excellent. In most, perhaps in all other respects, their character is faultless and their example wholesome. But this "fly in the ointment" mars fatally the symmetry of character. And it seems to be a constitutional trait, or blemish, —a certain omission, like that of the faculty for discrimination in men born colour-blind. And the worst thing about it is, that the mischief which results is not confined to themselves alone. Their friends are involved. Indeed, the results of their remissness radiate in an ever widening circle among all their friends and acquaintances. All must suffer, though one be to blame. Doubtless these failures bring much self-accusation, as well as confusion of face, to the delinquents themselves; and many, no doubt, are the promises, self-made, of amendment—made, alas, only to be broken. The usual helplessness of such reminds one of that graphic picture Victor Hugo has given us of the unfortunate fisherman caught in the quicksands on the coast of Brittany. The more he struggles to free himself, the deeper and more hopelessly he sinks, and the more powerless he becomes.

Among men who have become famous, nothing has been

more noticeable than their habit of turning every moment of
time to good account, and thus making every scrap available.
For upwards of half a century Jeremy Bentham, we are told,
devoted seldom less than eight, often ten, and occasionally
twelve hours of every day to intense study. This was the
more remarkable as his physical constitution was by no means
strong. He was a great economist of time. He knew the
value of minutes. The disposal of his hours, both of labour
and of repose, was a matter of systematic arrangement; and
the arrangement was determined on the principle that *it is a
calamity to lose the smallest portion of time.*

The following picture of Dr. Burney, busied with his celebrated work, "The History of Music," is from the pen of his
daughter : " The capacious table of his small but commodious
study exhibited, in what he called his chaos, the countless
stores of his materials. Multitudinous, or rather innumer-
ous, blank books were severally adapted to concentrating
some peculiar portion of the work. And he opened an
enormous correspondence, foreign and domestic, with musical
authors, composers, and students. And for all this mass of
occupation he neglected no business, he omitted no duty.
The system by which he obtained time that no one missed,
yet which gave to him lengthened life independently of
longevity from years, was through the skill with which,
indefatigably, *he profited from every fragment of leisure.*"

Youth is too apt to squander, fancying that, do what one
may, there will be enough left. It is only when the water
in the bucket begins to get low that many realize their loss.
When the rope becomes so worn that only a few strands
remain, the few begin to seem very precious. Great fortunes
have sometimes seduced their possessors to ruinous profusion.
Fatal mistake, always repented of, but always too late.

"When we have deducted," says Johnson, "all that is
absorbed in sleep, all that is inevitably appropriated to the
demands of nature, or irresistibly engrossed by the tyranny

of custom ; all that passes in regulating the superficial
decorations of life, or is given up in the reciprocations of
civility to the disposal of others; all that is torn from us by
the violence of disease, or stolen imperceptibly away by
lassitude and languor,—we shall find that part of our duration
very small of which we can truly call ourselves masters, or
which we can spend wholly at our own choice." Years rush
by us like the wind. We cannot see whence the eddy comes
or whither it is tending. In the words of old Herrick :—

> " Time flies away fast ;
> The while we never remember
> How soon our life here
> Grows old with the year
> That dies with the next December."

It was because Nelson attended to detail in respect of
time that he was so uniformly victorious. "I owe," he
said, "all my success in life to having been always a quarter
of an hour before my time." "Every moment lost," said
Napoleon, "gives an opportunity for misfortune."

Some one has called attention to the fact that our late
war illustrated on several occasions the military virtue of
celerity of movement; but the writer is of the opinion that
there was no instance of a campaign being decided by the
forced march of an entire army and consequent surprise of
the enemy. For this rapidity the first Napoleon was especially noted. In 1805 he swept suddenly, with a large corps,
across France, from Boulogne to the Rhine, and took the
Austrians so by surprise at Ulm that he almost finished the
campaign by a single blow.

When one takes into consideration the climate, one of the
most extraordinary marches, as well for the immediate and
remote effects of its rapidity as for the rapidity itself, was
that of Wellington in India, when, by going seventy-two
miles with only one interval of rest and sleep, he was en-

abled to gain the victory of Assaye. He thus describes it : "Starting at three in the morning, the troops went twenty-five miles, and halted at noon. Then I made them lie down to sleep, setting sentinels over them ; and at eight they started again, marching till one at noon the next day, when we were in the enemy's camp."

There is no man living, says Todd, who might not be a punctual man ; and yet there are few who are so to anything like the degree to which they ought to attain. It is vastly easier to be a little late in doing everything. It is *not* so easy to be a prompt, punctual character ; but it is a trait of inestimable value to yourself and to the world. The punctual man can do twice as much, at least, as another man, with twice the ease and satisfaction to himself and with equal satisfaction to others. Lord Brougham, who presided in the House of Lords and the Court of Chancery, who gave audience daily to barristers and found time to write reviews, to be at the head of at least ten associations which were publishing works of useful knowledge, was so punctual that when these associations met he was uniformly there when the hour of meeting arrived, and was in his place in the chair.

It has been wisely said that if one loves life he will not squander time, for that is the stuff life is made of ; and a distinguished authority has declared that whatever knowledge one does not solidly lay the foundation of before he is eighteen, he will never be master of while he breathes. The secret of success lies in this,—one must learn to plot like an old man and execute like youth. Remember always that the will is weak, not in resolving, but in executing. An officer of the Orleans regiment having been sent to Louis XIV. with a despatch announcing a victory, demanded the Cross of the Order of St. Louis. "But you are so young," objected the monarch. "Sire," rejoined the officer, "the men of the Orleans regiment are not in the habit of living long !" For

life in general, says a trenchant writer, there is but one
decree : " Youth is a blunder, manhood a struggle, old age a
regret." " But," he truly adds, and the fact is not without
encouragement and inspiration, " almost everything great has
been done by youth." The greatest captains of ancient and
modern times both conquered Italy at five and twenty.
Youth overthrew the Persian empire. Gaston de Foix was
only twenty-two when he stood victor on the plain of
Ravenna. Gustavus Adolphus died at thirty-eight. When
Maurice of Saxony died at thirty-two, all Europe acknowledged the loss of the greatest captain and the profoundest
statesman of the age. John de Medici was a cardinal at
fifteen, and was pope, as Leo X., at thirty-seven. Raphael's
Madonnas were all painted and his immortal works all
finished before thirty-seven. Sir Philip Sidney, said to be
the brightest figure of the Elizabethan era, and the most
complete embodiment of all the graces and virtues which can
adorn or ennoble humanity, died before he was thirty-two.
Francis Bacon, both admired and condemned, wrote a remarkable essay on the state of Europe when he was eighteen
years old, at twenty-nine was Queen's Counsel, and was
knighted at the age of forty-two. Edward Hyde, Earl of
Clarendon, entered Parliament at thirty-two ; was Chancellor
of the Exchequer and raised to the dignity of knighthood
before he was thirty-six. Gibbon entered Parliament at
thirty-seven, and two years later gave to the world the first
volume of his history. Chatterton died at eighteen, Shelley
at thirty, and Byron at thirty-seven. It is said that the
finest artillery officer in the late Confederate service was
Major Pelham of Stuart's cavalry, a young man of thirty-two.
Pitt commenced his long dictatorship at twenty-four. Alexander the Great died at thirty-three ; and Napoleon had
achieved all his victories at thirty-seven. At thirty-three
Jefferson wrote the Declaration of Independence ; and Hamilton helped to frame the Constitution of the United States

at thirty. But enough. Is it not quite manifest that the history of greatness is the history of youth?

It is the unexpected which always happens, we are told. It is a fact singular and striking enough, surely, when one thinks upon it, that, although a man can with skill and science and piercing intellect scan the most distant future, and predict with unerring certainty the very second when an eclipse, for instance, shall occur, he, at the same time, never knows what is just around the corner, and cannot possibly tell you what an hour may bring forth. "There occur from time to time in human life," says Arnold, "signal moments which become the landmarks of its history. These are indeed the momentous moments of life. They come upon us unawares. The air is charged with no sense of oppression and awe. There is no visible sign to the most observant or to the most superstitious. The 'moment' itself often comes in the most ordinary and commonplace guise. It is perhaps only a call, a letter, an interview, a sudden suggestion, a few minutes' talk at a railway station, and with suddenness and abruptness one section of life is clasped, and an entirely new page of its ledger opened up." But where is strength of character more finely manifest than in the power to deny one's self the most tempting present advantage for the sake of that dim and uncertain future which the soul instinctively feels has in store still greater reward?

There are several instances in the life of Webster during his practice at the bar showing the value of promptness in following one's convictions upon the instant. Once he was engaged in a case in behalf of a poor man who, he felt sure, had been defrauded by the villany of a wealthy resident of the town in good social position. And yet, though feeling so sure of the man's guilt, the proof at hand was miserably meagre, and, as he afterward declared, he was never in his life more badly prepared for a case. There was no evidence, and what to do he did not know. Just before the case was called, a friend of his client came and told Webster that he had just seen this wealthy man talking with a worthless fellow, and he had handed the latter a slip of paper in the entry. Webster thanked the man, and told him that was a pretty important thing to know, and asked him to say nothing about it. Presently this fellow was called to testify, and took the oath. During his testimony he used the words, "the said Brown" told him so and so. The unusual phrase from an ignorant man caught the quick ear of Webster, and it flashed upon him in an instant that he was being prompted from a written paper, and that this was the paper which had been handed him in the entry. "There sat Mason" (his great legal opponent), said Webster, "full of assurance, and for a moment I hesitated. The next instant, however, I said to myself, 'I will make a spoon, or spoil a horn!' I took the pen from behind my ear, drew myself up, and marched outside of the bar to the witness-stand. 'Sir!' I exclaimed, 'give me the paper from which you are testifying!' In an instant he pulled it out of his pocket; but before he had it quite out, he hesitated, and attempted to put it back. I seized it in triumph. There was his testimony in Bramble's handwriting! Mr. Mason got up and claimed the protection of the court. Judge Smith inquired the meaning of this proceeding. I said: 'Providence protects the innocent when they are friendless. I think I could satisfy the court, and my learned brother, who, of course, was ignorant of this man's conduct, that I hold in Mr. Bramble's handwriting the testimony of the very respectable witness who is on the stand.' The court adjourned, and I had nothing further to do. Mason told his client that he had better settle the affair as quickly as possible." Truly, promptness, as well as boldness, has "genius, power, and magic in it." A similar promptness once saved the life of the first Napoleon. During his Egyptian campaign his life was threatened by his disaffected

generals. Walking coolly among them, he said : "Soldiers,
you are Frenchmen ! You are too many to assassinate, and
too few to intimidate me." They walked away, saying,
" How brave he is ! "

One whose opinion is entitled to great weight has declared,
that, as far as one can decide at such a distance of time and
of scene, it seems all but certain that the rapid advance of
Hannibal on Rome after the battle of Cannæ, that of Henry
of Navarre on Paris after the battle of Ivry, or that of
Charles Stuart on London after penetrating as far as Derby,
would have changed the course of human history. Napoleon
used to say, that although a battle may last a whole day,
there were generally some ten minutes in which the fate of
the engagement was practically decided ; and his own marvellous career reveals the fact that neither his splendid
intellectual power nor his enormous force of will was so
potent a factor in his success as his prompt and perpetual
activity. On his return from Spain to Paris, he rode on
horseback eighty-five miles in five hours. After his victory
at Rivoli, he said, " The Austrians manœuvred admirably,
and failed only because they did not know the value of
minutes,"—a department of knowledge in which he himself
seems to have surpassed all men.

Let not impetuosity, however, betray you into imprudence.
Hurry and cunning, says Colton, are the two apprentices
of despatch and of skill, but neither of them ever learns his
master's trade. If after due precaution has been taken,
however, blunders do occur, be not dismayed. It is a well-
known truth in military science, that no battle is fought
without blunders. Good generalship practically consists in
the comparative fewness of them. Above all, never despair.
Among recent proverbs, or perhaps one should say, among
modern renderings of ancient saws, is one which certainly
commends itself for its quaintness as well as for the rare
vein of philosophy underlying it. It is this : " Don't cry

over spilt milk ; up, and catch the cow." It is never well to be too particular about carrying out one's ideal after any rigidly preconceived plan. One fertile in resources, if baffled or defeated in one direction, should be ready instantly to adopt whatever presents itself at hand. This has been the characteristic of all great leaders. In order to reach the mouth of the river, it may not be necessary to follow punctiliously all the windings of the stream. Be not too fastidious. Though plans be imperfect and achievement fall short of ideal, push on.

> " Ere *perfect* scheme of action thou devise,
> Will life be fled."

Schiller has written nothing truer than that.

This habit of promptness is invaluable to all public men. Others soon learn to rely upon such ; and a fine reputation in this regard is worth a great deal. The statue of Franklin was about to be unveiled in Printing House Square. The hour fixed was twelve o'clock. A few minutes before twelve it was noticed that all who were to take part in the ceremony were present save a certain well-known clergyman of the city. As the important moment approached, fears were expressed that there might be a disagreeable delay. At this juncture Horace Greeley interposed. " Gentlemen," said he, " there is no cause for uneasiness. I know the man. If Dr. —— isn't dead, or if some member of his family isn't dead, he'll be here in time." This was certainly reassuring. The confidence, however, was not misplaced. Just on the stroke of twelve the doctor entered, saying he would have been there at least some minutes earlier had he not been unexpectedly detained by a blockade in the street. Now, one cannot but feel that a reputation like that is worth having. "We are all so indolent by nature and by habit," says Todd, "that we feel it a luxury to find a man of real, undeviating punctuality. We love to lean upon such a man, and we are willing to purchase such a staff at almost any price. It shows, at least, that he has conquered himself." A very good rule laid down by the same author is this: When there are two things for you to do, one of which *must* be done, and the other is what you very much *desire* to do, *be sure to begin the former first.* Failure to observe this rule, most of us can doubtless testify, has far too often been disastrous to punctuality.

It does not surprise one so much that punctuality should be so striking a trait in the character of the clergyman to whom Mr. Greeley referred, when one discovers it to be the result not only of training and self-discipline, but of conscience as well; for in a prominent periodical, in writing upon this very theme, we find him classing a want of punctuality among "the minor immoralities." "Certainly," he says, "punctuality is among the highest virtues possible to man. The want of it shows a regardlessness of other people's property and other people's feelings. In business, no matter what his other qualities, if this be lacking all one's affairs are liable to get into disorder. If a man has no regard for the time of other men, why should he have for their money? What is the difference between taking a man's hour and taking his five dollars? There are many men to whom each hour of the business day is worth more than five dollars. It is no apology for one to say he does not intend to do harm. Thieves are not generally malignant."

It has been said of Howard the philanthropist, that he had never been a minute under or over the time of an appointment, so far as it depended upon himself, for six and twenty years; and that he never continued at a place or with a person a single day beyond the period fixed for going, in his whole life. This really seems like carrying things a little to the extreme, to say the least. Now, as regards this *punctiliousness,*—the appearing on the exact stroke of the clock, and never a minute over or under an appointment,—there may be, not unjustly, a difference of opinion. Always to be in season should be the inexorable rule; but after that, to make one's appearance a few minutes earlier would doubtless be quite as convenient many times as to rigidly compel one's self to appear on the exact stroke of the clock. A prominent American statesman, observes a writer in the *London Globe*, was said to take a pride in always knocking at any door within which he had an engagement precisely with the first stroke of the clock, or with the very tick of his watch. "Perhaps," he continues, "if that wondrous wise statesman had taken the trouble to 'tot up' all the odds and ends of time he must have wasted in securing this pettifogging precision, he would have found that, whatever he might have done for other people's time, he had really been as wasteful of his own as the veriest sloven in this way may be supposed to be on the showing of very exemplary people,—as wasteful, for instance, as Lord Palmerston, who was known to drop in to a public dinner four hours after the appointed time."

When Boswell gave his fashionable dinners in Welbeck Street, the guests were always given to understand that time must be observed to the minute, and that if they were not there, dinner must proceed without them. It was not often that folks came late, for most people can be punctual when they know it is expected of them. On one occasion, however, it happened to be the astronomer-royal who came in half a minute or so behind the appointed dinner-hour, and, as he no doubt expected, found the guests coming down the staircase to the dining-room. "I trust, Mr. Friend," said the host in greeting him, "that in future you will bear in mind we don't reckon time here by the meridian of Greenwich, but by the meridian of Welbeck Street." That sort of thing may be all very well when it is clearly understood that, in an auctioneer's phraseology, it is to be dinner-time "prompt;" but it is not every host who can muster the

hardihood for such rigidity, even though the guests may
not be astronomers-royal.   Most people would agree with
Dr. Johnson in his well-known dictum on the point.
"Ought six people to be kept waiting for one?" asked Boswell.   "Why, yes," said Johnson; "if the one will suffer
more by your sitting down than the six will by waiting."

Where one is known to be incorrigible, however, and
deliberately presumes upon his own importance or his host's
good-nature, the remedy is at hand, and simple.   Beau
Brummell was of this sort.   Among his other follies Brummell had that of choosing to be always too late for dinner.
Wherever he was invited, we are told, he liked to be waited
for.   He thought it was a proof of his fashion and consequence ; and the higher the rank of his entertainer, the later
was the arrival of this impudent *parvenu*.   The Marquis of
Abercorn had been repeatedly annoyed in this way.   At
length he resolved to bear it no longer.   Accordingly, having
again invited Brummell to dine, he gave strict orders to the
servants to have dinner on the table punctually at the time
appointed.   The servants obeyed, and "Brummell and the
cheese arrived together."   The "wondering beau" was
desired by the master of the house to sit down.   No apology
was made.   With the utmost coolness, however, the latter
simply added, "I hope, Mr. Brummell, cheese is not disagreeable to you."   It is said that Brummell was never late at
that house afterward.

Stuart Blackie, in his valuable little work on Self-
Culture, truly says : "Nothing commends a young man so
much to his employers as accuracy and punctuality in the
conduct of business."   And no wonder.   On each man's
exactitude in doing his special best depends the comfortable
and easy going of the whole machine.   In the complicated
tasks of social life, no genius and no talent can compensate
for the lack of obedience.   If the clock goes fitfully, nobody
knows the time of day ; and if your allotted task is a neces-

sary link in the chain of another man's work, you are his clock, and he ought to be able to rely on you. "The greatest praise that can be given to the member of any association," he continues, " is in these terms : *This is a man who always does what is required of him, and who always appears at the hour when he is expected to appear.*"

Appointments become debts. I owe you punctuality if I have made an appointment with you, and have no right to throw away your time if I do my own. The daughter of James Peale, the famous painter, relates the following incident to show that the wife of Washington emulated her husband in punctuality : " My father had an engagement to paint a miniature of Mrs. Washington in Philadelphia, the general being then out of town. He was obliged to go to her house, and the appointment for a sitting was arranged at seven o'clock in the morning. My father arrived at the house, and taking out his watch he found he was exactly on time. The thought then struck him that possibly it might be early to disturb a lady, and he decided to give ten minutes' grace before knocking at the door. He accordingly walked the pavement, and at the end of ten minutes pulled out his watch and rang the bell. He was ushered into the parlour, and Mrs. Washington accosting him drew out her watch and said she had given her orders for the day, had heard her daughter take her lesson on the harpsichord, and had read all the morning papers, and after all this had been waiting for him ten minutes." The Countess of Burford for the last few years of her life had to ride almost constantly on horseback upwards of sixteen miles to and from church ; yet neither frost, snow, rain, nor bad roads were sufficient to detain her at home, nor to prevent her being there before the worship began. The emphasis here placed upon this matter of scrupulous promptness in meeting an appointment may seem to some unnecessary, or at best not greatly important ; yet Dr. Fisk has declared, " I give it

as my deliberate and solemn conviction, that the individual
who is habitually tardy in meeting an appointment will
never be respected or successful in life."

Every one must have been impressed with the fact that
there are some men who seem to have no decision of character. Where this is lacking, promptness is out of the
question. Their manner in a great crisis is "like the
irresolution of the sea at turn of tide." What object more
pitiable than a man who never seems to know his own mind?
As Webster once said of an opponent, "This man neither
advances nor recedes, he simply ' hovers.' " Nothing can
possibly be more exasperating, under certain critical circumstances, than this perpetual vacillation. A man of this
stamp can never be said really to belong to himself. He is
for ever at the mercy of every chance current that may
overtake him. Perpetually swayed from his purposes, he
becomes a perfect football of fortune. Such, too, are ever
bemoaning their fate. Had circumstances been otherwise,
what might they not have done! Thus "days are lost
lamenting over lost days," instead of one's seizing lustily the
actual fact which confronts him, and compelling it to serve
him ; or smiting resolutely the circumstance which environs,
and making it his slave. How in contrast with this vacillation is the fine, prompt intrepidity of certain other men.
Their aims may be questionable ; their projects may indeed
be evil ; but half-hearted goodness is never a match for
evil in dead earnest. The very presence of a strong, prompt
man seems to make itself felt at once. Difficulties slink
away and cower out of sight like belaboured hounds. He
seems in league with the very "stones of the field." How
refreshing such a presence ! It is like a tonic. We love to
be near such. The very atmosphere seems charged with the
presage of success. Such men call forth our homage as if
by instinct the moment they appear. We rely on them at
once, without pausing to question why. This, doubtless,

accounts for the marvellous sway that certain bold, bad men
have from time to time held over their fellows in all ages
of the world. Not that this was necessary. Arm virtue
with the same weapons, and with its vantage-ground it
would inevitably win. But goodness and vacillating timidity can never hope to outwit vice and prompt, unerring
skill.

While Barry the painter was a young man residing at
Dublin, an incident occurred which strikingly illustrates the
character of the man. He was brought into contact with
some young men of dissipated habits, who on several occasions enticed him to form one of their tavern parties. As he
was returning home late at night from one of these carousals,
a sudden impression came to him of the folly of his course,
in thus wasting the time which might so much more properly
be employed in laying the foundation of his future re-
spectability and independence. Distrusting, perhaps, his
own power to carry out any resolution he might make to
deny himself the gratification which he had the means of
purchasing, and certain that the most effectual preventive
would be to rid himself of the means at once, he took all his
money, which was probably at that time no great sum, and
threw it into the Liffey, and then shut himself up with great
perseverance to his professional studies !

> " The flighty purpose never is o'ertook,
> Unless the deed go with it."

It was the sudden conviction of this truth that had come
home to the young painter. The resulting deed was not less
than heroic. Like Cæsar's, it was a burning of bridges.
Knowing this, one ceases to wonder at his subsequent
success. That might have been counted on as almost a
mathematical certainty.

Some one has declared the resolute casting out of a single
bosom sin to be equivalent to a liberal education. The same

might almost be said of the conquest of a single wasteful habit; for surely almost any man can understand somewhat of the reflex influence of every prompt conquest of that which is unworthy of himself. He has found it at war with his nobler self too often not to realize how persistently it tends to lower his ideal and mar his work. And doubtless he has also found each triumph to be to him as so much added capital. "There is no moment like the present," writes Miss Edgeworth; "not only so, there is no moment at all, no instant force and energy, but in the present. The man who will not execute his resolutions when they are fresh upon him, can have no hopes from them afterward. They will be dissipated, lost in the hurry and skurry of the world, or sunk in the slough of indolence." There is much truth in that. Surrounded as one is by so many distractions, impelled by so many motives for doing this or that or the other, where there are so many things one would *like* to do, if it were best, it becomes a matter of no small moment and concern to decide wisely as to that which shall receive one's attention and that which should be let utterly alone. In the realm of knowledge, for instance, the area has grown so vast that one must rigorously choose his specialty in order to be truly effective in any direction. "The secret of being learned," said Helvetius, "is bravely to determine to be ignorant of many things in which men take pride." Let one, for instance, read the best authors, and he may safely ignore the others. They are simply duplicates. It is best for one who wishes properly to understand what is *greatest* in human writings, says an eminent authority, to avoid mercilessly all second-rate matter, however good. "I have not read that book." Let one be frank and dare to make a confession like that, if he mean to get on. "The better is always an enemy to the best." The channel must be narrowed that the stream may flow in a rapid current and fall with great impression. It has well been said that the mechanical reading of all the standard literature would require more than three thousand years. Why should one attempt it just yet? The present writer once remarked to one of his instructors, a well-known Hebrew scholar, whom he sometimes met in a great library, that such places often exerted a depressing influence upon him, as the realization came that there were so many books in the world that one could never hope to read. "Ah, but that feeling never troubles me," was the instant and cheery response. "I know I never can read them all, but it is a comfort to feel that I can *browse around* as much as I please." What a wonderful sense of relief that remark conferred! It revealed a new standpoint. That man understood the art of "putting things." To know that we do not know what we do not know, and to know that we do know what we do know, says Confucius, that is wisdom indeed.

Hesitation is fatal to enterprise. It is right here that many men fail. They see their course, the way is plain; and yet they stand upon the brink and hesitate. Now, the only way for a man to do anything worth doing in this world is, as Sydney Smith says, to plunge in and scramble through as best he can. One of the famous rules of Alexander, and one to which he rigidly adhered, was, never to avoid doing anything because of the short bodily trouble it might occasion. It is easy to discern in this one great secret of his marvellous success. A certain morbid introspection seems to hold some men back. A man begins to analyze his motives, perhaps; or possibly all of his surroundings are not up to his ideal, and he begins to analyze these. Now, this analysis is like a wet blanket thrown upon the ardour of his resolves. Then self-consciousness comes in and floors him. It is probable that even the finest spirits have been conscious at times of a certain indefinable hesitation before making the important venture which is to win them success. The difference between them and those who

fail is, that the one promptly and resolutely conquers the
dread, while the other allows himself to be conquered by it.
"Nothing," said Mirabeau, "is impossible to the man who
can will. Is that necessary ? That shall be. This is the
only law of success." There is a fine and striking sentence
in the Book of Proverbs which most of us would do well to
remember : " Let thine eyes look right on, and let thine eye-
lids look straight before thee." Herein lie all the elements
of strength. Many a man has looked his soul in the face,
and, distrusting his own powers, has ignobly given up the
whole battle in despair, and made a failure of life, when
success was right at hand. A treacherous self-consciousness
was no doubt at the bottom of it. *Let a man forget himself
and how he is working altogether*, if he would succeed.

This singular apathy, or dread, or hesitation to which we
have referred, which comes upon even the rarest spirits at
times in such an unaccountable manner, is not usually
*fear*, to say the least. It is easy to see this, and to detect
the difference, although in what this difference lies one may
not be able exactly to tell. One thing, however, is evident.
The "native hue of resolution" has been "sicklied o'er with
the pale cast of thought." This, we say, is manifest. But
this is not *fear*. In proof of this, let a great crisis come
suddenly upon a man at such a juncture. The emergency
confronts him, and *must* be met. An accident has happened
to his neighbour; a fellow-man in great peril must be rescued.
The miners are imprisoned in the shaft. His comrades,
with death staring them in the face, are held fast in the
tunnel ; he *must* do *something*, and that *now*. Instantly
self-consciousness disappears. The soul is roughly shaken
out of its shrinking, cringing attitude, and springs at once
to the rescue. The deed of an unknown man becomes the
deed of a hero. His name is on every one's lips, and all
hearts are exultant at the revelation of the latent heroism of
which our poor, weak humanity is capable. Thus again and

again have men "forgot themselves into immortality." It is the forlorn hope that reveals the hero. The great crises of our lives drive us out of ourselves, and reveal the nobler soul which lay behind the weak, shrinking, unworthy timidity which held us back.

This peculiar hesitation of which we have spoken is doubtless a constitutional trait in many instances. At least, this is almost always true of men. It is rarely thus with women. Man is proverbially a reasoning animal, while woman is governed largely by her intuitions. Howells notes this difference in one of his fictions. "Our sense of details," he says, "our fatal habits of reasoning, paralyze us; we need the impulse of the pure ideal." This, he holds, we can get only from woman. Noting the contrast between two of his characters, he says : "He had a man's dark prevision of the means, and she had a heavenly scorn of everything but the end to be achieved." Certain great military leaders have seemed to combine both traits. No one, for instance, was more scrupulous in attention to details than Napoleon ; and no one, on the other hand, seemed to have a more exultant scorn of danger when the hour came for carrying out his plans. Grant, who resembled him more closely than any other military leader of modern times, was like him in this. Sherman, in a remarkable letter, honourable alike both to the head and heart of the writer, in which he pays Grant such a noble tribute, after referring to his careful preparation before a battle, goes on to say : "You then went into battle as if the event of possible defeat had never for a moment entered your thought. I can compare it to nothing," he beautifully adds, "but to the faith of a Christian in his Saviour. It was this that gave us confidence."

It must have cost Cæsar many anxious hours of deliberation, says Foster, before he decided to pass the Rubicon; but it is probable he suffered but few to elapse between the decision and the execution. "And any one of his friends

who should have been apprised of his determination and
understood his character would have smiled contemptuously
to hear it insinuated that though Cæsar had resolved, Cæsar
would not dare; or that though he might cross the Rubicon,
whose opposite bank presented to him no hostile legion, he
might come to other rivers which he would not cross; or
that either rivers or any other obstacles would deter him
from prosecuting his determination from this ominous commencement to its very last consequence." Let us never forget that a prompt action is an inspiration in itself. It is
contagious. Its influence is that of a clarion note or a bugle
call. It is Sheridan plunging the rowels into his steed,
halting the panic-stricken soldiers, and by his own indomitable
courage promptly turning the tide of battle and winning the
day. One finds a similar inspiration in certain short, sharp,
bristling sentences which hold within them truths that are
masters of the world. "In the hot haste of business, in the
perilous scenes of temptation, in the dark hours of pain and
sorrow, men will not listen to long arguments." The terse,
prompt, pregnant sentence is what men need.

Of the "dangerous ends" that wait upon "delays," whole
volumes might be written. The brakeman fails to signal
the oncoming train; the courier bearing the reprieve dallies
at the inn, carousing with his boon companions until the
life of the poor fellow which he held in his hands is the for-
feit paid. There is ten minutes' delay of the telegram, the
note goes to protest, and financial ruin stares the victim in the
face. Cæsar, on his way to the senate house, delays reading
the message which would have saved his life. Plutarch tells
us that when Archias, the polemarch at Thebes, dissolved in
wine and pleasure, received from his pontifical namesake at
Athens a full and particular account by letter of the con-
spiracy of Pelopidas and the exiles, who were even then
counting the minutes ere they struck the blow, although
the messenger expressly urged his excellency to read the

missive forthwith, as the contents were of instant import, Archias only smiled a tipsy smile and said, "Business to-morrow." Then he put the unopened letter under his pillow, and resumed his colloquy with his host, Philidas, who was in the plot, and who was taking good care to ply the polemarch with wine. Business to-morrow. Alas! for him no morrow was to come. Similar instances fill the pages of history. To guard against these perils of delay, most stringent measures have at times been adopted. We owe our familiar phrase "post-haste" to a measure of this kind. In the sixteenth century there were no post-offices in England; government couriers were the only bearers of letters, except the common carriers, whose principal business was the conveyance of parcels. These couriers were under martial law, and in the time of Henry VIII. were subject to the penalty of hanging for delay upon the road with their despatches. The letters of those days were consequently sometimes ornamented with the sketch of a gallows, with a courier thereon suspended. Underneath was the admonition : " Haste, post, haste ! Haste for thy life !"

There is no denying the fact that at times downright fear, a real want of moral courage, is at the root of many a failure. And fear is a very potent factor where it really exists. Perhaps no one is always and absolutely exempt. Dr. Johnson tells us that when Charles V. read upon the tombstone of a Spanish nobleman, " Here lies one who never knew fear," he wittily said, " Then he never snuffed a candle with his fingers !" But it is a man's own fault if he allow his fear to conquer him. Like Cæsar's officer, though with blanched cheek, one must advance with firm tread. Apprehension sometimes comes from looking too far ahead.

How few of us really live in the present ! Most of us are perpetually saddened by looking back upon the past, or filled with apprehension from looking forward into the dim and shadowy future. We are crippled in our exertions because we fail to seize vigorously upon the present. Let us learn to live *now.* Sydney Smith insists that the great remedy for melancholy is to "take short views of life." Why not? Surely it would rid a man of much of that needless apprehension so fatal to the fullest success.

The calmness of mind conferred by this habit of promptness is not to be overlooked. To say nothing of the dangers of delay, the serenity which is the inseparable companion of despatch is a luxury to which the disorderly man is an entire stranger. But it confers still more than this : it gives weight to character. That was a wise maxim of the Duke of Newcastle—"I do one thing at a time."

Hunt, the artist, in his entertaining little volume, "Talks about Art," among other valuable suggestions to young artists, says, "Vitalize your work. Look for the round, but look for the square within the round. Chop it out with an axe, and sand-paper it afterward!" Would not this secret, once learned and practised, *vitalize* all work? It is surely a secret which successful literary workers, at least, acquire early. Promptness seizes the burning, throbbing thought in the rough; chops it out rudely, it may be—it matters little so it be secured; then art may "sand-paper" it at leisure, caress it into beauty, and impart its nameless charm. Floors and flooring are of little moment, provided the pottery come out well glazed.

Many an interesting instance might be given to show the advantage to its possessor of ready wit and promptness in repartee. The apt reply, the prompt retort, has often enabled one to come off with flying colours, even in face of threatened defeat. A prompt and happy retort, moreover, if good-naturedly given, rarely fails to please even the one at whose expense it is given. But it must be prompt, to give zest. Even in literature, as Holmes wittily says, one finds it hard to get and to keep any private property in thought. "Other people are all the time saying the very things we are hoarding to say when we get ready." The brilliant "Autocrat," however, has certainly made sure of "saying" at least a few things before other people got the chance—in any event, before they improved it.

Charles Sumner, when in London, at a dinner given in his honour spoke of "the ashes" of some dead hero. "Ashes! what American-English!" broke in one of the guests. "Dust, you mean, Mr. Sumner. We don't burn our dead in this country."

"Yet," instantly replied Sumner with a courteous smile, "your poet Gray tells us that

'Even in our ashes live their wonted fires.'"

Mr. Sumner was not criticised again that evening. Surely one cannot fail to perceive at a glance the advantage conferred by prompt and ready response like this. And where in all literature will you find a better *bon-mot* than the reply of the young lady who heard her father severely criticised across a dinner table? The careless critic paused a moment to say, "I hope he is no friend of yours, Miss L——;" and quick as thought she replied, with the utmost nonchalance, "Only a connection of my mother by marriage."

After all, work as faithfully as one may, plan and execute as promptly as one possibly can, it is at best but little, comparatively, that one can do. It seems as if all one does is but a "rough draft," and that always there is something unfinished that ought to be done.

" Labour with what zeal we will,
Something still remains undone ;
Something uncompleted still
Waits the rising of the sun."

If life seem thus even to the most diligent, what must be thought of those who wilfully squander it? Let those who would achieve success take the lesson to heart, that only by prompt and strenuous endeavour are life's prizes to be won, and that for lost opportunities there is no resurrection.

# II

# Individuality.

"And how did Garrick speak the soliloquy last night?"

"Oh, against all rule, my lord; most ungrammatically. Betwixt the substantive and the adjective, which should agree together in number, case, and gender, he made a breach—thus stopping as if the point wanted settling; and betwixt the nominative case, which your lordship knows should govern the verb, he suspended his voice in the epilogue a dozen times, three seconds and three-fifths, by a stop-watch, my lord, each time."

"Admirable grammarian! But in suspending his voice, was the sense suspended likewise? Did no expression of attitude or countenance fill up the chasm? Was the eye silent? Did you narrowly look?"

"I looked only at the stop-watch, my lord."—STERNE.

Look well into thyself: there is a source which will always spring up if thou wilt always search there.—MARCUS AURELIUS.

LET it be noted that the subject of this chapter is not "Individualism," which, by far too often, is only another name for downright selfishness. Between that quality and individuality there is all the difference in the world. The latter is often winning and prepossessing, and always desirable; the former far otherwise. Moreover, we propose to show that this quality of individuality is not only not to be ignored, but is often invaluable to one who means to get on. Take an illustration. Europe had been "done to death." Books of European travel had flooded the market. The subject, worn threadbare, had come to be as "tedious as a tired horse" or a thrice-told tale, when an enterprising American conceives the idea of making the "grand tour," and telling about it in his own way. He does so. He puts his own intense individuality into his work. He travels over ground familiar to every one, and visits places which had been described a thousand times, but describes them in his own way. Every page, sparkling with wit, reveals the author's unique, original way of looking at things. The result is that Mark Twain and his "Innocents Abroad" become household words in two hemispheres, and the author's fame and fortune are made. Would you know the secret of it all? Find it in individuality. From the midst of a thousand platitudes and littlenesses this quality steps forth, and ere the dull and listless eyes of commonplace have perceived what it is doing, it has clutched success and won the prize.

It seems as if most of us dare not tread on ground where some one else has not already trod—dare not be original. Our own thought seems not worth the utterance, our own deed not worth the doing, simply because it is ours. Where were the Miltons or Shakespeares of the race, had these ideas been universal? The Chinaman ploughs with a stick because his father, and his grandfather, and his great-grandfather before him, ploughed with a stick ; and nothing can induce him to forsake the old familiar ruts and crooked furrows of his ancestors. But we are not Chinamen. Dare to believe that God sent you into the world to accomplish that which even an angel from heaven could not do so well. Individuality leaves the beaten track, but it is no iconoclast. It dares the unknown and unexplored. It appears, as the unexpected always comes, with a novelty and freshness that constantly surprise and charm us. Society always makes room for it, and its doors are opened wide. A thousand puerilities "strut their brief hour" to little purpose ; but individuality holds the "open sesame" before which men and barriers give way. How refreshing at times, amid the commonplaces and platitudes of society, to come upon a frank, sincere, and outspoken soul! We are naturally so afraid of one another and of one another's opinion, so restrained and cautious and imitative in our intercourse with one another, held under by the iron heel of custom, that when an ingenuous, untrammelled nature does appear, one having the unmistakable courage of his convictions, it is a great relief. We feel unburdened and rested. The impression is like that of the grateful breath of a June morning after the thraldom of winter's cold. We do not mean that independence of established opinion which asserts itself for the sake of being singular, which one sometimes sees. This is the counterfeit, and is instantly betrayed. A nature which is "nothing if not critical" is a very tedious affair. On the other hand, there is a certain outspoken honesty of opinion which is the soul of sincerity, and is always engaging. When a soul speaks from its centre, it is instantly recognized. The "accent of conviction" is unmistakable. And if sometimes opinions be wayward, or even mutinous, according to our preconceived notions of things, we give them place, and even welcome, because the manner of their expression relieves us and puts us at our ease.

There is a certain air of *abandon* about this quality of which we have spoken, that ever carries with it to the souls of others the assurance of sincerity. This always wins its way. Men may not acquiesce, but they will not censure. It is like Martin Luther's "Here I stand; I cannot otherwise!" And it is a curious fact that the spirit which is thus willing, if need be, to lose all, oftenest gains all. This quality in a man has a strange magnetic power, and wins upon every one, and that from the very start. While timid commonplace cowers cautiously in the background, fearing to venture, and fritters itself away in compliances and insincerities, individuality, with fine intrepidity, advances its line, stations its outposts, and reaches its goal. Its rights had never been acknowledged had they not been claimed; but its ends have been reached so naturally and easily

that we wonder how it was, yet cannot see how it could
have been otherwise. The eagle ever knows his eyrie.
There are certain men

> "Who walk up to fame as to a friend,
> Or their own house, which from the wrongful heir
> They have wrested, from the world's hard hand and gripe."

There is a cry in every human soul for its individuality,
—its own identity. It. had rather be itself than be an angel
and lose its own identity. What the world wants is individuality. If one have peculiarities, so called, let him be
thankful for them, so be that he train them to proper ends.
Have prejudices; settle some things once for all. Do not
have again to lay the foundation. Settle some questions,
and then go on. These very peculiarities may be strong
points in one's character. Only see to it that they be util-
ized in the right direction. Harness them up and make
them work for you, lest they make against you. Fire and
water are both admirable servants, but bad masters. So,
too, righteous indignation is a fine thing; but fretful, uncalled-
for anger is wasteful and exhaustive. Thus make your
peculiarities and idiosyncrasies perpetual avenues of delight,
rather than sources of annoyance to others.

It is curious, if not a little surprising, when one reflects
upon it, how many people are willing and contented to have
their thinking done for them; how many blindly and
slavishly follow the opinions of other people, made for them
ready at hand. But then, real thinking is, of course, hard
work, and the "toil of thought" exhausting. As George
Eliot says in "Middlemarch," "It is very difficult to be
learned. One gets so worn out on the way to great thoughts,
that one is often too tired to enjoy them." But all too
common is this tendency and willingness to which we have
referred. One easily falls into the slavish habit; and
because, forsooth, the thought he so blindly follows is

*printed,* it must needs be true. Ah, the talismanic influence of type! Instead of this servitude, begin early to think and act for yourself. Dare to differ with your author, if need be. Aim to find yourself in his book. As I pass through the market-place, I see a thousand things I don't want, and have no use for. Let me demand and take what is mine. A clever modern essayist has called attention to the habit which seems to be very general, of this mere adhesion to received opinion; and he declares that this habit in any matter is most mischievous, since it strikes at the root of independence of thought, and in literature tends to make the public taste mechanical. He further declares that there are certain books which are standard, before which the great majority of us bow the knee and doff the cap with a reverence that, in its ignorance, reminds one of fetich-worship. He thinks a good deal of this mock worship is due to abject cowardice ; that there is a great tendency in society to praise books which one has never read, simply because others praise them, and a deplorable absence of that independence of character, or individuality, which dares to differ upon occasion, and give voice to its honest conviction. He admires very much the courage of Charlotte Brontë for confessing that she couldn't find much pleasure in Miss Austen's novels, at the very period when everybody professed to adore them ; and he alludes to a similar confession of Miss Martineau regarding a very famous fiction. He accuses Macaulay of having (without probably intending it) done most to promote this hypocrisy in literature, but thinks Macaulay himself might have been a little more modest in view of the fact that his own reading in certain directions had been to so little purpose. "When Dr. Johnson is free to confess that he does not admire Gray's Elegy, and Macaulay to avow that he sees little to praise in Dickens and Wordsworth, why should not humbler folks have the courage of their own opinions? They cannot possibly be more wrong than Johnson and Macaulay were; and it is surely better to be honest, though it may expose one to some ridicule, than to lie." The more we agree with the verdict of the generations before us on these matters, the more, it is quite true, we are likely to be right; but the agreement should be an honest one. "As a rule," he continues, "I suppose even people in society (the drawing-rooms and the clubs) are not absolutely base, and yet one would really think so, to judge by the fear that is entertained by them of being natural."

The lesson of Longfellow's "Gaspar Becerra" cannot be insisted on too often,—"That is best which lieth nearest." In vain shall we seek outside of ourselves for that power which must come alone from within. Let one not make the mistake of supposing anything too profound or rich for popular appreciation. No train of thought, says Choate, is too deep or subtile or grand; but the manner of presenting it to untutored minds should be peculiar. It should be presented in anecdote, or sparkling truism, or telling illustration, or stinging epithet; always in some concrete form, never in a logical, abstract, syllogistic shape.

Who can estimate the amount of talent lost to the world for the want of a little courage? "There is one circumstance," says Sydney Smith, "I would preach up morning, noon, and night, to young persons, for the management of their understanding. Whatever you are from Nature, keep to it; never desert your own line of talent. If Providence only intended you to write posies for rings, or mottoes for twelfth-cakes, keep to posies and mottoes; a good motto for a twelfth-cake is more respectable than a villanous epic poem in twelve books. Be what Nature intended you for, and you will succeed; be anything else, and you will be ten thousand times worse than nothing." Elsewhere the same author divides mankind into classes, and among others whom he facetiously hits off is the class which he denominates "the Let-well-aloners, cousins-german to the Noodle, yet a variety,—people who have begun to think and to act, but are timid, and afraid to try their wings, and tremble at the sound of their own footsteps as they advance, and think it safer to stand still."

Of course, the secrets of eloquence were known to men long before the treatise on oratory or rhetoric appeared. What, indeed, is a treatise but the crystallized product of observations on results already achieved? The fearless thought was uttered, the dauntless heroism displayed, the thunder of the beak, the lightning of the eye, the melting pathos of speech, had all wrought their spell upon listening auditories long before the books appeared telling us how it should be done. What but individuality impelled the adventurous, self-reliant spirit to thus give voice to its emotion and its thought, and Columbus-like to brave the unexplored, while other men came afterward to tell how the success was won? So has it been in art, in literature, in science, everywhere. "Ancient Grecian art ascended by a stairway of two thousand years." The experiment comes first always. Again and again has the daring scientist, like Franklin braving the thunderbolt with his kite and hempen string, heroically taken his life in his hand before his brilliant achievement is recorded. There are heroisms of the laboratory no less than of the battlefield, and triumphs no less signal. That must be an enviable moment when the great chemist, after long waiting and patient experiment, scores his great victory and unlocks the hidden sources of comfort and enrichment to mankind. Whether in laboratory, or on the verge of yawning crevasse or Alpine glacier, it is individuality that dares.

Picture to yourself that voyage of Columbus over the unknown deep, and endeavour, if you can, to enter into his feelings as the strange seaweeds at length came floating by, and the birds of brilliant plumage were seen flitting around the ship, while the growing sultriness of atmosphere unmistakably betokened the approaching land. " What a moment was that when the first projector of an eclipse saw at length his daring prophecy realized, or when the great law of gravitation first revealed itself to Newton !" Is it easy, think you, for one to realize the impressions with which Leverrier " received back from Berlin the tidings that the predicted planet was found ; " or the feelings with which Copernicus upon his dying bed received the first printed copy of his immortal work? " He knows that in that volume he has rebelled against the sway of Ptolemy, which the scientific world had acknowledged for a thousand years......He knows that the world will be shocked by his innovations upon the popular philosophies ; but he knows that his book is true. He is dying, but he leaves a glorious truth as his dying bequest to the world." That was another such " moment," when that " great Columbus of the heavens," Galileo, first raised his newly constructed telescope to the skies, and saw fulfilled the grand prophecy of Copernicus as he beheld the planet Venus " crescent like the moon." Cannot one almost hear, through the wondrous silence of that starry night, a voice saying to his inmost soul, " O Galileo, no mortal has passed this way hitherto !"

" It is easy enough for sugar to be sweet and for nitre to be salt," and it has been justly observed that to think is the highest exercise of the mind ; to say what you think, the boldest effort of moral courage. But no man can express with spirit and vigour any thoughts but his own. This was the secret of Rousseau's eloquence. The principal of the Jesuits' College one day asked him by what art he had been able to write so well. " I said what I thought," was the terse reply. It would be well, doubtless, if men oftener had the courage to do this. In a recent number of London *Truth*, Labouchère strikes a blow at conventional art criticism. There are "Sir Joshuas," and "Lawrences," and "Romneys," and "Gainsboroughs," he says; "some are good, others are bad. There are landscapes by Poussin and others. What is their excellence? I am sure that I do not know." If people would only be sincere, he adds, ninety-nine out of a hundred would admit that they do not know.

One must learn to think for, and believe in, himself. He will find at every turn friends and relatives only too ready to volunteer advice, and urge him strenuously to the pursuit of this course, or that, or the other; but after adopting this or that course of life so zealously urged upon him, he will discover that these very friends have either mysteriously disappeared, or, if not indifferent, are utterly powerless to help him in the event of his defeat. Nay, rather let a young man fix firmly in his mind the conviction that no other man is either able or willing to help him. Let him consult his own adaptations, and follow the leadings of his own nature. Having found wherein his greatest strength lies, and the direction in which he is convinced, therefore, his greatest success must also lie, let him follow tenaciously the course thus deliberately marked out for himself. Let him hold inflexibly to this choice, and allow nothing to divert him from it. Even if he fail, he will then at least have the satisfaction of knowing that it is chargeable to his own account, and not, as is too often the case, to the folly of heeding the superficial and ill-considered advice of other people. Rest assured, however, in this course, instead of failure, the chances all point the other way.

In Sherman's remarkable letter to Grant, to which reference has elsewhere been made in this volume, occurs this notable sentence: "You are now Washington's legitimate successor, and occupy a position of almost dangerous elevation; but if you can continue as heretofore, *to be yourself,* simple, honest, and unpretending, you will enjoy through life the respect and love of friends and the homage of

millions of human beings." Who has not known certain
men of strong originality who always seemed to do naturally,
and as if by instinct, exactly what should be done, and in its
exact time and place,—that happy accomplishment which
others attain to only as the result of much experience, and
after prolonged and laborious effort? Quintilian mentions
one of this sort, who, being asked what rhetorical figure and
what thought are, replied : " I do not know ; but if they
have any relation to my subject, they will be found in my
declamation." These men are a law unto themselves. They
instinctively follow laws and rules without knowing it.
Bonaparte was one of them—men who spring at a bound to
a full and complete development without toiling through
the intermediate stages of learning, experience, and progress.
It has been justly said of Bonaparte, that in all things,
except, indeed, the possession of unlimited power,—for up
to that time he was not independent of the Directory,—he
was the same man at the beginning of his campaigns in
Italy as he was at the peace of Tilsit. " From the moment
of his crossing the Alps he had nothing to learn in the
art of war." Notwithstanding all his great determinations
were his own, Grant was never averse to availing himself
of the ideas of others, says Badeau ; "and as I must always
repeat," he adds, " no man ever learned the lesson of experience quicker or applied it more absolutely. But the
suggestions of others were simply presented, and either
accepted or rejected, as his judgment dictated ; he was
never persuaded. And if he took up an idea that he found,
it was so developed by his own mind that it became as
original in reality as if he had conceived the germ. Every
one who might be called an associate felt this. Sherman
resented the ascription to himself of the origin of the Vicksburg campaign, and has often told the story of his objection
to the movement with loyal and splendid magnanimity."
Men of this stamp, too, are shrewd and far-seeing, and

know their opportunity. They are full of enterprise and daring; and seem instinctively, also, to know their public. Depressed markets make little difference to them. In the midst of the worst depressions of trade one of these men will set his wits to work and invent something which every-- body feels he must have, even from motives of economy; and thus a demand is created, which, while it helps other people to save their money, enables him to *make* his at a very rapid rate. His duller companions look on in wonder and envy at the apparent ease with which the whole trans- action was accomplished and the fortune made which lay so nearly within their own grasp, and which they might have captured so easily had their faculties but been keen enough to see their opportunity. The fact is, the sicker the patient the greater the demand for certain remedies, if only the patient can be made to feel that the remedy will effect a cure, or even administer to his comfort, if you please. Thus, persons are often willing to pay a good round sum even for the sake of sympathy or simple cheer. And certain men have the sagacity to perceive this. As we have said, they know their public. Thus in the midst of the depressions of trade and the dulness of a hard winter Twain visits Washington, gives two of his characteristic readings, and departs a thousand dollars richer for his work. When Verdi was putting the finishing touches to "Il Trovatore," he was visited in his study by a privileged friend for whose opinion as critic he had the highest re- spect. He showed him his score, and played for him the "Anvil Chorus" on the piano. "What do you think of it?" said Verdi. "Trash," cried the connoisseur. Verdi rubbed his hands and chuckled. "And of this, and this?" he continued, playing. "Rubbish!" replied the candid friend. The composer arose and embraced his friend with a burst of joy. "What do you mean by this?" was asked, in natural astonishment. "My dear friend," responded

Verdi, " I have been composing a popular opera. In it I determined to please everybody except the great judges and classicists like you. Had I pleased you, I should have pleased no one else; but your disdain assures me of success. In three months ' Il Trovatore ' will be sung, roared, whistled, and barrel-organed all over Italy." Who doubts that Verdi understood his world? True, such power is rare, but men are willing to pay for rare things. Thus it happens that while platitudes and commonplace go a-begging, individuality, as we have said, finds a ready market even in the dullest times. It is surely worth something to have wares that possess, under all circumstances, a marketable value and steady demand. Who fails to see the significance of this factor in reckoning on success?

One of the most distinguished and vigorous writers of the day, himself a conspicuous instance of individuality, has declared : " Individual effort is, after all, the grand thing. A man alone can do more than a man with fifty men at his heels to fetter him. Committees are seldom of much use, and bodies and societies are sometimes a loss of strength instead of a gain. As some one has facetiously said, if Noah's ark had had to be built by a company, the keel would not have been laid yet." There is much truth in the old adage, that what is everybody's business is nobody's. Kingsley has strongly emphasized the essential nakedness of even the most favoured souls. Alone, he says, we must make our most important decisions in life, and alone we must go to the grave. The Germans call one of their greatest authors " The only," because they find none with whom to compare him. In one sense, and that a true one, the humblest man or woman may be called by the same title. When a great strong personality does appear, note how he takes hold upon his fellows. As Brooks declares, the thought, the feeling in the central man in a great city, touches all who are in it who think and feel. The very boys, he says, catch something of his power, and

have something about them that would not be there if he
were not in the town. Now, no man can assume such a
position; it must belong to him. The moment he attempts
to play the *rôle* which belongs to another, he gets befogged.
The mere imitator is a servile slave. Like the pupils of
Plato, who are said to have imitated his crooked shoulders,
the imitator is sure to pounce upon the very faults and
defects of his model, which, blemishes as they are, are yet
tolerated for the sake of the genius of their possessor, but
which even he would be infinitely better without. Phillips
Brooks has called attention to a passage in Macaulay's diary
which he thinks is full of philosophy. "I looked through
——," he says. "He is, I see, an imitator of me; but I am
a very unsafe model. My manner is, I think, and the world
thinks, on the whole a good one; but it is very near to a very
bad manner indeed. And those clear characteristics of my
style which are the most easily copied are the most questionable." In further illustration of the same, the distinguished rector of Trinity cites an instance which came under
his own observation. "The obtuseness of the imitator is
amazing," he says. "I remember going, years ago, with an
intelligent friend to hear a great orator lecture. The discourse was rich, thoughtful, glowing, and delightful. As
we came away my companion seemed meditative. By-and-
by he said, 'Did you see where his power lay?' I felt unable to analyze and epitomize in an instant such a complex
result, and meekly I said, 'No; did you?' 'Yes,' he replied
briskly; 'I watched him, and it is in the double motion of
his hand. When he wanted to solemnize and calm and
subdue us, he turned the palm of his hand down; when he
wanted to elevate and inspire us, he turned the palm of his
hand up. That was it.' And that was all the man had
seen," he adds, "in an eloquent speech. He was no fool,
but he was an imitator. He was looking for a single secret
for a multifarious effect. I suppose he has gone on from

that day till this, turning his hand upside down and down-side up, and wondering that nobody is either solemnized or inspired."

How accustomed one is to hearing mental products of all kinds spoken of as the author's children! How suggestive to speak of Handel's Messiah, Raphael's Madonnas, Gibbon's Rome, and Hume's England! Jeffrey once said to Macaulay, "Where on earth did you pick up that English style?" But a style like Macaulay's or that of any other great master of English is not "picked up:" it is the man him-self; it is the result of the training of the special power of the individual. The romantic attraction of Macaulay's style had numbered among his eager readers hundreds of thou-sands who seldom trouble historical tomes; and as for the permanent hold his solid genius had established on the reading world, Mr. Trevelyan sums up a page of figures with the statement that "within a generation of its first appear-ance upwards of one hundred and forty thousand copies of the History will have been printed and sold in the United Kingdom alone." Dr. Johnson's advice to give one's days and nights to Addison is well known. The study of the *dii majores* is of course valuable to a man; but, after all, they can only bring out and modify and perfect the native qualities which are already his. No absolute rules can be laid down by which one can acquire a fine style. It is *nascitur, non fit.* The study of the great spirits may awaken and inspire one, however. As Charles Kingsley says: " Bathe your spirit in their noble thoughts as in May dew; and feel thereby, if but for an hour, more fair." Or, as another English writer advises: "Analyze the special beauties of great authors. Acquaint yourself with Shake-speare; study his marvellous creations, his sublime thoughts, his great and varied powers of expression. Take down your De Quincey, and learn the resources of your mother-tongue. Compare Hazlitt's clear, cool, and somewhat hard English

with the delicate grace and humour of Charles Lamb, or
with the earnestness and enthusiasm, the manly vigour, and
the tenderness no less manly, of Charles Kingsley and Dr.
John Brown. Study Macaulay. The style of these men,"
he continues, "is not the expression of the mind merely,
but of the whole character." So is it always. It rests,
therefore, in great measure with ourselves whether our
style shall be good or bad. The permanence of our work
is almost entirely dependent upon the quality of the style.
"What we say may be very valuable, but unless we say it
as well as it can be said, a day will come when some one
else will say it better, and our work will be superseded."

This quality is the secret of that charm which our favourite
authors have for us. "I would prefer to think like Emerson, but to write like Holmes," was the response of a distinguished divine, when asked which of the two famous
authors' styles he would wish to have. There is a certain
individuality about every man's style, as about his features.
It has been truly observed that if an author has not been a
slave to others, his production will be as individual as himself. As his constitutional looks and organism differ from
those of all others, so will the construction and appearance
of his mental product differ also. The deportment or air of
the parent shows itself in the literary no less than in the
literal child. The style of Burke, for instance, differs vastly
from that of Johnson. And yet, who would willingly lose
either? In Burke, some one has said, we see the manly
movement of a well-bred gentleman; in Johnson, an equally
profound and vigorous thinker, the measured march of a
grenadier. "We forgive the great moralist his stiff and
cumbrous phrases in return for the rich stores of thought
and poetry which they conceal; but we admire in Burke, as
in a fine antique statue, the grace with which the large
flowing robe adapts itself to the majestic dignity of the
person." The individuality of the producer inevitably

appears in the production. A few notes heard, a few pencil-strokes seen, a few sentences read, quickly betray the composer, artist, or author.

> "Where'er the ocean inlet strays,
> The salt sea wave its source betrays ;
> Where'er the queen of summer blows,
> She tells the zephyr, ' I'm the rose!'"

The line of Apelles is not to be mistaken. Who, for instance, does not instantly recognize one of Boughton's pictures? Some subtle felicity of treatment or composition often reveals the identity of the artist and the special characteristic of his genius, or of his technical methods, which are unmistakable. "There would seem at first sight," says Macaulay, "to be no more in Milton's words than in other words. But they are words of enchantment. No sooner are they pronounced than the past is present and the distant near. New forms of beauty start at once into existence, and all the burial-places of the memory give up their dead. Change the structure of the sentence, substitute one synonym for another, and the whole effect is destroyed." Matthew Arnold bears witness to what we have just been saying, in a recent article concerning America. He refers to an "admirable essay of Sir Henry Maine," which, though not signed, "betrays him for its author," he says, "by its rare and characteristic qualities of mind and style."

We have already remarked that no one can assume the position of another. By this we would not be understood to mean that one must not study another, or the methods of others. The most individual of men have been the most familiar with the methods of other men. Webster, we are told, was able to recite from memory half the orations of Cicero ; and it has been asserted of Michael Angelo, the most original of modern artists, that he knew every statue and painting, and the excellency of every statue and painting, in

the world, of any master, past or present.  Other minds are
to native genius but so much nature, one among the many
ingredients in the common soil from which by its own elect-
ive chemistry it draws its life.  " Artists all over the world
go to Dresden and Florence and Rome to study the works
of other artists, and still they retain their originality.  The
artists of America collect their works annually in the Academy of Design in New York, and are themselves the most
frequent visitors, that they may comprehend the works and
methods of one another, and in some degree take to themselves the gifts of all."

   " People are always talking about originality," says
Goethe ; " but what do they mean ?  As soon as we are
born, the world begins to work upon us ; and this goes on to
the end.  And after all, what can we call our own, except
energy, strength, and will ?  If I could give an account of
all that I owe to great predecessors and contemporaries, there
would be but a small balance in my favour."  A most able
and vigorous modern thinker has declared that one who
cannot use the experience of others, and preserve at the same
time his own originality, misses a vantage that is hard to
over-estimate.  Newton was great, he says, not near so much
because of what he discovered as because of his ability to
bring together and combine all that others had observed.
" The original discoveries of Newton would have been an
impossibility to him had he not first comprehended what
others had wrought......In the power to digest and assimilate
the experience of others is the great difference between men.
The experience of a thousand men becomes the experience of
one man, and that one rises head and shoulders above his
fellows.  We do not abate one jot of our originality in learning from others.  To see a truth is to own it.  Where or
how originated, a thought is ours when we understand it.
The right of discovery has no validity in the domain of truth.
Bread and meat are ours when they turn to bone and muscle

in us. As has been said, no man eats veal and becomes a calf, or mutton and becomes a sheep. The individuality of every man's body is assured by the laws of digestion and assimilation, but not more so than is the individuality of the mind by corresponding laws. The great Swedish mystic uttered the most sublime of uninspired truths when he said, "The more angels the more room. True men are never crowded and never crowd. The healthy mind sees the truth, embraces, absorbs it, and forgets to think about him who uttered it." He further assures us that the world's progress is in its accumulations, and mentions the saying of Emerson, that nearly half the lines in Shakespeare's dramas are borrowed in whole or in part from the writings of others, but were so mastered by him that Shakespeare's originality was unquestioned. "Doubtless what we call Homer is a combination of the best in all poets that lived before him in Greece. Through him the streams flowed and became one, and were known ever after by the name of him in whom they were united. Let us fear the utterance of immature, half-understood thoughts, but not the lack of originality."

Could anything be more inspiring than contact with a master-mind? Let one read a few pages of Emerson, and fascinating as the author seems, and strong as the temptation is to go on with one's reading, does he not soon find rising up within him, stronger, if possible, than all else, the impulse to go out at once and do something worthy of himself ere the night shuts in? The most vigorous and powerful minds have ever acknowledged their indebtedness to others for kindling their own fires and inspiring them for their work. Byron himself, and Robertson, both confess to the habit of reading the production of some vigorous thinker to get their minds in working trim for their own intellectual tasks. Gray seldom sat down to compose without first reading through some cantos of the "Faerie Queene," it is said; and Corneille "fired himself" with the perusal of

"Lucan." One mind thus quickens another and illumines the path, and inspires us to enter; but, as has been truly said, every man who would ascend the hill of the immortals must for the most part walk alone, unaccompanied by mortal man.

The real help, then, which comes to us from great men would seem to lie in the fact that they evoke one's own life. Thus a man's mind may be roused by another, but he must "mould his own material, quarry his own nature, make his own character." And thus, too, it may happen at times, and often has, doubtless, that the pupil becomes at length even wiser indeed than his instructor. He may not always accept his conclusions, but he will own, "You awakened me to be *myself;* for that I thank you!" Wherever I find myself, either in nature or the libraries of the world, that is mine. I may find page after page dry as dust. At length I find in some brief sentence, perhaps, myself. I gladly throw aside as worthless whole pages which others might value. It is by the assimilation of all that is best around him, allowing it to enter into the very fibre of his being, and to become a part of his own life-blood, that one comes most surely to his own true individuality. Art thus becomes to him a second nature, like the polished manners of well-bred men, to which Schiller refers. True ease always comes "from art, not chance." It will often happen, doubtless, that one will find his own best thought anticipated by some former writer; but one need not be discouraged on this account. One possessed of resources of his own, and competent to think for himself, will neither, as Colton has put it, anathematize others with a *pereant qui ante nos nostra dixerint,* nor despair himself, but will rather go on, like John Hunter in physics, discovering things before discovered until, like him, he is rewarded with a *terra* hitherto *incognita,*—an empire indisputably his own, both by right of conquest and of discovery.

Holmes, in reviewing Edwin Arnold's "Light of Asia," remarked: "It is impossible for such an artist as Mr. Arnold not to remind us, whether by mere coincidence or unconscious imitation, of the great masters and the favourite authors...... These coincidences may amuse a reader, but they are of small account. All literature, we might say without unpardonable extravagance, lives by borrowing and lending. A good image is like a diamond, which may be set a hundred times in as many generations, and gain new beauties with every change."

It is curious to note how men of most marked individuality and most original methods have been perpetually influenced and swayed by some great predecessor. Each has the master in his eye. Napoleon dreamed of Julius Cæsar. Alexander the Great constantly slept with "Homer" under his pillow. The ideal hero of the Iliad helped to make the real heroes of later Greece. When Beaconsfield was asked in what style his official residence should be furnished and decorated, he said, pointing to a portrait of Sir Robert Walpole, one of the greatest and purest of England's prime ministers, "Furnish it for that portrait." What could be more beautiful than that utterance of Raphael just before he died,—"I shall see Dante"?

After all, it is but little that others can do for one, even though most willing to aid and advance him. One must early learn to depend on himself and his own unaided effort. Friends, affection, and human sympathy may accompany us to the beach, but each must set sail for himself and steer his own ship. No one can create heroism for another; it must be in himself. "We accompany the youth with sympathy and manifold old sayings of the wise to the gate of the arena," says Emerson, "but it is certain that not by strength of ours, nor by the old sayings, but only on strength of his own, unknown to us or to any, he must stand or fall." Like King Edward standing on the "little windmill hill," at the battle of Creçy, while his son, the Black Prince, was engaged in the hottest of the fray, the father can send encouraging words and admire the heroism of his son, but he cannot send him aid. He must win his own spurs.

A brave soul, moreover, is a thing that all things serve. Fearless intrepidity finds the way open as it advances.

> " The distant mountains that uprear
> Their solid bastions to the skies,
> Are crossed by pathways that appear
> As we to higher levels rise."

The great point, after all, is for one to be sure of himself. Let one assure himself, first of all, that he can do or say something which the world wants done or said, and then let him fearlessly act upon his conviction. As a recent writer has well put it in some words to would-be authors: "If you are planning to become an author, it will be wise to remember the advice of *Punch* to the young man contemplating marriage,—' Don't.' That is, don't if you can avoid it. Don't unless the pressure is so strong upon you that you can recognize yourself as really being 'called,' and that literature is to be the calling. Books must be written out of that which is in you; and if, without such calling, a man sits down and says to himself, 'Go to, let us make a book,' so surely will the end of that book and of that man —or woman — be disappointment and emptiness." The same might be said of music and painting. When a youth came to Mozart and asked him how he should begin to compose, the great man advised him to wait. "But," replied the youth, "you composed much earlier." "So I did," was the answer; "but then I asked nobody about it." The true poet wreaks his thought upon expression because he cannot help it. So with the artist. His finest conceptions will not leave him until he has revealed his thought

upon the speaking canvas. Men are thrilled with delight
as they stand before his completed work. Ah, could they
but see that which struggled for expression within the
artist's soul! Culture, training, polish,—all these are good,
but without this inner fire they are of little worth. It is the
personality behind all else which counts. It is this which
always takes the shortest road and the surest method. It
is truthful, simple, natural. True individuality will not
imitate, and cannot be imitated. There is as much difference between the genuine and its counterfeit as between
"the reverberation of thunder in an Alpine valley and the
tin-rattle of the theatre." "Through every clause and part
of speech of a right book I meet the eyes of the most
determined of men," says Emerson. "His force and terror
inundate every word ; the commas and dashes are all alive,
so that the writing is athletic and nimble, and can go far
and live long......It makes a great difference to the force of
any sentence whether there be a man behind it or no." It
is well known that certain famous actors and singers have
been made great simply by what is termed the "sympathetic"
voice. It was this that made Rubini so famous, and which
gave Gazzaniga the ability to sing "through your very
heart."

Garrick's individuality revolutionized the whole dramatic
stage. Men might condemn and criticise, but his perpetual
and unvarying success was their answer. And what was
his secret? He was true to nature,—true to himself. Mrs.
Clive was one night standing at the wing, alternately weeping and scolding at Garrick's acting ; and turning away in
anger, she exclaimed, "I believe he could act a gridiron!"
In King Lear, it used to be said that Garrick's very stick
acted. When Dr. Johnson was asked his opinion of the
reputation attained by this wonderful interpreter of Shakespeare, he replied, "Oh, sir, he deserves everything he has
acquired, for having seized the soul of Shakespeare, for

having embodied it in himself, and for having expanded its
glory over the world." Of Massena, Napoleon declared,
" He is not himself until the battle begins to go against
him ; then, when the dead fall in ranks about him, are
awakened his powers of combination, and he puts on terror
and victory as a robe." And Wellington once said of him,
"I do not know which was the best of the French marshals,
but I know that I always found Massena where I least
desired that he should be."

This power of individuality is often strikingly manifest in
great parliamentary leaders. It was pre-eminent. in Henry
Clay. "It would perhaps be impossible to find in the parliamentary annals of the world," says one whose own learning and large experience in public life give great weight to
his opinion, "a parallel to Mr. Clay in 1841, when at sixty-
four years of age he took the control of the Whig party
from the President who had received their suffrages, against
the power of Webster in the Cabinet, against the eloquence
of Choate in the Senate, against the herculean efforts of
Caleb Cushing and Henry A. Wise in the House. In un-
shared leadership, in the pride and plenitude of power, he
hurled against John Tyler, with deepest scorn, the mass of
that conquering column which had swept over the land in
1840, and drove his administration to seek shelter behind
the lines of his political foes." This strong personality,
as the same authority has shown, conquers often, both
against the right and the "heavy battalions;" as when
young Charles Fox, in the days of his Toryism, carried the
House of Commons "against justice, against its immemorial
rights, against his own convictions,—if indeed at that period
Fox had convictions,—and in the interest of a corrupt administration, in obedience to a tyrannical sovereign, drove
Wilkes from the seat to which the electors of Middlesex
had chosen him, and installed Luttrell in defiance, not merely
of law, but of public decency."

It was not adventitious circumstance that gave Secretary Chase his wonderful power over the financial destiny of the country in its hour of peril; it was the power of individuality and sheer moral courage. He had faith in the people. He dared to trust them. He did trust them. "When every other face was clouded, he stood in the sun. The people met him with an equal courage, and freely gave him all the money he wanted." Such power is the attribute of a commanding personality alone. This magnetism makes acts and words efficient, because courage and confidence are contagious.

" Each petty hand can steer a ship becalmed :
But he that will govern and carry her to her ends,
Must know his tides, his currents ;
How to shift her sails ; what she will bear in foul,
What in fair weathers ; what her springs are,
Her leaks, and how to stop them ; what strands,
What rocks do threaten her ;
The forces and the natures of all winds, gusts, storms, and tempests.
When her keel ploughs hell, and deck knocks heaven,
Then to manage her becomes the name and office of a pilot."

It has doubtless been noted by the observant reader that reference has repeatedly been made in these pages to the first Napoleon, and his life and character have been held up as illustrating in a striking manner many of those qualities which seem so essential to success. This has been done not blindly but advisedly, and after the most careful study of the man. While the author is not unmindful of the fact that many serious faults and blemishes serve to mar the symmetry of his character, and while the "fierce light which beats upon" his household relations in such works as the "Memoirs of Madame de Rémusat" must necessarily reveal many faults and foibles and much that is unlovely,— yet, with due allowance for these failings, he still believes that the instances are extremely rare in which are combined in any one man so many striking and admirable qualities,

and so many of those traits which inevitably command
success. No life, surely, will better repay careful and dis-
criminating study. Said an eminent man of middle age not
long since, "If I had read the life of Napoleon when I was
a boy, my own life might have been very different. It
would have filled me with an ambition to make the most of
myself." Not the least among other things for which he
should be honoured is his noble and striking testimony to
the divinity of Christ ; and, as Dr. Schaff justly observes,
the logical conclusion of this master-mind may well be set
over against the illogical denial of Christ's divinity by inferior minds. One surely discerns in this life how almost
inevitably unremitting study and a careful culture of all the
faculties lead to the highest places. Indeed, the hero of
Austerlitz himself realized that his greatest triumphs were
not those of his battle-fields. " I shall go down to posterity,"
said he, "with my Code in my hand." No one quality in
him, probably, was more striking than his marvellous individuality. Before this man imbecile kings, effete mon-
archies, shams of all kinds, went down. Thrones crumbled,
and royalty waited in his ante-chamber to know the will of
this master. One who had frequently seen him at St.
Helena relates that on one occasion, when Napoleon with
his suite galloped through the British camp on Deadwood,
the soldiers involuntarily and without orders fell into ranks
and saluted him. The orders given by the English Government were very explicit that Napoleon should not be recognized as *emperor*, but simply as *general.* When the emperor
was informed of this decree, he simply remarked, "They
may call me what they please ; they cannot prevent me from
being myself." Even Wellington thought his presence sub-
stantially equal to forty thousand men added to the strength
of an army. In Napier's opinion he was "the greatest
genius and the greatest soldier that ever lived." Wellington
himself once declared, "Napoleon was a very great man."

And upon another occasion, "It is no impulse of vanity which leads me to speak so highly of my opponent; for it was not I who beat him, but the determined bravery of the English troops and their unconquerable steadiness."

The Allies, despite their enormous preponderance of forces, would willingly shrink from meeting Napoleon in person. They hardly ventured on any movement where he was present except in overwhelming masses. When in 1814 he came to Châlons to withstand the flood of invasion, his generals hoped he was being followed by supports of troops. He coolly told them "No," and proceeded to encourage them by unfolding the boldness and profundity of his plans. But "the resistless might of Europe was setting in upon him, and even he could not achieve miracles." Men may ask,—

> " Upon what meat doth this our Cæsar feed,
> That he is grown so great?"

But the real secret lay far behind all, in the great personality, the intense individuality of the man. See the courage this confers as he fearlessly visits the stricken soldiers dying of the plague in the hospitals. Says Goethe: " Napoleon visited those sick of the plague, in order to prove that the man who could vanquish fear could vanquish the plague also; and he was right. 'Tis incredible what force the will has in such cases : it penetrates the body and puts it in a state of activity which repels all hurtful influences, while fear invites them." That there was no mere fustian about this man let Emerson's words testify. " We cannot," he says, "in the universal imbecility, indecision, and indolence of men, sufficiently congratulate ourselves on this strong and ready actor, who took occasion by the beard, and showed us how much may be accomplished by the mere force of such virtues as all men possess in less degree—namely, by punctuality, by personal attention, by courage, and thoroughness......His power does not consist in any wild, extravagant force—in any enthusiasm like Mahomet's, or singular power of persuasion; but in the exercise of common sense on each emergency, instead of abiding by rules and customs. The lesson he teaches is that which vigour always teaches—that there is always room for it. To what heaps of cowardly doubts is not that man's life an answer!"

Who has not been impressed with the power of this great quality to dwarf all its surroundings, however stately or grand? How the mere splendour of the most massive archi-tecture, for instance, fades before the greater splendour of a great orator's personality! All surroundings dwindle and become simply satellites of the central sun. It is curious, too, to note how men differ in this regard. As Père Arrius wittily declared, "When Bourdaloue preached at Rouen, the tradesmen all left their shops, the smiths their forges, and the physicians their sick, and flocked to hear the silver-tongued orator. But," he added, "when I preached there the following year, I set everything to rights again. Every man minded his own business."

How, too, this quality perpetually brightens our homes with its thousand artistic surprises and devices that fill us with ever renewed wonder and delight. What a charm it imparts to maidenhood! Though its piquant caprices may sometimes laugh to scorn the conventionalities, in spite of ourselves we are obliged to admire—indeed, we cannot help it; for innocence and charming originality are always allowed.

"Persons approach us," remarks a shrewd observer, "fa-mous for their beauty, for their accomplishments, worthy of all wonder for their charms and gifts; they dedicate their own skill to the hour and the company with very imperfect result......Then, when all is done, a person of related mind, a brother or sister by nature, comes to us so softly and easily, so nearly and intimately, as if it were the blood in our proper veins......We are utterly relieved and refreshed."

Hawthorne, in his "Scarlet Letter," touches a similar vein where he refers to that "mightier touch" of one coming after, awakening all the sensibilities and revealing the contrast between "the marble image of happiness and the warm reality." As with metals, so with men. The magnet has something to give; the steel is made to receive. Some men, it has been observed, have a penetrating and distributive personality that is felt as surely and swiftly as is the pungency of gums or the heat of fire; and others are made to be as responsive to them as clay. The indefinite word, in short, which comprehends all that draws and holds men is called "magnetism." We despair of getting a clear and full analysis of this subtile power; but it is enough, perhaps, that we know it when it exists, and are able to develop it where it is found. A visitor to Carlyle, who sought the great modern seer with much reverence, complained afterwards that "his presence, in some unaccountable manner, rasped the nerves. You left him feeling as if you had drunk sour wine or had had an attack of sea-sickness." Some one, on the other hand, describes the entrance of Dickens into a room as "the sudden kindling of a big fire, by which every one was warmed." The rare charm of Lord Houghton's social nature made itself everywhere felt, we are told. One whose tastes, by the way, were widely different, declared, "Whenever Milnes comes into a room everybody is in better humour with everybody else." As a recent authority has affirmed, this power is worth study by young people beginning life; for though intangible and almost indescribable, it is the strongest power which a man or a woman can possess.

The self-consciousness of greatness is one of its most singular and interesting characteristics. Never, says Legouvé, amid the fiercest agony, whether mental or physical, does a great artist lose self-consciousness; he is an eternal spectacle unto himself; great as may be his despair, he watches it with argus eyes. Rachel felt her own elegance as she posed for a young invalid; she seemed to herself a beautiful statue of Grief.

To sum up the whole matter, then, let us say: Dare to be yourself. Learn to think and act for yourself. Believe your own thought. To believe that what is true for you in your private heart is true for all men—that is genius, says Emerson. "Speak your latent conviction, and it shall be the universal sense. Take the place and attitude which belong to you, and all men acquiesce." Lay everything under tribute. Let all your studies, your observation, and experience contribute to develop only the more truly your real self, your true individuality. Aim ever to find yourself that which belongs to you in whatever direction, whether earth or sea or sky. All roads lead to Rome. Let all the roads you travel serve to bring you only the more surely to your distinct and true personality. In this way you shall arrive at that true independence which alone is of value. Richard Wagner, the composer, writing of himself, says: "My course of study under Weinlig was finished in less than half a year. He himself dismissed me from my apprenticeship, after having conducted me so far that I could solve the most difficult exercises in counterpoint with ease. 'That which you have gained through this dry study is called *independence*,' he said to me." And independence in thought and deed was ever one of Wagner's most striking and noble characteristics.

The little mind is timid and full of compliances, and must needs go with the crowd. The great soul dares to stand apart, and is "never less alone than when alone." Nothing, surely, is more remarkable than the appearance and achievements of gifted men. What trails of light or darkness have certain men left behind them! Blot out the names of the few great ones who have left their impress on the ages, and history would be a very tame affair. It was said of the first

Emperor Alexander of Russia, that his personal character was equivalent to a constitution; and of Montaigne, that his was worth more to him than a regiment of horse. "A man Cæsar is born, and for ages after we have a Roman empire." One Waterloo "changed the front of the world." The works of Raphael and Michael Angelo, the creations of Beethoven and Mozart, of Handel and the great masters, exercise for ever their magic spell, and leave humanity their debtors. The heroes of the race shrank doubtless from their work, as you are shrinking now from yours—from a sense of unfitness. At length, unable longer to resist the call of duty, "each forgot his weakness, and went and worked his fragment." So for each of us the duty waits. Our deed may not seem worth the doing, because so small. But it is our "fragment," and must be done; and no one else can do it for us. Let not life, then, be frittered away in vacillation and weak compliances, "like those meagre streamlets which seem to lose their way at every new impediment, for ever turning backward or creeping around; nor, on the other hand, emulate the headlong mountain torrent, boisterous and destructive." Let the ideal of your strength be rather that of the ocean, which, as one finely observes, in the calmest hour still heaves its resistless might of waters to the shore with an imperial consciousness of strength that laughs at opposition.

> "Practise thy spirit to great thoughts and things;......
> We can foretell the future of ourselves,
> And fateful only to himself is each."

# III.

## Application.

" It is not ease, but effort—not faculty, but difficulty, that makes men."

That cocoa-nut grove will not flourish which does not daily hear the steps of its owner in it.—HINDU SAYING.

> There is a fire-fly in the southern clime
> Which shineth only when upon the wing:
> So is it with the mind,—
> When once we rest, we darken.—BAILEY, *Festus.*

Seest thou a man diligent in his business? he shall stand before kings.—PROVERBS xxii. 29.

THERE is no concealing the fact that a very foolish notion is widely prevalent among young men respecting the dignity and value of work. The idea that the necessity for application is incompatible with the possession of great qualities, that the virtues of diligence and industry, forsooth, are inconsistent with great natural gifts, or some such foolish notion, has defeated many a man in the race of life, and done incalculable harm. The careful observer will not be long in discovering a certain class of men who have come to believe that if one is a " born genius " he will do great things anyway, and therefore there exists small need for exertion. The favourite idea of a genius, among these, appears to be that of one who never studies, or who studies nobody can tell when, and now and then strikes out at a heat, as the phrase is, some wonderful production. The notion seems to be that success is to be conquered by a sudden leap. " A masterly magazine article, a picture dashed off in fiery haste, some speech, or deed, or stroke of business ability, will certainly ere long, unless they are greatly mistaken, set the tongue of the town wagging, and carry them straight up the heights."

This "genius" is a character, as Dewey has justly observed, that has figured largely in the history of our literature, in the person of our Fieldings, our Savages, and our Steeles,—loose fellows about town, or loungers in the country, who slept in alehouses and wrote in bar-rooms, who took up the pen as a magician's wand to supply their wants, and when the pressure of necessity was relieved, resorted again to their carousals. Your real genius is an idle, irregular, vagabond sort of person, who muses in the fields or dreams by the fireside ; whose strong impulses—that is the cant of it—must needs hurry him into wild irregularities or foolish eccentricities; who abhors order, and can bear no restraint, and eschews all labour. This seems to be the favourite idea. What could be more absurd? And yet, " 'tis true, 'tis pity," so large is the number that complacently regard themselves as belonging to this class, that the consequences have been exceedingly disastrous. It must be admitted that certain brilliant fellows have at times lent colour to this conception, and, intoxicated for the time being with the homage of wondering companions, have no doubt willingly fostered the idea that their brilliancy was due to the sudden inspiration of the moment ; but the cunning deception has not always been proof against the prying curiosity of human nature, and the unmasking of carefully curtained windows and concealed lights has revealed these same geniuses tugging away, as if for dear life, far into the night even, at the very tasks which their less gifted companions were toiling over in the ordinary way. Even Sheridan's seemingly spontaneous and impromptu witticisms, as every one knows, were discovered to have been most carefully prepared beforehand,—all of which goes to prove that things are not always what they seem. Depend upon it, the most effective genius is the genius of hard work. Work, work, work, is the secret of all great achievement and distinguished success. We commend to those who are waiting for that happy moment of inspiration, that old story of the two men who set out together to reach a certain point. One trudged on steadily and securely afoot; the other, like Icarus, made himself wings and flew a furlong, when the sun melted the wax, and he came to grief. There are so many painters of one picture, writers of one novel, down there in the mud with him, some one significantly says. When Giardini was asked how long it would take to learn to play on the violin, he replied, " Twelve hours a day for twenty years together." If a man has failed, said a brave painter, you will find he has dreamed instead of working. There is no way to success in our art but to take off your coat, grind paint, and work like a digger on the railroad all day, and every day. The author of "Telemachus" was right when he sought to impress upon his pupil the fact that there was no royal road to learning, and that even the grace of God would not make a man a scholar. A man may be " superficially omniscient," as Charles Lamb expressed it, without much hard effort ; but there is but one pathway to thorough knowledge,—the republican one of labour and toil. What enabled William Pitt, when scarcely more than a boy in years, to command universal attention to his first speech in the House of Commons, and to extort from Burke the encomium, " He is not a chip from the old block, but the old block itself "? Such success is no accident ; it is the well-earned reward of many years of laborious and complete preparation. "That was a great moment when the king sent for Pitt as the only man who could make head against Fox, and resolved to govern through his means. The youngster accepted the post of

Premier. Without one moment's faltering he responded to the call. On the afternoon of the very same day on which that call was made, young Pepper Arden rose in his place and moved for a new writ for the borough of Appleby in the room of the Right Honourable William Pitt, who since his election has accepted the office of First Lord of the Treasury and Chancellor of the Exchequer. There was immediately a burst of loud and general laughter." It was not altogether unlike the moment when Disraeli sat down amid the derision of the House, saying the time would come when they would hear him. " Nevertheless, Pitt formed his cabinet, his majority increased, the influence of Fox declined, and at the age of twenty-four this heaven-born minister of state commenced his long dictatorship."

It may be a very good thing for a boy to have great natural talent, as has been well observed ; to be noted among his acquaintances as a very smart boy,—one who is sure to make his mark in the world. But it is still a very dangerous thing ; for it is a little curious that one seldom in after-life hears of these remarkable boys. They generally sink into very commonplace people, after all. Too often they are spoiled by injudicious flattery in early life. No boy, however talented, whose working power is not well trained, will ever accomplish much. In whatever line that work may be, he must apply himself to it with an intense purpose, —a tireless industry. It is astonishing what can be accomplished by constant repetition, and how easy this repeti-. tion makes any task. " Know thy work, and do it," says Carlyle, " and work at it like a Hercules. One monster there is in the world,—an idle man." How many are the men, for instance, who have accomplished anything memorable in the execution or creation of musical ideas, and established their pre-eminence in the musical world in any other way than by hard work? Students must rid themselves, observes a writer in one of our musical journals, of

the notion that talent is everything. Talent is nothing
unless joined with earnest and well-directed endeavour. A
German pianist, he tells us, during the first few years of his
course devoted thirteen hours every day to study.

What right, indeed, has any man to suppose himself
exempted from the old law of labour? "Limæ labor et
mora," as Horace says, are essential to all real success.
"Young gentlemen, remember that nothing can stand days'
works," said President Wayland. Of this almost omnipotent influence of simple, tireless industry, Sir Joshua
Reynolds has borne witness. He is one of the first men of
genius, says Horner, who has condescended to inform the
world of the steps by which greatness is attained. "The
confidence with which he asserts the omnipotence of human
labour has the effect of familiarizing his reader with the
idea that genius is an acquisition rather than a gift; while
withal there is blended so naturally and eloquently the most
elevated and passionate admiration of excellence that upon
the whole there is no book of a more inflammatory effect."
Some of the striking utterances of Reynolds in this direction
are well known. "Whoever is resolved to excel in painting," he says, "or, indeed, in any other art, must bring all
his mind to bear upon that one object from the moment
that he rises till he goes to bed." At another time he said :
"Those who are resolved to excel must go to their work,
willing or unwilling, morning, noon, and night ; they will
find it no play, but very hard labour." Like Reynolds,
Michael Angelo was a great worker, and so was Titian.
One of the latter's great works was eight years in hand, and
another seven. It has been truly observed that few realize
the amount of patient labour and long training involved in
the great works of the masters. They seem easy of accomplishment; but the arduous toil with which this ease has
been acquired is frequently lost sight of. "You charge me
fifty sequins," said the Venetian nobleman to the sculptor,

"for a bust that cost you only ten days' labour." " You forget," said the artist, "that I have been thirty years learning to make that bust in ten days."

A habit of application, one might safely say, is really of as much importance to almost any great man as is his genius. Not that any amount of application, as has been justly observed, can make a dull man brilliant ; but that without steady application a brilliant man might almost as well be dull, as far as anything that he is likely to accomplish is concerned. Indeed, some have even gone so far as to declare that perseverance is genius ; but this is hardly true. It may well be called, however, "the right hand of genius." That successful young real-estate broker seems to be marvellously fortunate. Every move he makes is a lucky one. With the utmost apparent ease he moves from one successful transaction to another. There is no fuss, no hurry, no demonstration, nothing done for effect ; yet his fine commissions continue to come rolling in, and men eager to secure his services wait their turn, as one after another is ushered into his private office. All this, to the superficial observer, seems very enviable, surely, and a vastly easy thing to do. But not all are aware that that genial and affable young broker has so thoroughly mastered his business that he has his hand continually on the pulse of the whole city ; that not a new street has been opened, that, indeed, there has been not one important transaction in real estate, not a single piece of property has enhanced in value, for many months, that has escaped his notice. That, added to a profound insight into human nature, and a knowledge of men, is a mastery of details, and a memory of facts, that would astonish an indolent man. Occasionally a transaction requiring apparently but a few hours' time rewards him with a handsome commission of thousands. Men observing only the brilliant result accomplished in so short a time exclaim, " A lucky fellow !" There was nothing lucky

about it. Behind that transaction was the generalship
that enabled him to manage men ; behind it, too, was the
sterling common sense and sound judgment that give men
confidence in each other ; and added to all this was a
certain keen sagacity, a shrewd observation which enabled
him to know when to move and when to wait, and an application to details which placed within his grasp every fact
having in any wise an important bearing on the transaction,
from beginning to end. Thus, while his rivals were slowly
making up their minds, he had already closed the bargain.
You may say it was a stroke of genius. It was rather
genius and application combined. This it was which enabled
him successfully to make head against the bright and eager
fellows who were watching for the chance. The same is
true elsewhere. That rising young architect at whose quiet
bidding appeared those elegant houses and magnificent public
buildings which seem at once a marvel of strength and
a dream of beauty, as he so readily and easily suggests to
you this or that tasteful design for your new dwelling, is
not simply giving you the cursory suggestions which have
come to him with the passing moment. Behind those ideas
which impress you as so fitting and beautiful is a knowledge
of all the architecture of all the periods, past and present.
That man is familiar with the work and methods of every
architect of note, and with every order of architecture from
the beginning down. And this power, we affirm, comes
from application.

Cæsar, a master in the art of speaking, as in many other
things, attained the position, Cicero tells us, by studious
application to the most intricate and refined branch of literature, and by careful and constant attention to the purity
of his style. And even the obstacles surmounted by Cicero
himself might well have daunted one not cast in heroic
mould. When in early years advised to give up public
speaking on account of the critical condition of his health,

" I resolved," he says, " to run any hazard rather than quit
the hopes of glory which I had proposed to myself from
pleading." That chapter from his life in which he gives us
an account of the pains and labour undertaken to improve
his natural abilities in this direction is full of encouragement
and vastly entertaining.

As every one knows, Clay and Choate and Everett all
subjected themselves to the most laborious training. Even
that most brilliant effort perhaps of Mr. Webster's whole
life, his famous reply to Hayne, was, as we now know, all
carefully prepared beforehand, though seemingly at the time
impromptu. " I was riding with him," says his friend
Harvey, " one morning in 1846 or 1847, to attend a cattle-
fair at Dedham, when the conversation turned on different
ways of preparing speeches. He said that no man who was
not inspired could make a good speech without preparation ;
that if there were any of that sort of people, he had never
met them. He added that it had often been remarked that
he had made no preparation for the Hayne speech. 'That
was not quite so,' said he. ' If it was meant that I took
notes, and studied, with a view to a reply, that was not
true ; but that I was thoroughly conversant with the subject
of debate from having made preparation for a totally different purpose than that speech, is true. The preparation
for my reply to Hayne was made upon the occasion of Mr.
Foote's resolution to sell the public lands. Some years
before that, a senator from Alabama introduced a resolution
into the Senate proposing to cede the public domains to the
State in which they were situated. It struck me at that
time as being so unfair and improper that I immediately
prepared an article to resist it. My argument embraced the
whole history of the public lands and the Government's
action in regard to them. Then there was another question
involved in the Hayne debate. It was as to the right and
practice of petition. Mr. Calhoun denied the right of

petition on the subject of slavery. Calhoun's doctrine seemed to be accepted, and I made preparation to answer his proposition. It so happened that the debate did not take place, because the matter never was pressed. I had my notes tucked away in a pigeon-hole, and when Hayne made that attack upon me, and upon New England, I was already posted, and only had to take down my notes and refresh my memory. In other words,' said Mr. Webster, 'if he had tried to make a speech to fit my notes he could not have hit it better. *No man is inspired with the occasion. I never was.'*" The inspiration of a great occasion is of little value to any man, unless behind it all lies the great fact of complete and thorough preparation.

One of the most successful of the great manufacturers of fine papers in this country owes his success largely to the fact that he has been familiar with the making of fine papers from his boyhood, having practically learned every item of the business by actual experience. He is thus in every respect master of the situation in his fine establishment. He knows the materials necessary, the exact quantity and quality required, and is perfectly familiar with every detail from the moment the crude ingredients enter the works, to the moment when the completed product, in beautiful sheets, rolls from the great "Fourdrinier," or leaves the calenders. That he should be defrauded, or imposed upon with impunity, is therefore out of the question. The moment he enters the establishment, be it night or day, he seizes a sheet of the paper, rapidly inspects and tears it. This test, under the eye of the master, is conclusive of all the rest. If fault or imperfection be discovered here—if it cannot pass this ordeal —some one is forthwith called to account. Who will say that the application which confers such mastery as this is of no moment? Old Captain Fox used to say that in his opinion the midshipmen at the Naval Academy ought to begin as coal-heavers,—at the very bottom of the ladder, and then work their way up. As it is, every one knows that no line officer ever comes to the command of a ship "through the cabin window." As a midshipman he must "learn all the ropes," and make himself perfectly familiar with every detail concerning a man-of-war, and the way to manage her in weather fair or foul. He is obliged to climb shrouds and to man yards, to set and furl sail in winter's storm and sleet as well as summer's calm. Thus he becomes the master. And thus, though in after-years he may not have this work to do, he thoroughly understands how it should be done, and the sailors know it too. There must be no risk of blunders in command to provoke the ridicule of the sailors or imperil all on board. Moreover, practised skill is ever at a premium, and commands appropriate recognition. Even the old tars pay it fitting deference. It was noticed during the naval operations of the Civil War that the old sailors obeyed with ready alacrity the orders of even young officers fresh from the Academy, while they were prone to question, if not to resent, those of the ablest volunteer officers placed in command. A certain clannishness, characteristic of old seamen, prompts them to yield a ready deference and cheerful recognition to the skill which they never hope to emulate themselves. Moreover, there is the consciousness which the trained officer has of his own superior power, which is the principal thing after all.

Few careers are fuller of inspiration or offer greater incentives to young men than that of Charles Dickens; and no one will deny that Dickens was a man of genius. But if any one imagines that this famous author relied upon his genius alone for his great successes, a study of his life will soon undeceive him. One night in London, while in the zenith of his fame, he was presiding at a meeting of the Newspaper Press Fund, and made reference to the hard work of his earlier years as follows: "I went into the gallery of the House of Commons as a parliamentary reporter when I was a boy not eighteen, and I left it—I can hardly believe the inexorable truth—nigh thirty years ago; and I have pursued the calling of a reporter under circumstances of which many of my brethren here, and my brethren's successors, can form no adequate conception. I have often transcribed for the printer from my shorthand notes important public speeches in which the strictest accuracy was required, and a mistake in which would have been, to a young man, severely compromising, writing on the palm of my hand, by the light of a dark lantern, in a post-chaise and four, galloping through a wild country, through the dead of the night, at the then surprising rate of fifteen miles an hour. The very last time I was at Exeter I strolled into the castle yard there to identify for the amusement of a friend the spot on which I once 'took' an election speech of my noble friend Lord Russell. It was in the midst of a lively fight kept up by all the vagabonds in that vicinity, and under such pelting rain that I remember two good-natured colleagues, who chanced to be at leisure, held a pocket-handkerchief over my note-book, after the manner of a state canopy in an ecclesiastical procession. I have worn my knees by writing on them on the old back row of the old gallery of the House of Commons, and I have worn my feet by standing to write in a preposterous pen in the old House of Lords, where we used to be huddled like so many sheep."

One is reminded of a somewhat similar reference in "David Copperfield" to these same hard-working days. "The man who reviews his life," he says, "as I do mine, in going on here from page to page, had need to have been a good man indeed, if he would be spared the sharp consciousness of many talents neglected, many opportunities wasted, many erratic and perverted feelings constantly at war within his breast and defeating him. I do not hold one natural gift, I daresay, that I have not abused. My meaning simply is that whatever I have tried to do in life, I have tried with all my heart to do well; that whatever I have devoted myself to, I have devoted myself to completely; that in great aims and in small I have always been thoroughly in earnest. I have never believed it possible that any natural or improved ability can claim immunity from the companionship of the steady, plain, hard-working qualities, and hope to gain its end. There is no such thing as such fulfilment on this earth. Some happy talents and some fortunate opportunity may form the two sides of the ladder on which some men mount; but the rounds of that ladder must be made of stuff to stand wear and tear, and there is no substitute for thorough-going, ardent, and sincere earnestness. Never to put one hand to anything on which I could throw my whole self, and never to affect depreciation of my work, whatever it was, I find now to have been my golden rules."

It has been truly observed that few things are more interesting, though few more difficult, than to trace the growth of a book from its first conception till it develops into full life and vigour. One is inclined often to ask, Was such and such a book composed under the influence of sudden inspiration, or was it the slow product of laborious thought? Was it written off at once without stop or stay, or was it corrected and revised with years of anxious care? Nothing is easier than for one to be deceived in his estimate of the toil implied in certain works seemingly easiest of achievement. Tom Moore used to declare that he never expected to get credit for half the toil expended on some of his airiest poems. It is true, as a rule, that work which is not subjected to careful revision is not likely to serve more than a temporary purpose. Much care, as well as never-ceasing diligence, is required on the part of those who aspire to do work that seeks a permanent place in the world of literature. James Payn, writing on success in fiction, frankly admits that it is quite true that some of the most admirable poems of our language have been written at a sitting, and under a strong impulse of the mind that falls little short of inspiration; but it is an error, he says, to suppose that whole novels in three volumes break forth from an author's imagination. Any one who has read with care the lives of our great novelists, he adds, must be aware indeed that quite the contrary is the case. The idea, it is true, may be born after that fashion, but the working it out involves toil and study, the reading of unattractive books, travel, and a hundred inconveniences abhorrent to the indolent mind. Unhappily the literary mind is naturally indolent. In many of what are called the inferior works of our great writers failure is distinctly to be traced, not to any falling off in the writer's powers, but to that disinclination to take pains which comes with advancing years, especially when accompanied with popularity. "Sure of his audience, the author is too often tempted to let this stand as it is, and that run as it will, rather than trouble himself, as of old, to make sure of his ground, to avoid discrepancies, or carefully to collect his threads together at the close of his weaving." Elsewhere he observes that among the items of success in fiction it may not be wholly degrading to allude to that of finance; and as indolence detracts from excellence in literature, it is also apt to diminish the profits to be derived from it much more than in other callings. "In no other will a man who is bent on success in it make it secondary, as men of letters so often do, to that of pleasure. The rising barrister, ambitious to rise higher as well as to fill his purse, will require something much more tempting than a fine morning to make him give up going to Chambers and pass the day in the country ; nor does he permit the convivialities of the evening to keep him till the small hours, and therefore to disorganize him for the work of the ensuing day. It is recorded, indeed, of the greatest wit that has ever set our tables in a roar, that he was wont to send round on 'soda-water mornings' to a fellow-scribe for 'ink,'—a euphemistic term implying a request that he would be so good as to do his work for him; but though the gentleman in question enjoyed a high reputation in letters, he could scarcely be said to have been a conspicuous example of material success. Even indisposition, which is often only another name for disinclination for work, should not be lightly permitted to interfere with literary labour. If once a man of letters permits the consideration of his not feeling quite in the humour to excuse his taking holiday, he will find that sort of inspiration occur to him pretty often. Of course there are many examples of writers that have done well for themselves in spite of this weakness, but they would have done much better if they had not given in to it. It is not too much to say that there have been more failures among men of high promise in letters through neglect of this common virtue of application than in any other calling."

It is true that no one can be taught to write a successful work of fiction; but it has been well observed that to suppose success in this direction comes by accident or impulse, that an author has only to sit with his pen in his hand and his eyes on the ceiling waiting for the happy moment of inspiration, is an equal mistake. Let it be remembered that without infinite capacity for taking trouble no good work is possible. An English author tells us that a voluminous writer once said to him, "Look at my manuscript. There is hardly a single correction in it, and this is my first draught. I never copy, and I rarely alter a line." "It would have been uncivil to say so," continues the author referred to, "but I could not help thinking that both author and public would have been none the worse if my friend had altered a good many lines, and recopied not a few pages."

This question of manuscripts is one worthy of careful consideration. Some one has well remarked that certain authors seem to think that any sort of "copy" is good enough for the press; but the truth of the matter is quite to the contrary. An untidy, useless, illegible manuscript is an offence to the publisher, dangerous irritation to the "reader," and to the printer an absolute cruelty. Many proof corrections, often made so wantonly and costing so much trouble and money, are also to be severely condemned. "Doubtless the *genus irritabile* has its wrongs from hard-headed and often hard-hearted men of business; but volumes might be written about the worry, the loss, the actual torment, that inaccurate, irregular, impecunious, and extravagant authors are to that much-enduring and necessarily silent class, their publishers." "For my sake, if not for heaven's," writes Dickens to one of his contributors, "do, I entreat you, look over your manuscript before sending it to the printer." And again: "Please keep, on abrupt transitions into the present tense, your critical eye." Colton affirms that the great cause of the delight we receive from a fine composition, whether it be in prose or in verse, is to be found in the marvellous and magic power it confers upon the reader, enabling an inferior mind, at one glance and almost without an effort, to seize, to embrace, and to enjoy those remote combinations of wit, melting harmonies of sound, and vigorous condensations of sense, that cost a superior mind so much perseverance, labour, and time. Moreover, an author by rewriting his own thoughts will be enriched beyond the mere weight of the words employed. Gibbon, we are told, rewrote his "Memoirs" nine times; Butler his "Analogy," twenty; Brougham the peroration in his plea for Queen Caroline, twenty; and Burke the conclusion of his speech at the trial of Hastings, sixteen.

As one contemplates the works of certain authors, one marvels at the toil of hand alone required to produce them. Perhaps the most remarkable example on record is to be found in the person of Lope de Vega. He "thought nothing of writing a play in a couple of days, a light farce in an hour or two, and in the course of his life he furnished the stage of Spain with upwards of two thousand original dramas."

Hallam calculates that this extraordinary man was the author of at least twenty-one million three hundred thousand lines. The most voluminous writer in modern times is, undoubtedly, Robert Southey, whose acknowledged works amount to no less than one hundred and nine volumes; in addition to which he contributed fifty-two essays to the "Annual Review," ninety-four to the "Quarterly," and to minor magazines articles without number. After Southey would come Voltaire and Sir Walter Scott.

It would, says Sydney Smith, in his "Culture of the Understanding," be a profitable thing to draw up a short and well-authenticated account of the habits of study of the most celebrated writers. It would go far to destroy the absurd and pernicious associations of genius and idleness, by showing that men of the most brilliant and imposing talent have lived a life of intense and incessant labour. We should discover that "rapt orations flowing free" have been worked out like mathematical problems; that fervid apostrophes have been compiled, and that laborious dissertations have been extemporized. Take Virgil, for instance. It was his custom, according to Donatus, to throw off a number of verses in the morning, and to employ the rest of the day in polishing and pruning them down. "It took him upwards of three years to compose his ten short Eclogues, seven years to write his Georgics, and upwards of twelve years to elaborate the Æneid, which he was so far from regarding as complete that he attempted to rise from his death-bed to commit it to the flames." Every line of Horace bears testimony to the fastidious labour of its author. There are, says Lord Lytton, single odes which must have cost the poet six weeks' seclusion from the dissipations of Rome. Lucretius's one poem represents the work of a whole life; and he has himself told us how completely he was absorbed in it—how it filled his waking hours, how it haunted him in his dreams. Nothing great and durable, says Tom Moore, has ever been produced with ease. Labour is the parent of all the lasting monuments of this world, whether in verse or in stone, in poetry or in pyramids.

A writer in "Temple Bar" furnishes a number of instances illustrative of this infinite capacity for taking trouble, of which we have spoken. Thucydides, he tells us, was at least twenty years in inditing his great work. That work is comprised in an octavo volume. Demosthenes made no secret of the pains he expended in forging his thunderbolts against Philip. So fastidious was Plato that the first sentence in the "Republic" was turned into nine different ways before he could satisfy himself. Pope would spend whole days over a couplet; Charlotte Bronté, an hour over a word; and Gray, a month over a short copy of verses. There is a poem of ten lines in Waller, which he has owned cost him a whole summer. Gibbon wrote the first chapter of the "Decline and Fall" three times before he was satisfied with it, and nearly a quarter of a century elapsed before the entire work was completed. John Foster, the essayist, would sometimes linger a week over a sentence. Addison was so fastidious that, Johnson tells us, he would stop the press to insert an epithet, or even a comma. Tasso toiled like a galley slave at polishing his stanzas. So morbidly anxious was Cardinal Bembo about style, that every poem on which he was engaged passed successively through forty portfolios, which represented its various stages toward perfection. How Petrarch laboured at his sonnets may be gathered from the following memoranda, which were found on the original manuscript of one of them: "I began this by the impulse of the Lord, 10th of September, at the dawn of day, after my morning prayers. ......I must make these two verses over again, singing them [*cantando*], and I must transpose them." "Three o'clock A.M., 19th of October: I like this." "Thirtieth of October, ten o'clock in the morning: No, this does not please me." "Twentieth of December, in the evening......I shall return to this again. I am called to supper." "Eighteenth of February, toward noon : This is now well ; however, look at it again." And this is the history of *one* sonnet. Sheridan's dialogue was little better than mosaic-work, painfully dovetailed. Gray, Miss Austen, Charlotte Brontė, and Charles James Fox were conspicuously distinguished by their morbid sensibility to the niceties of style. Some one speaking of Fox declared that he wrote "drop by drop." It is not a little strange, also, to find in this class old Izaak Walton, whose simple, homely diction was, it appears, the result of almost incredible labour. Even Goldsmith bemoaned the trouble his graceful periods cost him. "Every one," he once said bitterly, "writes better, because he writes faster than I." The account given by Rousseau of the labour his smooth and lively style cost him is so curious that we shall let him tell his own tale: "My manuscripts, blotted, scratched, interlined, and scarcely legible, attest the trouble they cost me. There is not one of them which I have not been obliged to transcribe four or five times before it went to press......Some of my periods I have turned, or re-turned, in my head for five or six nights before they were fit to be put to paper."

Hume wrote thirteen hours a day while preparing his " History of England." Montesquieu, speaking of one part of his writings, said to a friend, "You will read it in a few hours ; but I assure you it cost me so much labour that it has whitened my hair." We have already referred to Sheridan and the amount of labour expended on his comedies. It has been well observed that hardly any form of composition seems as easy as a good comedy, and yet such an estimate would be far out of the way. Take the " School for Scandal," for instance. How many of those who smile at the sparkling dialogue would believe the amount of thought and labour it cost? The characters were altered and recast again and again. Many of the speeches put into the mouths of Sir Peter and Lady Teazle, we are told, are so shifted and re-

modelled from what they were in the first rough draught that
hardly a word stands in the same order as originally written.

Coming down to more recent times, we find the same to
be true of our modern *dii majores.*  Dr. Holmes is said to
write very slowly and correct a great deal.  He is never
tired of mending or improving.  Longfellow was accustomed
to write very slowly, though with little difficulty of composition.  He used a lead pencil, and carefully weighed every
word before putting it down.  It is said he sent beautiful
manuscript to the printers, with hardly an erasure in it; but
by the time the "revise" was taken, very little of the original was left.  It is asserted that the whole of the "Divine
Tragedy" was rewritten after most of it was in type.  When
Tennyson sits down to write he gives strict orders that he
shall not be disturbed.  In his work he is deliberation per-
sonified, sometimes spending hours on a single line.  Emerson was accustomed to spend the forenoon in his study with
constant regularity.  He was a diligent, slow, and painstaking worker.  The best materials of his freshest hours of
thought were preserved, and slowly recast and put into form
in the quiet of his study.  His striking sentences are the
result of most persistent labour.  "They were all carefully
revised again and again, corrected, wrought over, portions
dropped, and new matter added.  He was unsparing in his
corrections, striking out sentence after sentence.  Even whole
paragraphs disappear from time to time.  His manuscript is
everywhere crowded with erasures and corrections.  Scarcely
a page appears that is not covered with these evidences of
his diligent revision."  One of his biographers tells us
that the published essays were often the results of many lectures, the most pregnant sentences and paragraphs alone
being retained.  "His apples were sorted over and over
again, until only the very rarest, the most perfect, were left.
It did not matter that those thrown away were very good,
and helped to make clear the possibilities of the orchard;

they were unmercifully cast aside. His essays were consequently very slowly elaborated, wrought out through days, and months, and even years, of patient thought."

Parton, writing of N. P. Willis, says for the benefit of young writers: "I may add that Mr. Willis never slighted his work, but bestowed upon everything he did, even upon slight and transient paragraphs, the most careful labour, making endless erasures and emendations. On an average he erased one line out of every three that he wrote, and on one page of his editorial writing there were but three lines left unaltered." Henry James is said to be very fastidious about construction, and rewrites until his manuscript is almost illegible. "I have never known," says one in writing of him, "a more painstaking author than Mr. James. Notwithstanding his great talents and acquirements, he has not an overweening confidence, even in his ability to construct a sentence properly. He corrects and revises every page until his manuscript is totally illegible to any one but himself." One of his friends asserts that George W. Cable is one of the most absorbed of literary workers. He is a thorough believer, he tells us, in the theory that labour is more powerful than genius. Like Pope, he makes corrections even when his manuscripts are in the hands of the printer. He once telegraphed to his publisher to change a certain sentence which he had found capable of improvement. Let aspiring young writers note that this extreme care about the little details of phraseology is a characteristic of all whose works do not sink into obscurity a few months after birth. "A flowing style appears spontaneous to the reader; but only those who have worked in the field of letters themselves know of the erasures, the turning of sentences and clauses, and the many rewritings that evolve the delights of the printed page. As old Ben Jonson said, ' Easy writing makes hard reading.'"

George Eliot is said to have worked harder on " Romola "

than on any of her other books. In her own words, "I
began it a young woman—I finished it an old woman;" and
yet but about seventeen months were consumed in writing
it.   One is reminded of Robert Stephenson's remark concerning the Britannia Bridge.   He declared that he grew
old ten years while he was building it.   For weeks before it
was finished he could get no continuous sleep, such was his
wearing anxiety.   He was initiating a new era of engineer-
ing, and was most wakeful and vigilant, that no element
might be overlooked in his careful computations.

Any one familiar with the rehearsals of a great oratorio
knows how "blue" and discouraging the outlook often seems,
particularly on the night of final rehearsal.   The singers are
tired and listless, mistakes are frequent, the patience of con-
ductor and chorus alike sorely tried, and a total depravity of
affairs in general seems to prevail.   Everything apparently
is "going to the dogs."   One unaccustomed to such a state
of things would instantly predict inevitable and signal failure.
How surprising to such shall seem the brilliant success when
at length the eventful night arrives!   Those wearisome
rehearsals have not been in vain.   Knowledge, accuracy, the
assurance and conviction of the manner in which each passage *ought* to be rendered,—in a word, the mastery of the
oratorio has been gained.   Drill and application have conferred it—these alone.   It needs simply "the breath of great
occasion" to give the finishing touch, the needed inspiration
—that is all.   And as the perfect harmonies of the "Creation"
or the inspiring strains of the "Hallelujah Chorus" surge
out over the vast and delighted assembly, one instantly perceives the significance and value of application and discipline
and drill.

One sometimes hears the familiar excuse given for inaction
that one is *waiting for his mood.*   This waiting for moods is
liable to rob one of many valuable moments.   Especially is
this true regarding young men.   It is safe to say that such

a state of mind should always be closely scrutinized. It may transpire that such an excuse is only another name for laziness. Anthony Trollope declared it all stuff and nonsense for one to wait for moods; and even Johnson maintained, as we know, that one could force himself to produce good work at any time, if he would only set himself doggedly at it. "Cogenda mens est ut incipiat," says Seneca. Compulsion, doubtless, must be often used. As has been truly observed, some of the best writing in the world is that which is done on our first-class daily journals. Yet, as every one knows, the "leader" must be written on the minute, and often, as for instance when an important telegram has come in late at night, against time. No journalist can habitually wait for a writing mood. No one, moreover, can realize more fully than an editor at the head of a great journal how all-important and invaluable to one in such a position is the possession of the utmost possible learning. Information on all sorts of subjects cannot be amiss, and no item of knowledge is liable to prove itself useless or superfluous to its possessor. "I was a college graduate before I was a reporter," said the editor of one of the great daily newspapers lately. "But if I could have stopped work after I had been two years in the office, and gone back to study international law, history, and languages, it would have been worth a large capital to me. A man does not know what he ought to know until he has been at actual work in journalism for a year or two." In this profession, as in every other, the increasing demands of the age require wide study and incessant work.

While it is undeniably true that the mind must often be driven to its task, it is also true, doubtless, that in works of the imagination the best results are only to be attained when the worker is in the best of moods. But genius is a law unto itself. Thackeray, it is said, would scribble page after page of manuscript, and tear each one up. In this style he would *court his mood* for an hour or two. Suddenly it would respond; then he would dash off a dozen or more pages at a sitting. Hawthorne's moods were capricious. There would be weeks, we are told, in which he could write scarcely a paragraph that he thought worth preserving. It is related of Lowell that he used to walk about the house talking to himself. He sometimes kept this up for days, and then suddenly retired to his study. When he reappeared, his work was finished.

It is curious to note in this connection what an aversion certain world-famous authors have had to entering upon their self-imposed tasks. They proved themselves splendid workers, but at the same time seem to have dreaded the work. Foster, the essayist, was one of these. While his brilliant essays were so successful and so much admired, he yet had almost to be driven to the task of composition. Charles Kingsley, that noble worker, once wrote in a book kept for the autographs of literary men, "Any sort of work," in answer to the question, "What do you dislike most?" Bryant may also be cited. Browne tells us that, although a journalist, and accustomed to daily writing, Bryant was not fond of literary composition, and seldom attempted it unless there was something he particularly wanted to say. Poetry with him was not only a labour of love, but a love of labour. He composed with the greatest difficulty, owing to an extreme fastidiousness that refused to be satisfied. Like Pope and Campbell, he was always anxious to alter and revise, and was ever finding what he conceived to be happier ways of expression. It is said he wrote "Thanatopsis" a hundred times, and that even after publication he had a copy of the poem with various changes from the published form. It used to be often asked why Bryant did not write more, but those who knew him well did not wonder. Poetry with him was "a mental agony." He took as much pains over his lines as Jean Jacques did over his prose, or Tennyson over his verse. He almost invariably, we are told, declined to furnish poems for college commencements, public occasions, and national festivals. The only instance, perhaps, of his departing from this established rule of his life was when he furnished two short poems to the "Ledger," for which Mr. Bonner paid him the unusual sum of three thousand dollars. "I know a score of clever fellows in the vicinity of Printing House Square," remarks Browne, in writing of him, "who would write a drama, half a dozen pieces of verse, a story, two or three columns of paragraphs, and a score of letters, to the country press, while Bryant was inditing a short poem. I am bound to say, however," he quietly adds, "his work would better bear critical examination than theirs." One is reminded by these instances of Grant's "Let us have peace," or of that declaration in his speech at London in 1877 : "Although a soldier by education and profession, I have never felt any sort of fondness for war, and I have never advocated it, except as a means of peace." The man of war, indeed, as Badeau says of him, always preferred peace. He never liked his profession. In England, when the Duke of Cambridge offered him a review, the courtesy was declined ; and Grant declared to his intimates that a review was the last thing he desired to see.

No man, says Inness, the painter, can do anything in art unless he has intuitions ; but between whiles one must work hard in collecting the materials out of which intuitions are made. Dante produces an immortal poem, in which both heaven and earth are brought under tribute, and which he says kept him lean many years, and involved immense study and toil. Such a masterpiece was a work of untiring industry as well as inspiration. Goethe said of one of his ballads, "Whole years of reflection are comprised in it, and I made three or four trials before I could bring it to its present shape." One of Tennyson's lines was quoted in his presence as a happy instance of a natural expression of a spontaneous thought, when the poet said, " I smoked a dozen cigars over that line ; " and Tom Moore confesses to almost incredible toil in collecting his material for " Lalla Rookh."

Then, too—one may as well admit it—men are naturally indolent. They love to take their ease, and are therefore averse to active effort. This capacity for mental labour, combined with reluctance to undertake it, is not uncommon. An indolent, capable man, as already noted, finds it painful to set his mind in motion. His inertia must be overcome by a force outside of himself. Poverty has often proved a great stimulus in this direction. Sir Samuel Romilly, the greatest Chancery lawyer of his day, we are told, worked up to an income of ten thousand pounds a year, equivalent to more than twenty thousand pounds in these days. When he began his professional life he had a small fortune, and thought of buying with it the lucrative position of the clerk of the court. But his father was in straitened circumstances, and the son generously turned the money over to him and went to work. His subsequent success at the bar, as he himself wrote, arose out of the pecuniary difficulties and confined circumstances of his father. When Lord Eldon began his practice at the Chancery bar as John Scott, Lord Chancellor Thurlow promised him a commissionership of bankruptcy. But the promise remained unfulfilled, for a reason which Lord Thurlow afterwards gave thus : " Jack, I withheld it as a favour to you. I saw that you had ability, but that you were naturally indolent, and that only want could make you industrious." Indeed, Lord Eldon himself used to say that the first requisite for distinction as a barrister was " to be not worth a shilling."

How many college-bred men seem to have derived little or no benefit from superior advantages enjoyed! And one need not often seek far to find the reason. They have shirked or idled instead of working. They have passed through the routine, it is true, and after a fashion have taken everything laid down in the college curriculum. But what has been achieved? What have they to show for it? A "sheepskin," perhaps, and possibly even that only by a stroke of singular good fortune. They have not added to their mental fibre; they have never really known what genuine study means; they have dreaded application, and since there is no other road to success, they have missed their way. Men who never enjoyed the privilege of a college education have far outstripped them. It has been truly said that the ranks of our thinkers and literary workers are constantly recruited by those who owe success to their own exertions. Many of our brilliant scientists, our most polished writers, are, as we say, self-made men. Howells was his own instructor; Hugh Miller had few opportunities of attending school, so called; Faraday never graduated at a university, yet he left a name of which all Englishmen are justly proud. Professor Gosse, of Cambridge University, England, we are told, was educated at home under the careful supervision of his mother, a lady of rare culture and force of character. Disraeli never went either to a public school or a university. If circumstances are such that a young man cannot avail himself of the advantages of a great school, let him not lose heart.

How large a majority of even college men, let us ask, know from actual experience what that sort of study means of which Bailey gives so graphic a portrayal in "Festus"? Some there are who will recognize the picture. Says Festus,—

> " I know what study is : it is to toil
> Hard through the hours of the sad midnight watch,
> At tasks which seem a systematic curse
> And course of bootless penance.
> &ast; &ast; &ast; &ast; &ast;
> Wring a slight sleep out of the couch, and see
> The self-same moon which lit us to our rest,
> Her place scarce changed perceptibly in heaven,
> Now light us to renewal of our toil.

This to the young mind, wild and all in leaf,
Which knowledge, grafting, paineth. Fruit soon comes,
And more than all our troubles pays us powers;
So that we joy to have endured so much;
That not for nothing have we slaved and slain
Ourselves, almost."

That kind of study always *tells*, and one may set it down as a rule that has few exceptions, that the successful man is one who has "disciplined himself and made a sacrifice." Nor let one conclude, because he cannot secure a whole day, it will therefore be of little use to save the fragments. Even an hour a day would in seven years be equivalent to well-nigh a whole year's study; and who will say that this is of small account? Moreover, what one learns thoroughly when young he retains through life. "Read Coke on Littleton again and again," was Lord Chancellor Eldon's advice to young lawyers. "If it be toil and labour to you,—and it will be so,—think as I do when I am climbing up to Swyer, or West Hill, that the world will be before you when the toil is over; for so the law will be, if you make yourself complete master of that book." As Lucretius puts it, a falling drop at last will cave a stone.

John Stuart Blackie declares that he never knew a man good for anything in the world, who, when he had a piece of work to do, did not know how to stick to it. And he refers to the poet Wordsworth as giving, in his "Excursion," as a reason for going on with his mountain perambulation when the sky began to look cloudy, that though a little rain might be disagreeable to the skin, the act of giving up a fixed purpose in view of a slight possible inconvenience is dangerous to the character. "There is much wisdom here," continues Blackie. "We do not live in a world in which a man can afford to be discouraged by trifles. A friend of mine, making the ascent of Ben Cruachan, when he reached what he imagined to be the top, found that the real peak was two miles farther on to the west, and that the road to it lay

along a rough stony ridge not easy for weary feet to tread
on. But this was a small matter. The peak was being
enveloped in mist, and it was only an hour from sunset.
He wisely determined to take the nearest way down ; but
what did he do next day ?  He ascended the Ben again, and
took his dinner triumphantly on the topmost top, in order,
as he said, ' that the name of this most beautiful of
Highland Bens might not for ever be associated in his
mind with bafflement and defeat.' "  This sort of a man,
depend upon it, will succeed in everything he undertakes.
Moreover, haste or shamming always betrays itself.  All
successful men come at length to know that there is a certain
quality of attainment, whether it be in art, or science, or
letters, which always and unmistakably represents, no
matter what the native genius, that " long scorning of
delights and living of laborious days " without which the
highest success is impossible.  Some seem to think that
success in painting, for instance, is something to be acquired
at a single bound.  They remind one of the illustration given
by Hunt, the artist, with a touch of quiet humour, concerning the parents of certain young ladies who are ever
anxiously on the look-out for evidences of elaborative and
accomplished work.  " This much-admired finish," says
Hunt, " is like the architecture that the countryman said
was going to be put on his house by a Boston man—
*after it was built.*"  Elsewhere he says, " Real finish must
be of the same quality as real beginning."  It is for ever
true that great artists win their matchless power only
through years of " that long travail of effort wherewith great
gifts have birth, and through the priceless discipline of true
training."  This confers the artist's skill and knowledge.
Then, at length, " strong and sure as the Atlantic tides
sweeping up the shore," comes the inspiration with all its
" hidings of power."
    The same rule of application holds in the business world.

Successful business men tell us that success in commercial life depends upon certain essential qualifications,—a character, for instance, in which are found indomitable resolution and power of rigid application. These are looked upon by the experienced as good as capital; sometimes better. " Without them the merchant will be beaten as the mercantile contest thickens and the heat of the business day advances. The young merchant can afford to be without coat and shoes (as many have been), but not without these grand and substantial elements of a business character." One of the most successful of English lawyers was Pemberton Leigh, Baron Kingsdown. In a privately printed work which he left—a most entertaining volume—he gives us his recollections in Parliament and at the bar. He retired from both at the age of fifty. He refused to be Solicitor-General; he refused to be Lord Chancellor. For twenty years he was one of the greatest judges of the final court of appeals. A peerage—he never took pay—was the only reward he would accept from his country. After the touching picture which he gives us of the poverty and hard work of his early life, he significantly adds : " It was the severe preparation for the subsequent harvest. I learned to consider indefatigable labour as the indispensable condition of success, pecuniary independence as essential alike to virtue and happiness, and no sacrifice too great to avoid the misery of debt."

It will be well for a young man to rid himself early of the idea that it is by books alone, or by books chiefly, that he is to advance in intellectual power. Many a man has loaded himself down so completely with the works of other men, that they have crushed out all originality in him and proved a useless burden. If a young man cannot go through college or university without losing all his native power and individuality ; if he have not strength enough in himself to make all else subservient to real growth, to assimilate the stores of learning offered him by other men, it were well to count the cost before engaging in such a venture. The main thing, after all, is not so much to cram one's self with other men's opinions as to have matured and well-digested convictions of one's own. The aim should be to train the working power in one's self. Carlyle, in a letter of advice to a young friend concerning the books he was to read, used these words : "Study to do faithfully whatsoever thing, in your actual situation there and now, you find either expressly or tacitly laid to your charge : that is your post. Stand to it like a true soldier. *A man perfects himself by work much more than by reading.* They are a growing kind of men who can wisely combine the two things,—wisely, valiantly can do what is laid to their hand in their present sphere, and prepare themselves, withal, for doing other wider things, if such lie before them." And let it not be forgotten that the surest avenue of escape from an uncongenial position, if a man find himself thus circumstanced, is not to lie down and bemoan his fate, but to throw himself so lustily into his work that it shall be seen by every one that his place is so manifestly more than filled, as to suggest his fitness for a larger field. It has been justly observed that the lawyer who rises to conduct a difficult case in his leader's absence, the surgeon who has a sudden chance presented to him, must have had long preparatory training before he can skilfully avail himself of any sort of emergency. He must have been *in the habit* of relying on himself. No way has been found for making heroism easy, even for the scholar, says Emerson. The world is nothing but a mass of means :

> " We have but what we make, and every good
> Is locked by nature in a granite hand,
> Sheer labour must unclench.
>      *     *     *     *     *
> The blowing winds are but our servants
> When we hoist a sail."

The extraordinary power of application which certain men have at times displayed seems truly marvellous. When Horace Greeley established the *Tribune*, Henry J. Raymond went into the office as associate editor, at the princely salary of eight dollars a week, and working, on an average, about thirteen or fourteen hours a day. Greeley, who was a perfect fanatic himself concerning labour, and who thought that a man only ordinarily industrious was a mere drone, actually urged Raymond not to work so much ; and he was the only person the editor-in-chief of the *Tribune* ever found it necessary to remonstrate with on that account. In September 1851, the first number of the *Times* was issued, Raymond being editor-in-chief, and it is reported that he had over twelve columns of his own matter in the initial issue. He was always a very fluent and easy writer, and it used to be said in the office, that if the days were a little longer Raymond would write up the whole paper. He was reckoned the most versatile writer on the New York press. One of his most remarkable perform-ances was his article on the death of Daniel Webster. It filled nearly fifteen columns of the *Times*, was written at one sitting, and in the incredibly short space of twelve hours.

While in Boston, during his second visit to America, Dickens kept himself strictly secluded from all but one or two old and intimate friends. He remained in his rooms at the Parker House, busily engaged all day in writing and study, except when engaged in taking his daily walk of six or eight miles. Much of his time was spent in the most laborious, painstaking study of the parts he was to read. The public, as we are assured by the best authority, had but little idea of the cost, in downright hard work, of mind, body, and voice, at which his readings were produced. In-deed, we are told that although Mr. Dickens had then read nearly five hundred times, he never attempted a new part in public until he had spent at least two months over it, in study "as faithful and searching as Rachel or Cushman would give to a new character." This, we are further assured, extended not merely to the analysis of the text, to the discrimination of character, to the minutest points of elocution, but the facial expression, the tone of the voice, the gesture, the attitude, and even the material surroundings were determined upon. He was so conscientious that he left nothing undone that time and labour could do to give to the public, that paid so much for the pleasure of hearing him, the full worth of its money. " I am come here to read," he said. " The people expect me to do my best ; and how can I do it if I am all the time on the go ? My time is not my own when I am preparing to read, any more than it is when I am writing a novel ; and I can as well do one as the other without concentrating all my power on it till it is done." Thus we see, as has been truly observed, that his consummate ability was not acquired, or acquirable, without great labour and perseverance. It often took him three months, we are told, to become perfect in a new scene ; and his bodily exhaustion after a night's reading was always great. The same painstaking conscientiousness is true of Salvini. " When I first became acquainted with him," says one of his friends, " I was of opinion that his interpretation of ' Hamlet' was based only upon the translated text ; but in the course of a very long conversation on the subject I discovered that he was well acquainted, through literal translations, not only with the text, but also with the notes and comments of our leading critics. The costumes worn by Salvini in ' Othello' are copied from those depicted in certain Venetian pictures of the fifteenth century in which several Moorish officers appear. It took him many years to master this *rôle*, and he assured me that he could not play it more than three times in succession without ex-periencing terrible fatigue. ' It is a matter of wonder to me,' he observed, 'that English actors can play a great character like this so many nights in succession, and above all that they retain self-possession while the fidgety noise of scene-shifting is going on behind them.' Speaking about dramatic elocution, he said : ' The best method is obtained by close observation of nature, and above all by earnestness. If you can impress people with the conviction that you feel what you say, they will pardon many shortcomings. And above all, study, study, study ! All the genius in the world will not help you along with any art unless you become a hard student. It has taken me years to master a single part.' "

Handel was an indefatigable worker, and so was Haydn. " Work," said Mozart, " is my chief pleasure." Meyerbeer worked fifteen hours a day, and the " Huguenots," the " Prophète," and his other brilliant works, bear witness to the value of their author's application to his art. Domenichino was once blamed for his slowness in finishing a picture which had been ordered. " I am continually painting it within myself," was his reply. Say what one may, the most effective genius is the genius of hard work. The first Napoleon was a tremendous worker ; he was never idle. At midnight, just before one of his most critical and decisive battles, "which had already been fought through in his own brain just as the thunderbolt of a hundred thousand men which he was about in a few hours to hurl from his right hand actually fought it through the next day," he was found sitting in his tent and drawing up an elaborate course of study for Madame Campan's young ladies' school !

It is curious to note the various expedients which have been adopted by hard workers in order to obtain that seclusion so necessary to securing the best results of one's work. M. D. Conway once, visiting Paris, found Mark Twain hidden away in Millet's studio finishing one of his books. It is told of Professor Anthon, that one summer, wishing to devote himself uninterruptedly to his "Classical Dictionary," he had a room fitted up in the attic of his residence, and callers were invariably told that the professor was "taking his summer vacation." It is related of Greeley that when he was writing his "American Conflict" he found it necessary to conceal himself somewhere, to prevent constant interruptions. He accordingly took a room in the Bible House, where he worked from ten in the morning until five in the afternoon, and then appeared in the sanctum seemingly as fresh as ever. Beggars, politicians, reformers, counsel-seekers, all pursued him so persistently that at length his sanctum on the editorial floor was demolished and a den prepared for him in the "impenetrable recesses in the vicinity of the counting-room." Many a one attempted to find him even there, but the result of the search was usually "a mingled groan and malediction, amid the howling darkness of the press-room,"—this, and nothing more.

Of all the heroisms of history, nothing is more striking than the record of the almost herculean tasks which have at times been performed under the inspiration of a pure and romantic attachment, or of that wifely affection which reveals so unmistakably "the beauty and strength of woman's devotion." In the account given by Sir William Napier of the immense service rendered him by his wife in the composition of his work on the "History of the Peninsular War," he tells us that when the immense mass of King Joseph's correspondence, taken at Vittoria, was placed in his hands, he was dismayed at finding it to be a huge collection of letters, without order, and in three languages, one of which he did not understand. "Many also were in very crabbed and illegible characters, especially those of Joseph's own writing, which is nearly as difficult to read as Napoleon's. The most important documents were in cipher, and there was no key. Despairing of any profitable examination of the materials, the thought crossed me of giving up the work, when my wife undertook, first to arrange the letters by dates and subjects, next to make a table of reference, translating and epitomizing the contents of each; and thus, without neglecting for an instant the care and education of a very large family, she did it in such a simple and comprehensive manner that it was easy to ascertain the original document in a few moments. She also undertook to decipher the correspondence, and not only succeeded, but formed a key to the whole, detecting even the nulls and stops, and so accurately, that when, in the course of time, the original key was placed in my hands, there was nothing to learn. Having mentioned this to the Duke of Wellington, he seemed at first incredulous, observing that I must mean that she had made out the contents of some letters. Several persons had done this for him, he said, but none had ever made out the nulls or formed a key; adding, ' I would have given twenty thousand pounds to any person who would have done that for me in the Peninsula.' " When we consider, says one in commenting upon the magnitude of the achievement, the immense deal of labour involved, the ingenuity requisite to bring order out of confusion, it stands as perhaps the most wonderful record of wifely love ever known. "No pleasure lured her from the task; no sunshine dancing without wooed her from the still solitude of the room where, patient, constant, unwearied, she pondered over the dark hieroglyphics, all for the love of him to whom she was so precious a helpmate, companion, and friend." The wife of Nathaniel Bowditch, the translator of Laplace's "Mécanique Céleste," was a woman of great piety and sweetness of disposition. He frequently declares that had it not been for her encouragement and sympathy he could not have carried on the work. Dr. Hitchcock of Amherst College pays a similar tribute to his "Beloved Wife," in the dedication of his "Religion of Geology."

It is undeniably true that in that fine quality which "hopes and endures and is patient," which is ever so prominent a factor in all distinguished success, womanhood is unsurpassed. In illustration of this, many notable instances might be given. Mrs. Reeves tells us that a certain prima donna refused to sit down at all on a day when she was to sing. " No, she would walk around the room, talking perhaps, singing perhaps, sometimes very busy with her needle and thread, but never sitting down the livelong day until the performance was all over. I remember well enough," she continues, "how, on the morning of a performance, Jenny Lind, Mr. Reeves, Mr. Goldschmidt, and myself were in the room ; and during the morning Jenny Lind and my husband were never still, passing each other, with music in hand, singing and practising, and intent on the work before them. 'Why, Jenny,' said Mr. Goldschmidt, 'you must have sung those songs many times ; surely there is no need of all this.' But remonstrance was in vain. Suppose you had called to see Jenny Lind," she adds, "on a day when she was singing. She would probably come into the room with a bundle of music in her hand, put it on a chair and sit down upon it, talk away pleasantly enough for a few minutes, turn to a passage in one of the pieces and hum it over. Having satisfied herself of her correctness, she would replace it and sit down again as calmly as possible, and resume the conversation at the point it was broken off." Who doubts that in this unwearied patience and persistence and application are to be found, in great part at least, the secret of that brilliant success of the "Swedish Nightingale" of which our fathers never tire of telling ?

We sometimes hear, says Legouvé, that certain great artists made their own voices. The expression is incorrect. No one can make a voice who has not one to start with, and this is proved by the fact that the voice is perishable. No voice would ever be lost, could it be made at will; but it may be changed, it may gain body, brilliancy, and expression, not only from a series of gymnastics adapted to strengthen the whole organ, but from a certain method of attacking the note. Additional notes may also be gained by study. On one occasion the famous Malibran, when singing the Rondo from "Sonnambula," finished her cadenza with a trill on D in *alt*, running up from low D, thus embracing three octaves. These three octaves were no natural gift, but the result of long and patient labour. After the concert some one expressed his admiration of her D in *alt*, to which she replied, "Well, I've worked hard enough for it. I've been chasing it for a month. I pursued it everywhere,— when I was dressing, when I was doing my hair; and at last I found it in the toe of a shoe that I was putting on." Von Bulow once declared that if he omitted practice for a single day, he himself could perceive the effect of it upon his playing; if he omitted it for two days, his friends could perceive it; and if for a longer period, the public would notice it. That old German inscription on a key, "If I rest, I rust," would seem to be as true of men as of iron.

Of the great musicians, Beethoven probably surpassed all others in painstaking fidelity and application. "Audacious and impassioned beyond every one," says Grove, "the moment he takes his pen in hand he becomes the most cautious and hesitating of men. It would almost seem as if this great genius never saw his work as a whole until it actually approached completion......There is hardly a bar in his music of which it may not be said with confidence that it has been rewritten a dozen times. Of the air, 'O Hoffnung,' in 'Fidelio,' the sketch-books show eighteen attempts, and of the concluding chorus, ten." Of many of the brightest gems of the opera, says Thayer, the first ideas are so trivial that it would be impossible to admit that they were Beethoven's if they were not in his own handwriting. And so it is with all his works. His favourite maxim was: "The barriers are not erected which can say to aspiring talents and industry, 'Thus far, and no farther.'" Mozart tells us that his melodies came to him of themselves, he knew not whence; and yet it is well known that Mozart was also a great worker.

Many have doubtless been struck with the graphic descriptions of natural scenery and surroundings in the works of William Black; but not every one is aware of the manner in which these well-nigh photographic delineations are produced. "We have known him in windy weather," says a recent writer, "shut up in the forecastle of a seven-ton yacht under full sail, diligently doing his hour's writing—he only works so much every day—while the *débris* of the forecastle was rattling around him and the ropes whistling above his head. Much of the fidelity of Mr. Black's descriptions of nature is due to the fact that they are actual transcriptions taken down at the moment under all sorts of difficulties." The world calls these persons men of genius. But no native ability relieves them from the necessity of earnest and persistent application to whatever they undertake. How little conception has the public generally of the infinite pains taken by some of our great lawyers when an important suit is pending, or how faint an idea of the amount of labour performed! Men look on and marvel as they perceive how unmistakably and how easily, to all appearances, the great advocate proves himself master of the situation; but few have any adequate idea of the secret of it all, or of the amount of toil involved. A lawyer of large practice is compelled by his cases to master subjects in almost every department of knowledge. An incident illustrative of this is told in the life of Lord Lyndhurst. He was employed as counsel in a case which related to Mr. Heathcote's famous invention of the bobbin-net machine. That he might conduct the case successfully, he determined

to understand the working of the machine. Accordingly
he went to Nottingham, and took his place in the mill at
one of the looms. He did not leave it till he could make
a piece of bobbin-net with his own hands, and understood
perfectly the details of manufacture, as well as its principles.
When the case came on in court he produced a model machine
and worked it with such ease and skill, and explained the
nature of the invention with such clearness, that judge, jury,
and spectators were alike astonished. He gained the case,
because, in the opinion of all, he had mastered the details and
principles of the invention. It is related of Daubray, a
French actor, who was to play a butcher's part in a recent
piece, that he rose early every morning for weeks to visit the
market and observe how the butchers cut their meats. The
famous Gavarni spent his days in observation of the manners
of different social classes. He even got his tailor to have
him arrested, that he might make a study of the prisoners in
a Paris jail. His restless eyes were ever on the watch for
material. He sat frequently on a bench in the Tuileries, or
before a café, with a pencil concealed in his hand and his
little book at his side. *Never be afraid of taking pains!*
What finer motto could a young man adopt than that? Rest
assured of one thing,—if you will not take pains, pains will
take you, as Whately wittily observes.

According to all accounts Meissonier, the great French
artist, possesses this splendid trait. It was he who received
from A. T. Stewart sixty thousand dollars for one of his
paintings. He almost always paints from a model. " Here,"
said he to a visitor recently, as he took up a small wax figure,
" is the model of a horse prancing. It would have been impossible to draw direct from nature, so I had a horse brought
around here and made to prance while I modelled him in
wax. It was a terrible job. I had the horse brought here
every morning for four weeks, before the image was perfect;
but it is finished now, and I can draw from it at my leisure.

You see, too, I had a miniature set of harness made and fitted on the image, so as to have every strap and buckle just right. Here is another figure of a horse rolling upon the ground as if struck by a shot. It is for a battle scene. I had them throw a horse down and make him roll and struggle while I modelled him, and they had to do it more than a score of times."

Wherein lies the secret of the great superiority of certain well-known products in the market over others apparently the same, but which one finds upon examination to be far inferior? One of the leading New York dailies some time since gave an admirable answer to this question, as follows: "Simply because they are made by people who know more than any other people in the world engaged in the same work. They put more brains into their work than others do; they are intelligent enough to know the value of care, intelligent enough to be conscientious about employing it, intelligent enough to know how to employ it with skill to produce the best results." And does it not pay?

Two or three generations ago a member of a family now well known in Massachusetts determined to develop the industry of paper-making in this country. By application, persistency, and thrift he laid the foundation of a great fortune. His sons and grandsons, inheriting the same fine qualities, and maintaining the highest standard of excellence in manufacture, received the contract for making the first "Greenbacks," and now send their elegant papers to all parts of the world. In a eulogy on Jeremiah Mason, before the Suffolk bar, Mr. Webster said: "I will not say of the advantages which I have derived from his intercourse and conversation all that Mr. Fox said of Edmund Burke; but I am bound to say that of my own professional discipline and attainments, whatever they may be, I owe much to that close attention to the discharge of my duties which I was compelled to pay for nine successive years, from day to day, by Mr. Mason's efforts at the same bar. *Fas est ab hoste doceri;* and I must have been unintelligent, indeed, not to have learned something from the constant displays of that power which I had so much occasion to see and feel."

No young man need bemoan the fact of his having but a meagre library. It has often been the case that the finest work has been done by possessors of the fewest tools. In fact, in these days it would seem that one's danger lies in just the opposite direction. Amid the multiplicity of cheap books, one is in danger of becoming surfeited, and allowed little opportunity to think for himself, or to thoroughly digest any one of the many works thrust upon him. The reading and re-reading of a single volume has been the making of many a man. The thorough mastery of one great book will at times reveal powers of thought in the student of which he never dreamed. One is apt to dissipate his strength if he attempts to spread himself over too large a surface. Instances are not uncommon of a single picture, for instance, thoroughly mastered, having a great influence in the training and development of an artist's genius. To a Velasquez, a portrait of the Duc d'Olivarez, which the Earl of Elgin lent him, that he might study it while yet a young artist, Sir Francis Grant ascribed much of his after success.

Let a young man, then, at the outset of his career resolve that he will, by all fair means at his disposal, conquer his place in the world, and deserve success even if he does not reach it. Let him neither shrink nor shirk, but make up his mind to pay full price. "The gods sell anything and to everybody at a fair price." Let him not despise recreation, but not give it undue prominence in his calculations; learn to regard it rather as a means to an end. "Rest is not what I want," said an eminent surgeon, "but strength." Moreover, to secure one's right to amusement and recreation, as Lord Brougham says, one must pay an honest price, which is a good day's work. Learn, like Cæsar, to count nothing done if anything remains to be done. Remember always that without the desire and the pains necessary to be considerable, you never can be so. "What a wretched, insignificant, worthless creature any one comes to be," writes Sterling to his son, "who does not as soon as possible bend his whole strength, as in stringing a stiff bow, to doing whatever task lies before him!" Life, it has been asserted, begins with renunciation, and "the angel of Martyrdom is brother to the angel of Victory." Have a purpose in life, a distinct aim, some goal of honourable achievement ever before you, and let nothing daunt or turn you aside. Be not easily repulsed. A publisher once wrote to an agent, "If you work hard two weeks without selling a book, you will make a success of it." The idea was that by so doing he would show himself to have that perseverance which would enable him to triumph over all obstacles, and would insure him success in any undertaking. This is what Greeley termed the "genius of persistence." Remember, too, that we "acquire the strength we have overcome." Great success, depend upon it, is ever the fruit of great labour. Moreover, if wealth and royalty even are not exempt, why should any one expect to be? Francis Joseph of Austria is one of the hardest of workers. He is always at his desk at five o'clock in the morning. Signing papers, and other business, keeps him occupied till eleven o'clock. Then he has a lunch. He then returns to work, remaining till four o'clock. At that hour he dines. The two young Vanderbilts,—Cornelius and William K.,—the present heads of the family, are both great workers. One is first vice-president and head of finance of the Hudson River Railroad; the other is second vice-president and master of transportation. Each knows his business thoroughly. The most striking thing about either of them, it is said, is the fact that they work as hard as if they were hired by the job,—which they are by the way,—and that they are perfectly democratic, and accessible to anybody who has business with them. When Cornelius was twenty he was made a clerk, at the bottom of the ladder, and his youngest brother, William K., was put at work in the same office the next year. "For more than eighteen years now they have bowed down to it in that great concern, and they are far better trained than their father ever was in all the details of the business."

When the famous light-house, Pharos, was built, its architect was commanded to place the king's name upon it. He did so, but first cut his own name deep in the rock and covered it with cement. When the latter had hardened he inscribed thereon the name of the king. The storms and billows at length wore this away, leaving the name of the architect permanently carved in the solid rock. The superficial student is simply working upon cement; the real worker, the true scholar, upon the solid rock. The results achieved by the one are but transient and fleeting; the work of the other shall endure. "Life is short, art long, opportunity fleeting, experiment slippery, judgment difficult." These first words of the medical aphorisms of the wise Hippocrates, as Blackie tells us, were set down as a significant sign at the porch of the benevolent science of healing more than five hundred years before the Christian era; and they remain still the wisest text which a man can take with him as a directory into any sphere of life. "Thy life," says Carlyle, —and he never wrote anything finer nor more true,—"wert thou the pitifullest of all the sons of earth, is no idle dream, but a solemn reality. It is thy own. It is all thou hast to confront eternity with. Work, then, like a star, unhasting, yet unresting."

# IV

# The Single Eye.

"The undivided will......
'Tis *that* compels the elements, and wrings
A human music from the indifferent air."

"The wind never blows fair for that sailor who knows not to what port he is bound."

"Do right, and fear no one. Thou mayest be sure that with all thy consideration for the world, thou wilt never satisfy the world. But if thou goest forward straight on thy way, not concerning thyself with the friendly or the unfriendly glances of men, then thou hast conquered the world, and it is subject to thee."

"If thine eye be single, thy whole body shall be full of light," is the familiar declaration of Holy Writ. Words more true were never uttered. Is not here one secret, at least, of the vast difference in men as regards success in life? There are many men alert and active enough, if that were all, but somehow all they do amounts to nothing. They seem perpetually running to waste. They form great projects, and toil terribly, but there is no great underlying purpose. It is this which makes every stroke tell. One can see with half an eye that something more than mere activity is needed. Of what avail to fill your granary with the fruits of harvest if it is all to be destroyed by rats and vermin? A man ought not merely to act, but to act with a purpose. Purpose and persistency are ever essential to the highest success. It was said of the first Napoleon that in conversation he always went directly at the heart of a subject, whatever it might be. With an unerring instinct in investigation, he would strike at the soul of a mystery, and unravel it, caring little for unimportant particulars. However this may have been concerning his conversation, we know that it was pre-eminently true concerning his conduct of the art of war. He won his victories chiefly by rapid concentration of his forces on a single point of the enemy's line. A wise and eager hunter is sure to select the fattest of a herd, and, leaving the rest, to pursue and capture that one. The value of a burning-glass lies in its power to focalize a mass of sunbeams on one point; and the secret of success in any direction consists in having one thing to do, and doing it. A vigorous writer calls a lack of purpose among men mental shiftlessness. Nothing is more noticeable in men who have achieved great ends than a certain persistency which nothing seems able to daunt. Defeated, perhaps, times without number, they yet clung to their ideal, pursuing by night and by day the object dear to their hearts, until at length they were crowned with success. It is for ever true that the martyrs of one age become the heroes of the next. Contumely, slander, ridicule, abuse—what are these to a soul throbbing with a great ideal? They are simply not to the purpose; they must stand aside. There are men, moreover, as Emerson says, who rise refreshed on hearing a threat. What sight more thrilling than that of a human being absorbed, taken possession of by some grand conception, and forgetting everything else until the daring achievement is wrought? It is "the quiet lightning deed" that these men prize, not "the applauding thunder at its heels which men call fame." The fame is sure to come, but not because it is run after, as Longfellow has well said. Before such men civilization strides onward; remote nations become neighbourhoods; rivers are spanned, mountains tunnelled, broad oceans become ferries, and the world itself is transformed into a vast whispering-gallery. The products of every clime are at our very doors. Comforts, conveniences, and even luxuries come trooping into the homes of the common people, and men bask in the sunshine of prosperity, forgetful often that it was simply the single eye, the strenuous purpose of a great soul, that wrought it. It is well for us that such souls are not easily daunted or intimidated. Fulton can well afford to bide his time, even though his great achievement be looked upon for the day as simply his folly. To-morrow sets him right. Stephenson remonstrated with by his sceptical neighbours, and triumphantly asked if it would not be embarrassing should a cow invade the track, quietly replies that it would be embarrassing indeed "for the coo." Field crosses and recrosses the stormy Atlantic. Ten years of defeat and failure cannot daunt him. On the heels of all comes the unlooked-for barrier of a great civil war. At length that cable is laid, and Europe and Asia are at our very doors. The labours of Hercules, indeed! Mr. Field in his great enterprise, we are told, crossed the ocean nearly fifty times. His perseverance conquered; and now ocean telegraphy unites all continents, and brings the East and the West together to talk around one fireside. Then, too, if ever a moment approached the sublime, it was that in which the veteran Morse sat at his instrument on the stage of the great hall in New York and sent his message around the world. It would be difficult to find an instance to equal it in grandeur. Never, surely, has man approached so near to divinity in his control of material forces as this. There is that within the soul of these men which sleeps not night or day until its end is gained. As Gilfillan finely said of Napoleon, he was profound, as well as brilliantly successful. Unlike most conquerors, his mind was big with a great thought which was never fully developed. He was not raised, as many have stupidly thought, upon the breath of popular triumph. It was not chance that made him king, or that crowned him, or that won his battles. "He was a

*cumulative* conqueror. Every victory, every peace, every
law, every movement, was the step of a giant stair winding
toward universal dominion. All was systematic, all was full
of purpose, all was growingly progressive. No rest was
possible. He might have noonday breathing-times, but there
was no nightly repose. 'Onward!' was the voice ever sound-
ing behind him. Nor was this the voice of his nation, ever
insatiate for novelty and conquest; nor was it the mere
'Give, give' of his restless ambition. It was the voice of
his ideal, the cry of his unquenchable soul. He became the
greatest of warriors and conquerors, or at least one of the
greatest, because, like a true painter, he came down upon
the practice of his art from a stern and lofty conception or
hypothesis to which everything must yield. As Michael
Angelo subjected all things to his pursuit and the ideal he
had formed of it, painted the Crucifixion by the side of a
writhing slave, and, pious though he was, would have broken
up the true cross for pencils; so Napoleon pursued his ideal
through tempests of death-hail and seas of blood, and looked
upon poison and gunpowder and men's lives as merely the
box of colours necessary to his new and terrible art. When
we try Napoleon," he continues, "by human standards, and
compare his scheme with that of other conquerors, both seem
transcendently superb. He saw clearly that for Europe
there was no alternative between the surges of anarchy and
the absolute government of one master mind. He saw that
what was called 'balance of power' was a feeble and useless
dream, and that all things in Europe were tending either to
anarchy or a new absolutism; either to the dominion of
millions, or of that one who should be found a match for
millions. He thought himself that one. His iron hand
could in the first place grasp the great sceptre, and his wise
and powerful mind would afterward consolidate his dominion
by just and liberal laws. 'On this hint he spake'—in
cannon. This purpose he pursued with an undeviating

energy, which seemed for a season sure and irresistible as one of the laws of nature."

It seems amazing to the casual observer that any one man could exert so prodigious an influence over his fellow-men. Power like this has a singular fascination for all of us. The wizard enchanter engraved his name not only on the stones and marbles of the capital, but on the very heart of France. "Cut an inch deeper," said a member of the Old Guard to the surgeon who was probing his wounds, "and you will find the emperor"—meaning in his heart. Now, what was the secret of this man's power? One secret, surely, was his marvellous faculty of concentration—the single eye. A keen observer would have discovered this trait when the obscure and untitled boy was studying mathematics at Brienne no less truly than when, a few years later, all Europe was trembling under the measured tramp of his armies.

Take another instance. Two hundred years ago, in north-western Europe, a conglomeration of barbarous tribes were striving each for the supremacy. Presently a man appears —a man with a great purpose. He was of the Romanoff family. His own right arm and trusty sword were all his equipment. But he resolves from the first to make himself master of the situation. He is determined his country shall be respected among foreign powers. This one purpose takes full possession of him. To compass this end he leaves no stone unturned. He travels abroad to gain the requisite knowledge. We find him in London perfecting himself in matters of government, finance, and commerce. Again he appears working at the trade of a common ship-carpenter at the naval yards of Saardam in Holland. He perfects himself in all the accomplishments requisite to a great ruler. He is determined to lift up his people socially and politically. He puts a premium on skill and learning wherever found. By liberal rewards he induces men of rare accomplishments in all directions to reside in his dominions. No price is too

great, no toil too arduous, so long as his end is gained.
Now, note the result. "The silent rivers and widespread
lakes of Muscovy are suddenly made white with the sails of
trade; her vast plains are covered with waving crops of
golden grain. The magnificent city of St. Petersburg, with
its marble palaces, arises like magic out of the icy swamps
of the Neva. A powerful navy issues from the unfrequented ports of the Baltic, and Europe is astonished by
the sudden apparition of a gigantic sovereignty, with its
powerful and disciplined armies, its numerous and well-ap-
pointed fleets, entering into a fierce and victorious conflict
with the veteran troops of Sweden, headed by Charles XII."
And all this due to the concentrated might of one man—
Peter the Great!

It is this "undivided will" which works miracles. It is
men of this stamp who "change the front of the world."
How in contrast to these appears the Jack at all trades and
master of none one sees on every hand! The attempted
versatility of certain men reminds one of the sign in an
obscure London shop window—"Goods removed, messages
taken, carpets beaten, and poetry composed on any subject;"
or of that one in Paris of a certain Monsieur Kenard, who
announces himself as "a public scribe, who digests accounts,
explains the language of flowers, and sells fried potatoes."

All who have watched the careers of their schoolfellows
must have noted how often the brilliant member of his
class has succeeded in after life only in making of himself
a brilliant failure; while the commonplace plodder, whose
horoscope was far from bright or promising in those earlier
years, has easily overtaken and passed his more favoured
rival. One need not look far to find the secret of it all.
With those who have failed there is almost sure to be found
the inevitable factor of shiftlessness. Easily dissatisfied,
they have drifted from one vocation to another, veritable
rolling stones, until all purpose and energy and stamina have

disappeared, and they have finally found themselves forced by sheer necessity into the occupations and drudgeries of mere menials. It is the old story of the lump of gold continually bartered with ever-increasing ill fortune until the poor old grindstone, received in final exchange, is precipitated by a crowning stroke of ill luck into the stream. Many a man of respectable parts to begin with has thus frittered his life away. One must learn to take into reckoning "the long result of time," and not alone mere present gain. May we not discover right here, too, an explanation of that which has often puzzled more than one of us—namely, the fact that so many men of fine scholarship and much erudition are so often inefficient, and fail to impress themselves in any wise upon their fellows? They have stores of learning, but it is like lumber in a garret—it is not available. They seem not to know how to use it or to make it effective. And so they remain apart from the great, busy, throbbing life of men, like driftwood or leaves that have been whirled into an eddy by the rushing tide, and left behind; or like stranded ships upon a bar, splendidly built and finely equipped, but comparatively useless unless some power can be found to float them. Or, to change the figure, they remind one of the great Corliss engine at the Exposition—perfect in every part, but useless until the band is on and the connection formed. Somehow, with most of these men, the band is never on.

How ponderous that mass of wheels and rods and levers on yonder railway! How immense the weight, how motionless! Who can stir it? But stay! Let the engineer once open that throttle, and see!—she stirs! she rouses herself! All those mighty, hidden forces, which remind one more of omnipotence than all else which the hands of man have chained, begin to assert their sway, and lo, what power! Alas! in these men of whom we are speaking, this force, so essential, seems for ever lacking. The one great requisite never comes. The omission is a fatal one. It is the presence of a great, controlling, all-absorbing purpose, that shall make effective all the rest. It is the single eye; it is the undaunted will, bringing into subjection all the other powers, and making them pay it tribute. Storrs has given us a fine picture of this. "See the lawyer," he says, "before a jury in a case where his convictions are strong and his feelings are enlisted. He saw long ago, as he glanced over the box, that five of those in it were sympathetic with him; as he went on, he became equally certain of seven: the number now has risen to ten; but two are still left whom he feels that he has not persuaded or mastered. Upon them he now concentrates his power, summing up the facts, setting forth anew and more forcibly the principles, urging upon them his view of the case with a more and more intense action of his mind upon theirs, until one only is left. Like the blow of a hammer, continually repeated till the iron bar crumbles beneath it, his whole force comes with ceaseless percussion on that one mind till it has yielded and accepts the conviction on which the pleader's purpose is fixed. Men say afterward, ' He surpassed himself.' It was only because the singleness of his aim gave unity, intensity, and overpowering energy to the mind."

It is this faculty, then, of throwing ourselves with undivided power upon the immediate work in hand, whatever it be, of which we speak. This power enables a man to forget himself and his surroundings, to lose sight of all that preceded and all that shall follow the one great absorbing task which has come with the hour and confronts him. As Sydney Smith says of study, the only valuable kind is "to read so heartily that dinner-time comes two hours before you expected it; to sit with your Livy before you and hear the geese cackling that saved the Capitol, and to see with your own eyes the Carthaginian sutlers gathering up the rings of the Roman knights after the battle of Cannæ, and heaping them into bushels; and to be so intimately present at the actions you are reading of, that when anybody knocks at the door, it will take you two or three seconds to determine whether you are in your own study or in the plains of Lombardy, looking at Hannibal's weather-beaten face, and admiring the splendour of his single eye." This is concentration— this is power, and the source of still greater power. This attribute it is that sends the soul straight to its object. It is Demosthenes swaying his listening auditory. He tells them of their wrongs, of the injustice done them, of the tyranny of their oppressor, until, swayed to and fro, rocked with swelling passions and emotions like a forest rocked beneath the sway of the storm when the whirlwind is abroad, they cry out in passionate utterance, with curved lip and blanched cheek and clenched fist, " Let us march against Philip !" It is Brinsley Sheridan resolved on the impeachment of Hastings, and bringing every point to bear in that marvellous speech until he carries the day. It voices itself in Perry's famous " We have met the enemy, and they are ours !" Its presence is unmistakable, and where it exists success may be predicted with almost the certainty of fate. Napoleon, being told that the Alps stood in the way of his armies, exclaims, " There shall be no Alps !" and the wondrous road of the Simplon is built. Given this attribute in a man's character in its fullest manifestation, and there is no limit to his possibilities of accomplishment. It takes possession of the boy Warren Hastings, as he lies upon the grass under the trees of the old ancestral estate at Daylesford, which had passed into other hands, and confers a power that makes the dream of this boy one of those dreams that come true.

Lowell, in one of his " Biglow Papers," makes the Rev. Homer Wilbur say : " People are apt to confound mere alertness of mind with attention. The one is but the flying abroad of all the faculties to the open doors and windows of every passing rumour; the other is the concentration of every one of them in a single focus, as in the alchemist over his alembic at the moment of expected projection. Attention is the stuff that memory is made of, and memory is accumulated genius." It is well to keep this in mind. Doubtless one great obstacle to this singleness of aim, or concentration, is the mistaken impression that one must know almost everything. One thus, by attempting to spread himself over too large a surface, soon finds that he is able to do nothing really as it should be done. Here was the one striking weakness of Coleridge; and Sir James Mackintosh, according to all accounts, must be placed in the same category. Curran, the Master of the Rolls, said to Mr. Grattan, "You would be the greatest man of your age, Grattan, if you would buy a few yards of red tape and tie up your bills and papers." Sydney Smith, referring to the remark, declares that this was the fault or the misfortune of Mackintosh. "He never knew," he tells us, "the use of red tape, and was utterly unfit for the common business of life. That a guinea represented a quantity of shillings, and that it would barter for a quantity of cloth, he was well aware; but the accurate number of the baser coin, or the just measurement of the manufactured article to which he was entitled for his gold, he could never learn, and it was impossible to teach him. Hence his life was often an example of the ancient and melancholy struggle of genius with the difficulties of existence."

Matthew Arnold has truly said that we have not time nor strength to deal with half the matters which are thrown upon our mind, and they prove a useless load to us. A paragraph recently went the rounds of the press, headed, "Never Forget Anything." This prompted a rejoinder from one of the most brilliant representatives of New York journalism on "The Use of Forgetfulness." It is an old proverb, he says, "Da mihi, Domine, scire quod sciendum est." And he further notes the instance of the great Grecian general Themistocles, who, when some one spoke to him of an art of memory, answered, "Teach me rather to forget......This happily illustrates," he continues, "the disparity between what we receive in our minds and what we have use for. The truth is, the great want of the day is concentration. Instead of acquiring that which we can digest and retain, our education is undertaken as if our life were endless, and our power of attention and recollection inexhaustible. It is not the omnivorous reader who makes his mark in the world or best does his work, but the man who concentrates his faculties on those especial subjects which come up before him in his life-work. When Agassiz was asked for his opinion touching a matter which bore upon the chemical analysis of a plant, he replied, 'I know nothing about chemistry,' and refused to give an opinion. He was a naturalist, not a chemist. It would be well to imitate the example of the great naturalist. Life is short; time is fleeting. The channels of knowledge run wider and deeper than ever before, and multiply a thousand-fold. It is but an infinitesimal part of the vast treasury of knowledge that man can grasp and use. The mind itself can retain but a given quantity; and just as we thin out the useless books of our libraries that we may appropriate the space to volumes of lasting worth, as we pull up the weeds in our garden that the flowers may find room to grow, so it is well for us to get rid of our mental weeds, and by using the means of forgetfulness relieve ourselves of the useless rubbish which encumbers the mind and hinders the growth and development of a true culture."

If you have anything to say, condense it; make it brief and strong. When the famous Dr. South was asked if he was going to preach a short sermon, he said, "No; I have not had time to prepare one." A clear, condensed statement, in the pulpit or out of it, means hard work and thorough preparation. "If you want to do substantial work, concentrate ; and if you want to give others the benefit of your work, condense."

The fact is, in order to attain to the highest success, one must learn early in his career that there are many things that are to be resolutely pushed aside. The vision becomes blurred, the energies weakened, by attempting to compass too wide a field. "It is always good to know something," was a wise utterance of one of the wisest of men. But by this he did not mean to assert that mere indiscriminate knowledge is always good. It is undeniably true that division of attention is with most men death to enthusiasm and success. "Beauty," declared Michael Angelo, "is the purgation of superfluities." To know, then, what wisely to omit, what resolutely to exclude from the realm of one's knowledge, is no small achievement. It is this that reveals the master. The laboured and useless acquirements of some men, and their ponderous and inefficient movements, remind one of Sir Robert Peel's description of a certain kind of eloquence, — "The smallest possible quantity of common sense enveloped in the greatest multitude of equivocal words."

One, then, must rigorously choose and maintain his specialty, in order to achieve any real success. This single-ness of purpose reveals itself at once. It is manifest in all that a man does. It is not easy of imitation. The bold front, the confident mien, may be assumed, but no one is deceived by it. One easily discovers a lurking falter in the tone, a hesitancy in the speech, a something in the glance which brings betrayal. All sincere and simple souls speak and act from the centre. While others are vacillating, they go directly to their object. Where the single eye is wanting, there is a tremor in the lip, a lagging in the gait, an in-decision, subtile but unmistakable, in the whole presence and air and bearing. There is "mud behind the eye." The "open sesame" of the true prince is honoured at once, but woe to the pretender. How many are the might-have-beens! Right here, probably, lies the secret of many a failure. These took one hand to their work, instead of throwing their whole strength upon it and their whole heart into it. How many such might have been giants who are only dwarfs! How many a one has died "with all his music in him!" How many a mute inglorious Milton sleeps unknown because of failure just here! It is a lamentable fact, but one which must often have been noticed, that the children of those who have raised themselves to social position and influence by their own personal effort, almost invariably waste what their parents have saved. Superior advantages and brighter prospects are on the side of the children. There appears no good reason why they should not occupy even a higher place than their wise and persevering fathers. In reality they come to nothing. Take that case of the younger Cicero, for instance, or the son of Chesterfield;—the one with all his advantages a mere "dry pump with no suction;" the other, little more than a blockhead: in both, the great purpose wanting. There is much truth in that remark of Cassius :—

> " The fault, dear Brutus, is not in our stars,
> But in ourselves, that we are underlings."

One is perpetually reminded by some men of the remark once made concerning a certain personage, that he had spent all his life in letting down empty buckets into empty wells, and was frittering away his age in trying to draw them up again.

In contrast with such, what an inspiration is the fine spirit so noticeable in certain men! By them life's Gordian knots are instantly severed. Perplexities and vexations vanish like fog before a bracing nor'-wester. Surveyed from a certain standpoint, history itself seems but a record of the capacity or incapacity of a few individuals. Blot from

its pages the few great names which mark epochs, and what
is left seems surprisingly small. The history of the world
shows us that men are not to be counted by their numbers,
but, among other things, "by their clear and steady resolution of either ceasing to live or of achieving a particular
object; which, when it is once formed, strikes off a load of
manacles and chains, and gives free space to all heavenly and
heroic feelings."

See how this spirit manifests itself in all great souls,
from Saint Paul down. "This one thing I do;" "None of
these things move me." Here was the secret of that simple
soul which something had "compelled to be seraphic." So
of Socrates. "A voice had spoken in his soul, and he
obeyed it; he would do nothing else but obey it. He was
irresistible." See it in Pelopidas and Epaminondas prefer-
ring death rather than surrender their great purpose of
humbling Sparta. Note it in Pompey. It was not necessary for him to live, he said, but it was necessary that he
should be at a certain point at a certain hour. In Cæsar
and Napoleon we discover the same trait. And coming
down to the greatest soldier of these modern times, we find
the same spirit voicing itself in "I propose to move immediately upon your works;" and again in the words since so
familiar, "I shall fight it out on this line if it takes all
summer." Speaking of this very trait, Sherman, in that
remarkable letter to which reference has already been made,
says, "I repeat, you do M'Pherson and myself too much
honour. At Belmont you manifested your traits,—neither
of us being near. At Donelson, also, you illustrated your
whole character. I was not near, and M'Pherson in too
subordinate a capacity to influence you." After referring to
his bravery, unselfishness, and honesty, he further says,
"But the chief characteristic is the simple faith in success
you have always manifested......This faith gave you victory
at Shiloh and Vicksburg. Also, when you have completed

your best preparations you go into battle without hesitation, as at Chattanooga,—no doubts, no answers; and I tell you it was this that made us act with confidence. I knew that wherever I was you thought of me, and if I got into a tight place you would help me out if alive. My only point of doubt was in your knowledge of grand strategy and in books of science and history; but I confess your common sense seems to have supplied all these." What was this "common sense," to which General Sherman thus refers, but the very quality of which we are speaking,—that single eye which pierces through all surroundings, however chaotic, and sees at a glance what to do and how to do it; that simplicity of pur- pose which carries the soul straight to its mark; that un- erring instinct of victory which compels success? Wherever one discovers great achievement, he is sure to find behind it this inevitable simplicity of purpose. Rest assured that nothing great will ever be accomplished without it. It is true that at intervals certain men appear who seem capable of great accomplishment in almost any direction; equal to any amount of work, however arduous or varied,—men of phenomenal talent and great versatility, like Da Vinci, for instance; but these are the rare exceptions which prove the rule. Let a man devote five years of persistent study and application to any one thing, and he will be surprised to find with what ease and comparative pleasure the task which at first seemed so arduous and irksome may be performed. Truly has Fuller declared that he that sips of many arts drinks of none; and Bacon, in his "Letter of Expostulation to Coke," observes: "You, having a large and fruitful mind, should not so much labour what to speak as to find what to leave unspoken. Rich soils are often to be weeded." Ad- vice like this might well be heeded by some of our more voluminous authors. One might then hope to avail himself of what is most valuable in them, and yet have time for something else besides. "Why cannot authors," some one asks, "take the time and trouble to condense their wisdom and learning; for, really, who of the most diligent of their readers can hope to master even the truly valuable works of our great writers? There is Carlyle, for instance, with his thirty octavo volumes, and Ruskin with twenty. Both have amply illustrated the beauty and strength of the English language, but years alone are sufficient to do justice to these many volumes. Who doubts that each of these volumes might, not unprofitably, be cut down one-half; or better, that all might be condensed into a few handy volumes of reasonable size?" It has been well said of Ruskin, that were he to set forth and illustrate in a single volume the philosophy of art which he has spread over a score of volumes, there would be some possibility of a busy world acquainting itself with his principles and his spirit. But when one remembers that there are a hundred other eminent names besides, each with twenty, thirty, fifty, or a hundred volumes, all worthy of reading and study, one is simply overwhelmed, and is compelled to implore future writers, at least, to sift and resift their ideas and words, so that they may be brought into as small a compass as possible. Harriet Martineau condensed all that was valuable in the "Positive Philosophy" of Comte into a single volume; and Froude tells us that the great Spinoza compressed into three volumes the whole of his system of speculative philosophy, which was the work of a lifetime, and which revolutionized all previous systems. Had he been like certain others we know, he might have left mayhap a hundred volumes for dust and the moths. The voice of experience, the pressure of the times, the demand of the age, the conspicuous examples of failure and of success, all combine to emphasize the truth that a man must go straight to the mark if he would win.

When Louis Napoleon started off for the German campaign, the enthusiastic Parisians, we are told, removed his horses and drew his carriage through the thoroughfares themselves. But it was all a farce. Presently came Wörth, and Metz, and Sedan. The Emperor is a prisoner, the Empress is fleeing by stealth to England, and the eyes of the French people are opened. The *purpose* behind the German bayonets was more than a match for French display. The secret is the same in all realms, whether of art, or science, or what not. Hunt, in his "Talks about Art," gives emphasis to the desirability in a painter of that simplicity of eye which is the only simplicity which can and must be learned. "Think all you can. Put in as little hand work as possible, and as much intelligence. Permit yourself the luxury of doing it in the simplest way." Of similar import were the strong and noble words of Ex-Secretary Evarts to a body of theological students : " In trying cases, lawyers make little of their knowledge of Justinian and Coke. So the learning of the clergy should not be produced in sermons to the poor and weak and wicked. The learning should be assimilated into the growth of the mind, and the winged words of the preacher be sent at the foe in front, and not scattered among the squadrons on the sides." In the same vein, also, is the excellent advice of a fine authority on literary composition : "Say the most possible in the least space. Pitch right into your subject. Make the title and first sentence so that it must be read ; and so of the second, no matter what has preceded or is to follow." This has the true ring. The great fault with much would-be fine writing seems to be, that its author, to begin with, had nothing to say, and then has taken for ever to say it. It is wonderful what power and control over one's faculties may be acquired if one persistently keeps the one great and supreme object before the soul. The mind is naturally a vagrant, prone to wander into all sorts of by-ways, unless kept steadily and resolutely to its purpose and to its work. " Wool-gathering " is its proverbial characteristic. Once under control of a great purpose, however, all lesser objects can happily be placed under tribute as vassals. The night before the celebrated battle of Pharsalia, which was to decide the fate of the known world, Brutus was in his tent reading and making notes from his author with the pen.

There is nothing more striking than this power of concentration possessed by certain men,—that disciplined self-control which knows how to create its own solitude at will. It is indeed no small accomplishment,—the learning " to command one's time and think one's own thoughts amid the most feverish environments." But some of our finest treasures of English literature have been created amid surroundings most busy and distracting, and seemingly most unfavourable. Some of the most laborious literary undertakings have thus been prosecuted. It was in the midst of engrossing political duties that Niebuhr carried on his historical labours. In the intervals of a busy mercantile life Roscoe produced his Histories of Lorenzo de Medici and Leo X. It was in the midst of a restless and feverish career that Scaliger, Buchanan, and Erasmus accomplished their gigantic tasks. Or, take for instance in these modern times that lovely creation, Edwin Arnold's " The Light of Asia." It came not from cloister or solitude, but right from the heart of busy London, born amid the throng and uproar of the great metropolis, its author editor-in-chief of one of the great London dailies,—*The Daily Telegraph*, a paper with an average circulation of a quarter of a million copies. That this writer of " leaders," addressing every morning so large a circle, should have produced from out the hurly-burly of his daily occupation such a poem, is indeed a marvel. As Channing of London well says, " That amidst the responsibilities, interruptions, anxieties, harassing cares, and ever varying distractions of such a life, a poet could evoke, in his few hours for quiet thought, an epic in eight books on one of the loftiest themes for spiritual contemplation, and one of the purest ideal types of a heavenly human life known in history, is certainly a surprising instance of concentrated power." And the same writer further affirms, that to his certain knowledge the book was only conceived, begun within the year, and was perfected and published during one of the most disturbed and trying periods that the nation had passed through for a generation at least. Power like this is to be coveted. To be able, as Byron has felicitously put it, thus to steal from "all one has been or yet may be," and lose one's self entirely in the present duty, is certainly invaluable to a busy man. Charles Kingsley possessed it in a marked degree. In that charming volume, "Letters and Memories" of his life, we are told that his holidays were few and far between in his life of labour, but when they came, he could give himself wholly up to them, thanks to his " blessed habit of intensity," which he declared had been his greatest help in life. " I go at what I am about," he used to say, "as if there were nothing else in the world for the time being. That's the secret of all hard-working men ; but most of them can't carry it into their amusements." As Thomas Hughes said of him, his was " a spirit of fearless and manly grappling with difficulties ; a spirit of vigorous, prompt, and rigorous carrying out of whatever was taken in hand ; a spirit of generous and hearty co-operation with fellow-workers, a wide range of interest,—not meaning by this, scattered, desultory thought, but thought like Napoleon's, ready to be concentrated at once where the battle must be fought."

Many a failure in life has been due to the fact that there has been more than one object present to the mind, a double vision in place of a single picture before a single eye. Secondary considerations have been allowed to confuse the mind and thwart the purpose. Expediency has been consulted until the native thrill of resolution has died out. Simplicity of purpose suffers not from the loss of energy, which is inevitable where there is a scattering of effort. Forty years ago a young mechanic took a bath in the river

Clyde. While swimming from shore to shore he discerned a beautiful bank, uncultivated, and he then and there resolved to be the owner of it, and to adorn it and build upon it the finest mansion in all the burgh, and name it in honour of the maiden to whom he was espoused. "Last summer," says a well-known American, "I had the pleasure of dining in that princely mansion, and of receiving this fact from the lips of the great ship-builder of the Clyde." That one purpose was made the ruling passion of his life, and all the energies of his soul were put in requisition for its accomplishment. It has been well said, that a steady gaze, a settled purpose, an unwavering earnestness, a simple motive, will carry a man rapidly and pleasantly to his goal, and spare him many troubles by the way. Instead of being diverted by the distractions, or misled, as loiterers through life are sure to be, by surrounding allurements, the simple-minded worker discharges his duty and presses forward unaffected by the hindrances by which others are delayed. Thoroughness in work or character is priceless. It is this which gives completeness to accomplishment, whether the thing achieved be great or small; and this is all-important. In its finest manifestation, the great undertone which pervades it is always this: "Whatsoever thy hand findeth to do, do it with thy might." One-half the failures are due to a lack right here. Nothing can take its place. Neither sagacity, nor keenness of instinct, nor absorbing toil and devotion to one's interests will avail where this is wanting. It is not so much the amount of work men do, it has been said, which kills them, as the way in which the work is done. Strains and bruises come from "dead lifts."

It is interesting to note the sway of a great purpose over the soul, and its power to win men from minor considerations, which, with men generally, count for so much. The love of fame and the love of money, for instance, have great influence with most men. But the response of

Agassiz, when urged to devote a portion of his time to lecturing, on account of his great popularity and the amount of money he would be sure to make, shows how little hold this consideration had upon him : "I have no time to make money !"—a characteristic reply. So of Beethoven. On a certain occasion, despondent on account of his increasing deafness, and almost tempted to put an end to his life, he said, "Art—she alone, she held me back. Oh, it seemed to me impossible to quit this world before I had accomplished all of which I felt myself capable, and therefore I preserved this unhappy life." How, too, the strength of a great purpose has enabled men to triumph over obstacles and to scorn difficulty and danger ! See Locke subsisting on bread and water in a Dutch garret ; and Murray, the famous linguist, learning to write by scribbling his letters on an old wool-card with the end of a burnt heather-stem. Professor Moore, we are told, when a young man, being too poor to purchase Newton's "Principia," borrowed the book, and copied the whole of it with his own hand. Samuel Drew used to tighten his apron-strings "in lieu of a dinner ;" and Heyne slept many a night upon a barn floor with only a book for his pillow.

To accomplish anything, one must have an object ; he must keep his eye fixed on that. To be great in any direction, one must concentrate all his strength. Divide him, and you conquer him ; concentrate his powers, and he becomes invincible. Alexander, his heart throbbing with a great purpose, conquers the world. Hannibal, impelled by his hatred to the Romans, even crosses the Alps to compass his design. While other men are bemoaning difficulties, and shrinking from dangers and obstacles, and proposing expedients, the great soul, "without fuss or noise," takes the step, and lo "the mountain has been levelled, and the way lies open." Let the man, then, who would succeed, throw his whole being into one work ; let him pursue it with relentless will and energy. Let him scorn difficulty and danger, and brave defeat. Let him adopt the motto which the Scottish editor posted in his *sanctum sanctorum,* "Nothing is worse for those who have business than the visits of those who have none." Let him have one dominating, ruling, all-pervading purpose, and compel all else to pay it tribute, and, rest assured, he will not long remain in doubt as to results.

# V.

# Ḥabit.

How use doth breed a habit in a man !—SHAKESPEARE.

For use almost can change the stamp of nature.—*Ib.*

"Man is a bundle of habits."

I trust everything under God to habit, on which in all ages the law-giver as well as the schoolmaster has mainly placed his reliance,—habit, which makes everything easy, and casts the difficulties upon the deviation from a wonted course.—LORD BROUGHAM.

A MAN'S success in life depends so largely upon the habits which he forms at a very early period, that nothing would seem to be more important than to have the strongest possible conviction of this wrought into his mind at the very outset. "I feel as if it were not for me to record, even though this manuscript is intended for no eyes but mine," says Dickens in "David Copperfield," "how hard I worked at that tremendous shorthand, and all improvement appertaining to it......I will only add to what I have already written of my perseverance at this time of my life, and of a patient and continuous energy which then began to be matured within me, and which I know to be the strong point of my character, if it have any strength at all, that there, on looking back, I find the source of my success." The great tendency with all of us is to form habits, to run in grooves. Fortunately this great controlling principle in human nature has its good side. If it indeed be true that

"Ill habits gather by unseen degrees,
As brooks make rivers, rivers run to seas,"

it is also true—and the thought has comfort in it—that by
the blessed law of compensation this deep-rooted tendency
works for good as well as ill; that life's sternest duties and
requirements, however arduous at first, become at length,
by their continued performance, not only easy, but a source
of real pleasure.

A modern essayist has somewhere declared, and it seems
to us a singularly wise remark, that no one's example is so
dangerous to us as our own; for when we have done a certain thing once, it is so much easier to do it again.    Habit
forms itself by repeated action.    Habits are like paths
beaten hard by the multitude of light footsteps which go to
and fro.    No reason can be given why the fact of having
done a thing should increase the tendency to do it; all reason stops at this point,—it is not possible to explain it.
The pain annexed to the interruption of the habit, we are
told, is the means by which obedience to the law is secured.
Nature is too good a legislator to pass any act without
annexing a smart penalty to the violation of it.    No one
thing concerning it is more curious than this very fact, that
though we feel, possibly, no pleasure in doing that to which
we have become accustomed, we do feel great pain from not
doing it.    A habit is something which we *have*.    That is
what the word means.    As some one has wittily observed,
it often becomes something which has us.    Sometimes men
shorten distances by "cutting across lots," as it is termed.
Where they do this, a narrow strip of grass about a foot or
fourteen inches wide will soon be destroyed, and a narrow
strip of ground about the same width beneath it will be
trodden hard,—and that is a path.    In the same way men
form habits.

This curious physical impulse of habit has been noted by
Dr. Combe.    "A tendency to resume the same mode of
action at stated times," he says, "is peculiarly the characteristic of the nervous system, and on this account regu-

larity is of great consequence in exercising the moral and intellectual power. All nervous diseases have a marked tendency to observe regular periods ; and the natural inclination to sleep at the approach of night is another instance of the same fact. It is this principle of our nature which promotes the formation of what are called habits. If we repeat any kind of mental effort every day at the same hour, we at last find ourselves entering upon it without premeditation when the time approaches."

The proclivities which develop and harden into habits are apt to reveal themselves early, and when properly encouraged and patronized they have often resulted in brilliant achievement. Take for instance the simple propensity for whittling. Sam Cunard was a Scottish lad of Glasgow. He was clever and facile in all sorts of inventions. These he wrought out with his jack-knife. This seemed his only talent. For a long time it brought him neither money, credit, nor reputation. But at length there came a special demand for his peculiar talent. The great ship-builders and owners, Burns and M'Ivor, wanted to increase their facilities for transatlantic navigation,—for carrying foreign mails in particular. They consulted Sam. He at once set his wits and knife at work. The result was a model of the first steamship of the celebrated Cunard Line. All their magnificent ships have been built from that one model, without material alteration. This company, as every one knows, has now a great fleet of capacious steamships doing service in every sea and employing many thousand men. Surely Sir Samuel Cunard's jack-knife had wrought well. That Scottish lad's whittling propensity enabled him to retire from active life with an ample fortune, with the honours of knighthood, and the pleasure of knowing that he left his appreciative patrons more largely enriched even than himself, and the whole world greatly benefited. Napoleon's boyish passion for his mimic cannon only foreshadowed the terrible execution of his artillery in later years. Those crude charcoal sketches of Sir Joshua Reynolds's boyhood, under which his severely practical father had written, "Done by Joshua out of sheer idleness!" foreshadowed the future greatness of the man. The same may be said of that portrait of the sleeping infant, drawn in red and black ink by the boy West while yet only seven years old. The truant Tom Gainsborough wandering along the green lanes and past the hedgerows of Sudbury, and seating himself amid the flapping dock-leaves to draw, betokened even then "the first English painter of English landscape." One of his paintings to-day is worth a fortune to its possessor; indeed, one of them was but recently sold for the sum of ten thousand guineas. So, too, of many another youth it may in truth be said, "the child is father of the man."

It has been said that we come into the world a bunch of susceptibilities. The noiseless years pass on, and we emerge into maturity "a bundle of iron habits." Ten thousand influences are perpetually at work upon us; invisible powers mould and fashion us. We look into a man's face and receive a certain impression, but all of the real man is out of sight. The habits of thought which are transforming his life and character are hidden; yet they leave their impress just as truly as the sculptor leaves his upon the marble block. Note him at his work. A stroke here, another there, a thousand gentle touches, and presently you perceive that the curve of the lip, the play of the nostril, the expression of the eye, have all been growing under his hand, until at length the striking countenance, powerful, impressive, grand, stands out before you "the artist's thought severely beautiful, fixed for ever in the solid stone." So with men. The lofty aspiration, the benevolent thought, the sympathy, the incorruptible integrity, all reveal themselves. There are some faces that need no letter of commendation. Like the shining face of Moses descending the mount, the countenance betrays the luminous secret. Contrast with these the bleared visage, the sodden look, the dull and lifeless expression of this other, and see what evil habit has wrought in the features of the prodigal.

Every man carries within himself to a great extent his own destiny. Undaunted will, unflinching energy, ever and everywhere make their mark and bring success. In business, who is the man that succeeds? The man who thinks clearly, who plans wisely, and executes promptly and with untiring energy. "Is there one," says the eminent John Hunter, "whom difficulties dishearten? He will do little. Is there one who *will* conquer? That kind of man never fails." Difficulty and hardship bring out and develop the latent powers. It is the habitual blow on blow which makes the arm of the blacksmith so strong. We are unconsciously educated by our surroundings, our habitual associations, as well as by our habits of thought. Our companions, our books, the conversations of every day, leave their impress for good or ill. We are not the same to-day as yesterday. In the chamber of the boy who ran away to sea was found the picture of a splendid ship under full sail. It hung upon the wall. It greeted him every time he entered the room. When he awoke in the morning his eyes turned to it,—his thoughts dwelt upon it. The desire to be a sailor became at length the ruling passion of his life. That picture was the secret of it all. This it was that at length became the occasion of his flight.

The law is universal. We see its influence in every direction. "There is no degree of disguise," says a distinguished essayist, "which human nature may not be made to assume from habit. It grows in every direction in which it is trained, and accommodates itself to every circumstance which caprice or design places in its way." Many persons wonder why men of great fortune continue to labour, instead of resting and enjoying themselves, and attribute it to mere

love of gain. They forget that long habit becomes second
nature ; that such men find rest in constant occupation, and
that the enjoyment prescribed for them would be the severest
punishment that could be inflicted. Take the case of A. T.
Stewart or William B. Astor, for instance. A few years
since, Mr. Stewart spent regularly fourteen hours of the
twenty-four behind his desk in his private office, working
daily harder than any one in his employ, and as unapproach-
able as the Grand Lama. Even those who succeeded in obtaining an interview achieved it only after running such a
gauntlet of interrogations and cross-questions at the hands of
the various personages set for the great merchant's defence
that they were not likely soon to renew the attempt. For
more than fifty years William B. Astor was a daily worker
at his desk. Sentence such men as these to idleness, and
before many years, not to say months, they would in all prob-
ability be in their graves. Long-continued habit has made
their work a second nature, and without it they would be
utterly wretched and unhappy.

Habit increases our facility for work. It is the secret of
skill in all realms of human endeavour. It gives rapidity to
the fingers of the knitter, and confers the wonderful execution possessed by the master musician. The rapid *click*,
*click* of the nimble type, dropping like leaden hail from the
practised hand of the skilful compositor, is the result of this
same all-prevailing law. Statesman, artisan, editor, all find
their work easier as they repeat their efforts, just as the persistent habit of lifting heavy weights made Winship the
modern Hercules that he was. The skill of the Japanese
juggler and the marvellous feats of the gymnast are due to
the same law.

It is all important to remember, too, that unless the habit
of doing what a man proposes to do at any given time has
been securely built up, it is liable to break down upon the
application of a severe test, and often at a critical moment,

when he needs it most. Never did West Point stand so high in public estimation as during the war, when "the superiority of men educated systematically, and in all military matters, was established beyond controversy. This was seen especially in unexpected movements and emergencies. The civilian might fight one battle, and fight it well; but the next might take him by surprise, and end in a signal but unnecessary defeat." When the great crises come, the real power and stamina which long training and habit have wrought hold a man unflinchingly to his post. Under ordinary circumstances the captain of an ocean steamship may seem a very genial, easy-going man; but let danger threaten his noble vessel, and the real character of the man begins to display itself. The habits of promptness and decision, of sleepless vigilance and energy, which long discipline has conferred are revealed. You will find him at his post, hour after hour, undismayed by the terrors of darkness or the fury of the storm. Fidelity and discipline have a marvellous power. The last thing heard as the waters closed over the ill-fated *Arctic* was the sound of Stewart Holland's gun.

The cultivation of a habit of attention to little things is invaluable to a man. Wellington was remarkable for this. All the petty details of military service and camp life received his closest attention. To this scrutiny of minute matters rather than to genius his success is traced. He had the rare distinction, it is said, of never losing a battle. No fragment of information escaped his memory or attention, no matter how apparently unimportant.

Some writer has aptly observed that one ought to know something about everything and everything about something. Harvey, speaking of Thomas H. Benton, says: "Mr. Benton had all sorts of knowledge. He seemed to have acquired more political facts than even John Quincy Adams. He had a wonderful memory, and read almost everything. During the discussions on the Oregon Bill, Mr. Benton made

a speech, as did many other members; and near the close of
the debate, Mr. Webster was about to speak, and wanted to
get a book, *of which he had an indistinct recollection*, for some
geographical fact to illustrate a point in his remarks. It was
something he had seen a great many years before in a book
which was now probably out of print. He only knew the
name of its author, but he set to work to find it. He asked
Peter Force, who had collected a great political library at
Washington; but Mr. Force could not find it. He then got
the librarian of Congress to hunt for it; but he had no
success. Mr. Webster was about giving it up in despair,
when it occurred to him to speak to Benton. He went to
him and said, 'You know everything, colonel, and where
everything is. Have you any recollection or knowledge of
such a geography, such a book, or such an author?' The
colonel stopped a moment to think, and then replied, 'I
know what you want; I'll see if I can find it.' An hour
afterwards, Mr. Webster, having left the Senate, returned
to his seat, and there, lying on his desk, was an immense book,
with a leaf turned down to the place that he wanted to find,
although he had not said a word as to the particular *part* of
the book he wished to consult. Without any suggestion of
his, Mr. Benton had guessed at what he wanted, and turned
down the leaf. 'I looked up from my desk to his,' said
Webster, 'and there he was, bowing to me as if to say,
"That's it." I do not suppose there was another man who
could have found that book for me.'"

It is related of George the Third that on one occasion when
Mr. Justice Park was present, the king said of him, "It is
wonderful to think that this little head contains the whole law
of England." "Not so, sire," replied the judge; "it but contains *the knowledge where the law may be found*." These are
notable instances, truly. On the other hand, there are men
whose knowledge is so confused as to remind one of the woman
who had "a place for everything and everything in *that* place."

This ability to recall at will where to find what one wants strikes the key-note of all really serviceable memory. One may cultivate the habit of memorizing like a parrot, but this is of less use than is generally supposed. "What we most want ready and available is the power and the science, not the tools. A mathematician is such still, without his formulæ and diagrams. The oldest judge remembers the rules of law, though he forgets the case in point; and the ablest counsel are allowed refreshers." Some one has well said that it is the ignorant, not the wise man who tries to tell you all he knows. It is the poor, not the rich man who stops to count and jingle his shillings. "The scholar does not con every page of his library daily or during a lifetime. The millionaire does not daily convert all his property into shillings and pence and enumerate them; but the scholar and the millionaire, in times of emergency, know what and where are their resources, and fear no bankruptcy or sheriff, which is no small satisfaction."

The first great requisite in cultivating the habit of memory is *attention.* Indeed, it has been declared that the art of memory is the art of attention. "What thou dost not know thou canst not tell." In reading history, for instance, lay the volume aside now and then and see if you can give a clear and concise account of what you have read. Use the best and most expressive words you can command. Fox once said of Pitt that he had not only a word but *the* word,—the very word to express his meaning. Let this be your aim. One great secret is *a thorough determination to remember.* "They can who believe they can" is true here as elsewhere.

A habit of classification is of immense value. Let one learn to have "pigeon-holes" in his brain, if we may be allowed the expression. As facts come under his observation, let him classify them by putting those which are related to each other by themselves, and others which are also related by themselves. One easily remembers that which interests him. He thus comes presently to have a vivid conception of a subject, whatever it be, and *conception* is the quality for which we call a man "clear-headed." The author recalls a most striking illustration of the value of this habit as exemplified in the person of a distinguished scholar. The modesty of the man was unmistakable; and yet, as one listened to him, while there was no effort to shine, yet one caught such glimpses of the vast stores of information at his command that Goldsmith's lines seemed verified :—

> " And still they gazed, and still the wonder grew
> That one small head could carry all he knew."

Tennyson is said to have brought this habit to great perfection. It is related of Sumner that at one period of his senatorial career he had the impression that his memory was not serving him as it should. He accordingly procured an immense historical chart, hung it in his room, and formed the habit of committing a certain portion of it to memory every morning. This he compelled himself to do. It was a sort of mental gymnastics.

Joseph Cook affords perhaps one of the most notable illustrations of prodigious memory. A well-known general of our army, who knew Cook in his boyhood, and was his classmate, related to the author an incident of the latter's early life which appears not a little remarkable. It seems the students were to prepare orations, and two or three weeks' time had been allowed them for this purpose. On the morning of the day for delivery Cook came to his classmate's room to inquire concerning them. He had not done a stroke of work on his. He found his friend had prepared a very elaborate production, having spent days in its preparation. Cook proposed that they proceed to the grove and rehearse it. This was done. He held the manuscript during the rehearsal, after which they returned. The afternoon came, and Cook being first called upon, proceeded to the stage, and as a boyish trick gave the whole of his friend's oration, *verbatim et literatim,* from beginning to end. His only opportunity for committing it had been the brief interval mentioned. Such power seems indeed phenomenal.

Actors, we are told, have by the constant use of the memory accomplished some remarkable feats. Some years ago John Ryder, in England, undertook to memorize a copy of a London newspaper and recite it in public; and he did it, reciting the whole paper from beginning to end. The comedy of "The Game of Speculation" was translated from the French, rehearsed, and produced at the Lyceum Theatre in London in four days. Charles Matthews, who played the leading part, Affable Hawk, and who is on the stage throughout four long acts with hardly any intermission, committed the character perfectly to memory in twenty-four hours, or, to use his own words after the first night, "I swallowed the whole dose, and don't think I spilled a drop." When the curtain rose on the first production of "Pizarro," the last act of the drama was not written; and Brinsley Sheridan wrote off the fifth act in the green-room, the call-boy taking it from him and then distributing it to the different actors as the first four acts were being played, to be studied by them as best they could.

It is doubtless true that certain men of eminent abilities may dispense with rules. They are a law unto themselves, and instinctively follow rules without knowing it. But for the majority the diligent cultivation of desirable habits is indispensable; and few things are more important to one than the habit of observation. It is astonishing how many of us go about with our eyes open and yet seeing nothing. One great secret of the vivid character of the descriptions of Macaulay is the zeal with which he visited and made inquiries in the localities where many of the events took place which he has recorded. At Weston Zoyland, a village in Somersetshire about four miles from Bridgewater, celebrated

as being the scene of the Duke of Monmouth's defeat at the
battle of Sedgemoor, the historian was well known.   He
resided at an humble inn in the village for some weeks,
occupying his time with minute investigations in the neighbourhood, and while the facts and impressions were fresh in
his mind writing that portion of his narrative in a little room
which is still shown to the rare visitors to the locality.

We find the same method of work in writers of fiction.
When Sir Walter Scott was driven one day by a friend to
look at a ruined castle about which he wished to compose a
story or reproduce a legend, his friend saw him take out
his note-book and write the separate names of the grasses
and wild flowers which grew amid the ruins; and on his
friend expressing his surprise, he said that it was only by
such means a writer could be fresh ; otherwise, in all his
stories he would be mentioning the same kinds of flowers.
This "ignominious love of details" is doubtless the secret
of much of an author's success, after all.   Vernet, we are
told, was a perfect master of water when young, because he
studied the water itself constantly ; but when fame and age
came upon him, and he grew careless and neglected this
water study, he lost the faculty and worked by "a false and
uniform pattern."   Never forget that it is because you have
acquired the habit of " looking out for other people's thoughts
and illustrations that you have thoughts and illustrations of
your own."   Whitefield, it is said, was conversant with life
from the humblest mechanic to the first characters in the
land.   He let nothing escape him, but turned all into gold
that admitted of improvement.

As an illustration of the perfection to which this habit of
minute observation may be brought by training, we may
cite the fact that some years ago there was at Washington
a character familiar to the frequenters of the great balls and
receptions, whose duty it was to receive the hats and outer
garments of the guests as they arrived, and who had so

trained himself in this direction that without the use of
checks or memoranda of any kind he, on their departure,
with unerring accuracy would return to each of the hundreds
of guests his or her own property in every instance, and a
mistake was never known.

One will find the habit of carrying note-books to have
been a characteristic of most successful men. It was a con-
firmed habit with Beethoven. Grove tells us that he went
"nowhere without his sketch-books." In these books every
strain that occurred to him was written down at the moment.
He even kept a book by his bedside to record anything that
suggested itself. Abroad or at home it was all the same;
only out of doors he made his notes in pencil, and traced
them in ink on his return to the house. It seems as if he
placed no reliance whatever on his memory. He began the
practice as a boy, and maintained it to the last. In the
sale catalogue of his effects more than fifty of such books are
included. They are made of large, coarse music-paper, oblong,
two hundred or even more pages, sixteen staves to the page,
and are covered from beginning to end, often margin and all,
with close-crowded writing. Locke, Parr, and Gibbon always
read with commonplace-books beside them; and the same
method was adopted by Butler, the author of "Hudibras."
Pope always carried a note-book with him, and never hesitated
to jot down anything which struck him in conversation.

It is quite common for men of affairs, lawyers, editors,
statesmen, and men of letters, to have a system of this kind.
The great painters had the same habit. Leonardo da Vinci
always carried a sketch-book in his girdle. A certain writer
says of him: "He was so much pleased when he encoun-
tered faces of extraordinary character, or heads, or beards,
or hair of unusual appearance, that he would follow any
such more than ordinary attraction through the whole day.
He always carried with him a little book, in which he noted
down the features he met, eyes and mouths, noses and chins,

necks and shoulders, and at home would combine them to make up such heads as he wanted. Moreover, he often invited people from the lower orders to his house, amusing them and sketching their faces. For the sake of his studies he even accompanied criminals to the place of execution." Hogarth, it is said, would sketch on his finger-nail the face of any one who impressed him particularly in the street. This may account for the astonishing variety of the countenances in his drawings. Gainsborough in his morning walks made collections of broken stones, herbs, and fragments of glass. These were his memoranda. Then in his studio he formed a landscape model upon the table, expanding these objects into rocks, trees, and water.

No one, probably, ever brought this habit to greater perfection than Garfield. He had, we are told, a large leather-bound blank-book, arranged with indexes and classification divisions for the name, author, page, and subjects of books, wherein he hoarded scraps from his fugitive readings. His plan for preserving his memoranda he had matured with much thought, and he credited it with having much to do with the success of his extemporaneous speeches, the like of which, as every one knows, for wealth of information have not been heard in either branch of Congress for many years. It was a common saying in the reporters' gallery that when Garfield chose to cram on a subject, there was no man in Washington who could stand before the deluge of facts with which he would overwhelm all opposition. In his large memorandum - books there were many hundreds of pages filled with scraps, annotations, picked sentences, incidents, and witticisms, from a collection of authors and newspapers, representing the best thought in the literature, modern and ancient, of almost the entire world. Besides these quotations there were numerous thoughts of his own upon the innumerable things he had read during the course of his prolonged studies, and which he embalmed in black and white "when the 'idea divine' was warm and living in his brain." All were arranged in the nicest order, and through the series of books one could follow the trail of the great debater's readings, it is said, from their beginning. Thus, for the year 1859 you would find the first annotations on financial subjects at first somewhat straggling, and mixed in with more or less of the classic poets; then they become more frequent, until they outnumber all other topics. In addition to his scrap-book he had a large case of pigeon-holes, holding perhaps fifty boxes, labelled, " The Press," " French Spoliation," " Tariff," " Geneva Award," " General Politics," " State Politics," " Public Men," " Parliamentary Decisions," " Anecdotes," " Electoral Laws and Commission," etc. These were filled with the choicest references and bits of current literature on the various special topics, and were continually replenished from every product of the printing-press. The wonderful comprehensiveness of his readings, and the closeness with which he followed such a great number of public questions, was remarkable. It was this that enabled him to prepare in an hour's time to speak with detailed intelligence upon any question that might be sprung in the House of Representatives. It was this, too, which made him so formidable an antagonist; for by running over his memoranda on any subject which came up for debate he was almost sure to find just the thing he wanted—some ugly fact, perhaps, which his opponents had forgotten, because none of them had taken the trouble to preserve it "in the cold exactness of black and white." Garfield's references covered a greater range of public questions, probably, than those of any other public man in America. Indeed, it has been justly observed that it is doubtful if there was a debater in any of the European countries that could boast a broader literary culture than he possessed.

George Alfred Townsend's versatility in writing of public men is due in great measure, doubtless, to a similar system.

He is said to have a stock of scrap-books running back for twenty years, filled entirely with personal items; and there is hardly a man that the newspapers have spoken of during that time that Townsend cannot find something interesting about in his compilation.

The plan of George Bancroft, the historian, is probably more extended than that of any one else in this country. He works on a special subject, however, and has a score of stenographers and bookworms especially trained for the purpose, "as large as the editorial force of a respectable newspaper."

Emerson's habits in this direction are well known. He was accustomed to jot down his thoughts at all hours and places. The suggestions which came to him from his readings, conversations, and meditations were transferred to the note-book he carried with him. His mind being always alert, many a gem of thought was thus preserved. Who has not heard the story told of his wife suddenly waking at night, while as yet his habits were unknown to her, and anxiously inquiring, as she heard him moving about, if he were ill. "No; only an idea," was the response, as he proceeded to jot it down.

Verdi's habit is to jot down the ideas, as they arise in his brain, in the pages of his note-book, on the backs of old letters, odd visiting-cards, or anything, in fact, that comes to hand; then in the seclusion of his study the new work takes shape and consistence. Visitors, or society in any form, are said to be fatal to his work and paralyze his genius.

While many of the great creators of our literature have seemed thus in many points to agree in their general habits of preparation, their methods of actual work, when they have fairly settled themselves down to the task of giving shape and form to the products of their imagination, and bestowing upon them "a local habitation and a name," have differed greatly. Some, for instance, have laid great stress

upon plots, while others have seemingly paid little or no
attention to the plot itself, but have made the personages
their strong point—just as some lawyers emphasize the
points of law, while others make herculean efforts to carry
the jury, as Choate was wont to do. This latter course was
a marked characteristic of Dickens. The development of
a striking personage in the story seemed to wholly absorb
him, so much so that it has been said that he lost his own
identity for the time being in that of the creations of his
brain. His characters seemed to possess him, and he would
go wandering around at times as if in dreamland, while
under the pressure of this intense consciousness of their
reality—literally haunted by them day and night. As for
his plots, however, as has been aptly observed, they resemble
a highroad that winds, now into a green lane, now up a
steep hill, and now down to a broad valley, while one is left
utterly puzzled to tell how he arrived there. He was accustomed to seize at once upon the first ideas that came to him,
and to commit them to paper without elaboration. He was
at infinite pains afterwards, however, to revise and correct
both manuscript and proof.

Alphonse Daudet's stories, it is said, were all begun with
the climax and its participants, and from that point worked
back to the opening of the tale. Then the story was rewritten, the characters developed, and such incidents introduced as suggested themselves. They were written with
a purpose, but it was never known to the author when a
story was begun what characters would enact the incidents
leading to the catastrophe. It was a working back from
effect to cause. Théophile Gautier believed in long prefaces.
It was an epigram of his that his "greatest novel would be
all preface." Charles Reade did not approve of them. He
declared that many a clever story was ruined by a preface.
His theory was that the tale ought to tell itself, without
prologue or epilogue. A recent writer has given us a

delightful glimpse of Reade's own habits of work. He usually kept his stories on the stocks, he tells us, for a year or more. His method of nursing the youngling was peculiar. The chapters were roughly blocked out on separate sheets of paper. Then they were numbered and arranged in their order, or dropped between the leaves of a large scrap-book. Then the process of fecundation began : an incident was added to one chapter, a bit of description to another, and a scrap of dialogue found place on still another sheet. Then the shifting of scenes, incidents, dialogues, and whole chapters began. The matter in chapter *five*, for instance, found place in *eleven ; eleven* became *seven ; seven* was lodged at *five*, and so on. The work was growing all the time. Details were evolving themselves from the mass of facts. A new character was suggested. His course was traced roughly through the chips of this literary carpenter shop. He was hinted at, for example, in *three ;* he appeared in *six ;* he became necessary to the story in *nine*, and so on to the climax. A few important chapters were roughly written out, or dictated, then pinned together and replaced in the book or stowed in a pigeon-hole. Again more changes and transpositions. Finally the sheets, and scraps pinned or gummed to them, were all taken out and gathered into a stack. Then the author rapidly shuffled them over and grasped the story as a whole for the first time. When the story had reached this stage it was as good as written. Mr. Reade then settled down to seven or eight hours' manual labour a day, and in three months the book was advertised.

The prose fictions of Charles Kingsley (with one exception, "Alton Locke") were never copied. His usual habit was to dictate to his wife as he walked up and down his study. He was accustomed to master his subject thoroughly out in the open air, in his garden, on the moor, or by the side of some lonely trout-stream, and never to put pen to paper until the ideas were clothed in words ; and these, save occasionally in some of his poems, he rarely altered. Godwin, we are told, wrote "Caleb Williams" backward, beginning, on principle, with the last chapter and working up to the first, on a plan similar to that of Daudet, to which reference has been made. Charles Lever had remarkably little of the professional author about him. His biographer tells us that no panegyric about his last book would have given him as much satisfaction as an acknowledgment of his superiority at whist. He hated especially the drudgery of copying and revising.

Cooke tells us that when Emerson desired to write an essay he would turn to his note-books and transcribe all his paragraphs on the proposed subject, drawing a perpendicular line through whatever he had thus copied. These separate jottings, written perhaps years apart and in widely different circumstances and moods, were brought together, arranged in such order as was possible, and then welded together by such matter as was suggested at the time. Alcott says he once went to his study and found him with many sheets of manuscript scattered about on the floor, which he was anxiously endeavouring to arrange in something like a systematic treatment of the subject then in hand. He has also given us quite an entertaining account of Emerson's manner of preparing his essays. After referring to his remarkable diligence in securing everything which interested him for his commonplace-book, he tells us concerning these gathered treasures that they all had an intrinsic value, but they needed a setting. He did not let any of these sentences drop. How then shall these pearls be arranged and strung together? He employed no magic in this; they were gems when he had set them. That was his art. He copied them on paper, and saw how they would come together. One jewel after another was examined until he found one which he thought would do in a certain place. "There is no ordinary coherence in his essays. Each paragraph is complete in itself. Whatever he wrote was finished and good, but he considered every sentence well before it was put on paper. It was slept upon, dreamt on, and then written. You can't read one of his books at a sitting and get any good out of it. Each word, almost, must be pondered over."

Writing of the author of "The Scarlet Letter," one who knew him well says: "Though Hawthorne was humility itself in his estimate of his own powers, yet when once he was under the influence of his Muse, not all the criticism of ancient and modern times could have made him swerve by so much as a hair's-breadth from the path along which she led him. When he was at work he was in a region by himself,—alone with his art,—into which the voices of the exterior world could never penetrate, nor its presence intrude. The work being done, however, and sent forth, the worker would return to a colder and more sceptical state, in which he took, as it were, the part of the world against himself, and led the attack. So little is known of the man that it has always been the custom to paint his portrait from the same palette which he himself used for his pictures. But it is important to remember that the man and writer were, in Hawthorne's case, as different as a mountain from a cloud."

It is curious to note how many poets have first clothed their thoughts in prose. A recent authority assures us that the original form of the Æneid was a prose narrative, which was afterwards gradually versified, the poet writing at first fluently, and then laboriously polishing his lines till he had brought them as near perfection as possible. Thus, too, Goldsmith worked at "The Traveller" and "The Deserted Village," and Johnson composed "Irene," Butler his "Hudibras," and Pope the "Essay on Man."

When Balzac was engaged in writing his novels he used to send off the skeleton of the story to the printers, with huge blank spaces for the introduction of conversations, descriptions, and the like, and on receiving the printed sketch would shut himself up in his room, drink nothing but water and eat nothing but fruit and bread, till he had completed the work by filling up the spaces. Southey usually had three and sometimes four of his works passing through the press at the same time, and would give to each its allotted space during the twenty-four hours. Wordsworth used to go to bed on returning from his morning walk, and while breakfasting there dictate the lines he had put together on the march. One, at least, of Rossini's operas was composed in bed. He was at that time young, poor, and unknown, and lived in wretched quarters. He never wrote his overtures till the very last minute, and then apparently only because necessity compelled him.

Not every one can hope to bring himself under such perfect discipline and control as Anthony Trollope tells us he achieved, but doubtless many of us might approximate it. " It is my custom," he says, "to write with my watch before me, and to require from myself two hundred and fifty words every quarter of an hour. I have found that the two hundred and fifty words have been forthcoming as regularly as my watch went." While all may not be equal to this, few realize, who have not had the experience, how much may be accomplished by strict method and the systematic using of every fragment of time. Amid all the occupations of his busy life, Mr. Beecher declared at the banquet given to Froude, the historian, on the occasion of his visit to this country, that he accomplished the entire reading of the latter's " History of England " during the few spare minutes in which he had from time to time been kept waiting for his dinner. Longfellow's translation of the " Inferno " was the result of ten minutes' daily work at a standing desk in his library while his coffee was reaching the boiling point. " So soon as the kettle hissed," says Ward, " he folded his portfolio, not to resume that work until the following morning. In this wise, by devoting ten minutes a day during many years, the lovely work grew, like a coral reef, to its completion."

Instances are common in every-day life of men who cannot think to good purpose when shut up in a room with a pen, and who find their best inspiration in wandering about the streets and hearing what they want in the rattle of cabs and the seething of life around them, like the scholar of Padua whose conditions of work are given by Montaigne as a curiosity : "I lately found one of the most learned men in France......studying in the corner of a room cut off by a screen, surrounded by a lot of riotous servants. He told me—and Seneca says much the same of himself—that he worked all the better for this uproar, as though, overpowered by noise, he was obliged to withdraw all the more closely into himself for contemplation, while the storm of voices drove his thoughts inward. When at Padua he had lodged so long over the clattering of the traffic and the tumult of the streets, that he had been trained not only to be indifferent to noise, but even to require it for the prosecution of his studies."

Buffon declared himself utterly incapable of thinking to good purpose except in full court dress. This he always put on before entering his study, not even omitting his sword. On the other hand, there were few coats more threadbare, we are told, than those of Victor Hugo. Buffon did not deign, except in lace cuffs, to occupy himself with the humble animals whose history he was writing. It was his habit, also, to have his hair in such elaborate order that, by way of external stimulus to his brain, he had a hairdresser to interrupt his work twice, or when very busy, thrice a day. Haydn used to declare that if when he sat down to his instrument he had forgotten to put on a certain ring, he could not summon a single idea. How he managed to summon ideas, as some one aptly remarks, before Frederick the Second gave him the said ring, we are not informed.

But even these trivial instances of caprice, it has been well observed, help to suggest that when the fancy is called upon, the ordinary conditions of straightforward work must be considered at an end. Fancy dictates the terms on which she condescends to appear. Of Dickens we are told that "some quaint little bronze figures on his desk were as much needed for the easy flow of his writing as blue ink or quill pens."

At the time when Niccolo Machiavelli composed the works which have immortalized his name, he was living in obscure retirement, where his only companions were rustics. He himself says, in a letter to his friend Francesco Vettori, that he trifled away his days, but his nights he gave to intense study. "When evening closes in," he says, "I return home and shut myself up in my study; but before entering there I cast off on the threshold my rustic dress, covered with mud and dirt, and put on clothes fit for courts and senates; and thus attired, I enter the ancient courts of the ancient men, where, being by them affectionately received, I feed on that food which alone is mine, and for which I was born." While Haydn arrayed himself for his task in full court costume, his peruke sprinkled with powder, his wrists enclosed with delicate ruffles of fine lace, his fingers covered with rings of precious stones, Oliver Goldsmith loved best to write in dressing-gown and slippers.

Some men need active influences as their form of mental stimulus. Alfieri could work best while listening to music or galloping on horseback. Washington Irving's favourite studio was a stile in some pleasant meadow, where with his portfolio on his knees he formed his graceful periods. When Hazlitt had a work in hand he invariably went into the country to execute it, and almost always to the same spot,—a little wayside public-house called "The Hut," standing alone and some miles distant from any other house, on Winterslow Heath. It is the habit of Dumas the younger, when he has a new work in hand, to flee from

Paris to the château of Salneure, that he may write in quiet. "It may seem surprising to some that an author so Parisian, so bold, so fond of raillery, and so observing, should flee from his models and seek to write amid the silence and the poetry of the country such positive, aggressive, and lively works as bear his name."

This influence of one's surroundings is a very potent one. An intensely interesting chapter would be one giving an account of the novel circumstances under which certain of the most famous works were produced. Some of them we know. Shelley composed the "Revolt of Islam" while lying in a boat on the Thames at Marlow; Keats, his "Ode to the Nightingale" in a lane at Hampstead. Burns composed his magnificent lyric, "Scots wha hae wi' Wallace bled," while galloping on horseback over a wild moor in Scotland, and "Tam o' Shanter" in the woods overhanging the Doon. The greater part of Arnold's "Roman History" was written in his drawing-room with his children playing about him, and lively conversation, in which he frequently joined, going on around the table on which his manuscript rested. Priestley and Beddoes are said to have been fond of writing under similar circumstances. "What would to nine men out of ten be an intolerable distraction was to them a gentle and welcome stimulus." Johnson's "Vanity of Human Wishes" was composed as he trudged backwards and forwards from Hampstead. Some of Fielding's comedies were scrawled in taverns. Byron tells us that he composed the greater part of "Lara" at the toilet table, and the prologue on the opening of Drury Lane Theatre in a stage-coach. "Among all the distractions of the events they describe, Cæsar committed to paper the immortal 'Commentaries.' Moore's splendid Eastern romance 'Lalla Rookh' was written in a cottage blocked up by snow, with an English winter howling round." Longfellow's "Wreck of the Hesperus" came into his mind as he was sitting by his fireside the night after a violent storm. "He went to bed, but could not sleep. The 'Hesperus' would not be denied; and as he lay, the verses flowed on without let or hindrance until the poem was completed." Victor Hugo in his long walks would prepare the work of the morrow, and as his memory was prodigious he had only to write out what that dictated. He often related to his friends that in his youth, during a rainy winter, he was occupied with his "Marion Delorme." He had chosen, as a place of exercise under shelter, the Passage du Saumon. The first act, a marvellous commencement full of passion, poetry, and fire, was the work of two afternoons spent in promenading in this passage of dingy shops where were sold, side by side, stockings, straw mattings, and butchers' caps.

Authors do not often invite us behind the scenes. "Genius, like the Nile, keeps its springs secret." Yet we are favoured with occasional glimpses, nevertheless. As one perceives the utter and deliberate ignoring of all hygienic laws (at least as they are commonly received) on the part of many of these,—the turning of night into day and day into night, the reckless use of stimulants of all kinds, with other similar indiscretions,—one ceases to wonder that the significant designation, *genus irritabile*, should be given the unique race. A simple narrative of the way in which much imaginative work has been done would, as has well been said, read like an attempt to keep up the action of brain-fever by artificial stimulus. "Balzac preached to us," says Théophile Gautier, "the strangest hygiene ever propounded among laymen. If we desired to hand our names down to posterity as authors, it was indispensable that we should inmure ourselves absolutely for two or three years; that we should drink nothing but water and only eat soaked beans, like Protogenes; that we should go to bed at sunset and rise at midnight, to work hard till morning; that we should spend the whole day in revising, amending, extending, pruning, and polishing our night's work, in correcting proofs, or taking notes, or in other necessary study."

Byron affords an illustration of the tendency which one often finds to put one's-self "out of working condition" in order to work the better. "At Distati," says Moore, "his life was passed in the same regular round of habits into which he naturally fell." These habits included, as we are told, very late hours and semi-starvation, assisted by cigars and tobacco, and in the evening by green tea without milk or sugar. Schiller was a night-worker and a coffee-drinker. Not only so, but he used an artificial stimulus altogether peculiar to himself. He found it impossible, according to the well-known anecdote, to work except in a room filled with the scent of rotten apples, which he kept in a drawer of his writing-table, in order to keep up his necessary mental atmosphere. This at first glance seems really odd ; and yet who of us has not at times realized the potency of certain odours in recalling most vividly associations of the past ? The fragrance of new pine lumber or cedar shingles, for instance, or the burning of autumn leaves in the crisp morning air, recalls most vividly some of the brightest associations of youth. Doubtless by this same law of association this seemingly trivial influence brought back to the brilliant poet the memory of certain rare hours, and perpetually renewed for him the familiar atmosphere, flooding the mental horizon with its nameless charm.

Shelley's habit of continually munching bread while composing is not mere trivial gossip, we are assured ; and to mention in passing a modern instance in this direction, it is said that Jay Gould, the Wall Street magnate, has been known to have two sticks of peppermint candy placed regularly each morning on his office desk.

"That night, and not morning, is appropriate to imaginative work," declares a competent authority, "is supported by a general consent among those who have followed instinct in this matter. Upon this question, which can hardly be called vexed, Charles Lamb is the classical authority." Some one has asserted that he would hold a good wager that Milton's "Morning Hymn in Paradise" was penned at midnight. There have been two great imaginative writers, however, of the very first rank who believed that "the highest and freest work can be done under the healthiest conditions of fresh air, early hours, daylight, and temperance—not abstinence." One of these was Goethe, the other was Scott. Goethe and Balzac were the very antipodes of each other in their way of working. Mr. Lewes gives the account of Goethe's day at Weimar, as follows: "He arose at seven o'clock. Till eleven he worked without interruption. A cup of chocolate was then brought, and he worked on again till one o'clock. At two he dined. His appetite was immense. Even on the days when he complained of not being hungry, he ate much more than most men......He never dined alone. There was no dessert or coffee. Then he went to the theatre, or else received friends at home. By ten o'clock he was in bed, where he slept soundly......Like Thorwaldsen he had a talent for sleeping......No man of business or dictionary maker," adds Mr. Lewes, "could make a more healthful arrangement of his hours."

Dumas the younger is a morning worker. His habitual good-humour proves that his health is fine. "He is hungry immediately on rising, and attacks a good plate of soup with the eagerness of a rustic. After that he seats himself before a large secretaire and writes until noon in negligent dress." Hugo was an early riser, but he did not live on soup. "Before noon he lived only on his thoughts. He wrote much, and his heart was in his work." Lamartine was another early riser.

George Sand always wrote at night. "Lady of the manor during the day, devoted to her guests, making preserves, and engaged in needlework, it was at one o'clock in the morning, when the château was fast asleep, that this genius awoke and gave us 'Mauprat,' 'François de Champi,' 'Consuelo,' and a hundred other works."

If Balzac's may be taken as a type of the artist's life, Kant's may be taken as the type of the student's. While usually very methodical, there was one point in Kant's character which illustrates the need of the mind for artificial conditions, however slight they may be, when engaged in "dreaming." During the "blindman's holiday," between his walk and candle-light, he sat down to think in twilight fashion, and while thus engaged he always placed himself, it is said, so that his eyes might fall on a certain old tower. This old tower became so necessary to his thoughts, that when some poplar trees grew up and hid it from his window he found himself unable to think at all, until, at his earnest request, the trees were cropped and the tower brought into sight again. The elder Dumas, we are told, had to forbid himself, by an effort of will, to leave his desk before a certain number of pages were written, in order to get any work done at all; and Victor Hugo is said to have locked up his clothes while writing "Notre Dame," so that he might not escape from it till the last word was written. In such instances as these it has well been observed that the so-called "pleasures of the imagination" look singularly like the pains of stone-breaking.

These glimpses vouchsafed us from time to time reveal unmistakably the fact that the strange race to whom the world owes so much have been "compassed" to a surprising degree with whims and oddities, and ruled by habits and idiosyncrasies not a few.

It would be exceedingly interesting to know how long it takes for "use" to "breed a habit in a man." In this respect men differ greatly. Habits seem to attach themselves to certain men as readily as burrs or cockles fix themselves to one's clothing in passing through a neglected field, and to be shed almost as readily; almost every day displays some new trick or mannerism. Others cling with the tenacity of barnacles to the hull of an ancient ship. Habits seemingly most trivial, yet excessively annoying, have at times gained the ascendency over men of unquestioned power. What more amusing, for instance, than Dr. Johnson's habit of touching the posts, and of always placing his right foot first over the threshold?

While one recognizes the presence of this strange, occult power within him, this mysterious tendency in one's nature to repetition, holding within its viewless grasp such untold possibilities for evil as well as good; while it is also true that the finest natures have yielded to its baleful influence, as De Quincey's opium and poor Lamb's "wet damnation" testify; while on every hand are the bleaching bones of the victims of this demon who first clutches the soul and then destroys it, this mutinous sailor that *scuttles* the very ship on which he has taken passage,—it is yet a reassuring reflection that this same power may be harnessed to work *for* a man as well as *against* him. Let no one, then, fear to undertake the acquisition of any habit which seems desirable; for it *can* be formed, and with more ease than one may at first suppose. The habit of saving and improving every fragment of time, for instance, is invaluable. In the gold-room of the Philadelphia Mint there is a perforated floor through which pass the dust and filings of the gold, the aggregate value of which is thirty thousand dollars every year.

The inflexible rule of regularity soon becomes an all-important factor. Charles Dickens sat at his desk for three hours every morning, no matter whether he wrote a word or not. Habits become at length part and parcel of the man himself, inwrought in the very fibre of his being, betraying themselves at times in the very latest utterances of the lips. Lord Tenterden expiring with the words, "Gentlemen of the jury, you will now consider your verdict," Napoleon's "Tête d'armée!" and Chesterfield's "Give Dayrolles a chair," are striking examples of this.

Habit thus becomes destiny. "God gives us the power to form habits, that we may crystallize victories. All improvement in the eye of the painter, in the tongue of the orator, in the hand of the artisan, is the gift of habit. It is a channel worn in the substance of the soul, along which our purpose and our ability run with increased facility." The formation of a habit reduces to this simple direction : Apply yourself to any course marked out for yourself industriously, punctually, and persistently, and you prevail. Having this marvellous power at command,—*use it!*

# VI.

# Health.

For life is not to live, but to be well.—MARTIAL.

"A brilliant intellect in a sickly body is like gold in a spent swimmer's pocket."

O blessed health! thou art above all gold and treasure; 'tis thou who enlargest the soul, and openest all its powers to receive instruction and to relish virtue. He that has thee has little more to wish for; and he that is so wretched as to want thee, wants everything with thee.—STERNE.

THE author wishes he could be sure of making this chapter so interesting that its perusal might not only confer pleasure but profit as well. He is fully aware that no subject could well seem more hackneyed. At the same time, he is also persuaded that no subject touched upon in the whole volume has so important a bearing upon the success of any man. One may possibly escape the commonplace even in the treatment of so trite a theme. Nor let it be supposed that the writer is an advocate of "sawdust puddings," or that he looks with any degree of allowance upon "cant," which he abhors. He gives assurance, moreover, that the chapter shall not be, if he can help it, a morbid one, at least. Happily, as regards himself he can say that

> "Good digestion waits on appetite,
> And health on both."

Yet observation and experience have both proved to him what an enemy to all a man's best interests ill-health is. He

11

has seen men in the great army of letters, and others in the full tide of business prosperity, compelled to drop out of the ranks at the very moment, perhaps, when success was just at hand. He has known men of most brilliant parts and rarest attainments hampered and trammelled for years for the same reason, and cut off at length in middle life with their great projects all unfulfilled.

Well does the author remember a certain evening when one of the most brilliant and accomplished of scholars called around him in his library a group of students, and in an impressive manner urged upon them the vast importance of caring for their health. Nor was the influence of his words lessened by the knowledge that the advice came from the depths of a bitter experience on the part of the one who gave it ; and the counsel was still more strongly emphasized when in a few brief months that brilliant life went out just as the fruits of years of scholarly research were about to be given to the world.

Now, if health be not invaluable, and of paramount importance to a man, what means that first inquiry of all nations when one man meets another? The very first salutation of all, in slightly varying phrase, concerns a man's health. Its loss is the subject of most anxious concern and solicitude among friends; and yet we go on abusing it, apparently without a thought of its inestimable value,— violating its laws until compelled by stern necessity to use wisdom when perchance too late.

Blackie has called attention to the fact that great men have often overworked themselves by foolishly attempting to do that which might just as well have been left to subordinates. Every one can see how foolish it would be in a great military leader, on whom the lives of thousands and possibly the fate of a whole campaign depends, to unnecessarily expose and hazard his life in some insignificant encounter. That remonstrance of the people when David had

mustered his army for battle, and declared that he would
surely go forth with them himself, was not without meaning. "Thou shalt not go forth," said they: "for if we flee
away they will not care for us; neither if half of us die,
will they care for us; but now thou art worth ten thousand
of us." And they were right. The health of every one is
of vast moment to himself, but there are many reasons why
the health of a professional man seems to be and really is
more valuable than that of some others. Louis XIV., saun-
tering in the garden of Versailles with his courtiers, saw
Mansard, the architect, walking through one of the alleys.
He soon joined the old man, and Mansard took off his hat,
as was strict etiquette in the presence of his sovereign; but
the king lifted up his hand in friendly reprehension, and said,
"Pray keep it on. The evening is damp, and you may take
cold." The courtiers, who were all standing bareheaded
around the king, stared at each other at this extraordinary
show of courtesy. But Louis, observing their surprise, said,
"Gentlemen, you are amazed; but learn this: I can make a
duke or a marquis with my own breath, but God only can
make a Mansard."

Herbert Spencer, in his after-dinner speech at the great
banquet given him in New York City just before his departure for home, said: "Along with your kindness there comes
to me a great unkindness from Fate; for now that, above all
times in my life, I need full command of what powers of
speech I possess, disturbed health so threatens to interfere
with them that I fear I shall very inadequately express
myself. Any failure in my response you must please ascribe,
in part at least, to a greatly disordered nervous system."

Dickens also, when he gave his famous "Readings," during his second visit to America, was sadly out of health.
He was thus obliged to deny himself many a pleasure, and to
decline the most flattering invitations of a social nature. In a
letter written to his friend, Mr. Philp of Washington, he said:

"I was on the point of writing to express to you my regret that I must forego the pleasure of dining with you while at Washington." Then referring to his indisposition, he added: "It is so oppressive, and would, but for occasional rest and silence, be so incompatible with my readings, that my only safe course is to hold to the principle I established when I left Boston, and gloomily deny myself all social recreations. I am bound to disclaim the least merit in this virtuous-looking self-denial. I retire to the cloister as discontentedly and growlingly as possible."

And poor Carlyle,—that Prometheus with a vulture for ever at his heart,—who has not felt a throb of sympathy at the spectacle of this strong spirit struggling through the long years against such odds? May not much of the bitterness and apparent ill-humour of this man be easily accounted for by the fact that his whole nature was warped and distorted by the pangs of his perpetual and incurable malady; and should not corresponding allowance be made? In his talk to the students at Edinburgh he said, with an earnestness wrung from the depths of his own bitter experience: "Finally, I have one advice to give you which is practically of very great importance. You are to consider throughout, much more than is done at present, and what would have been a very great thing for me if I had been able to consider, that health is a thing to be attended to continually; that you are to regard that as the very highest of all temporal things for you. There is no kind of achievement you could make in the world that is equal to perfect health. What to it are nuggets or millions?" As has been truly said, Carlyle here but voices the common feeling of overwhelming, irreparable mistake that vast numbers are called to undergo. "No pangs of physical suffering would have wrung from this man such words as these, but the fact that he had been crippled in his work, that the clearness of his vision had been dimmed, and that a hue not natural to himself—a hue partial, distempered, morose—was spread over all that he had done.   It is late before we learn that the whole of man goes into his work.   Poet, orator, philosopher, or man of business, his body follows him and holds the pen, and shapes the thought, and imparts its quality to all that he does or says."

How true it is, as the Italians have it, " He that has good health is rich, though he knows it not."   But where you find one man thoroughly well, you will find a hundred who are not.   And the sad thing about it is that we are so reluctant to learn from the experience of others.   It seems as if each must needs learn the bitter lesson for himself before he can be made to feel and believe its truth.   And thus advice like that of Carlyle and others, so invaluable if youth would only heed it, is apt to go for little, if it be not wholly disregarded.

One thing, however, is certain: the man who aspires to be a master of the situation must have a care for his reserves. What a vast difference there is in men in this regard !   Some men seem utterly reckless as to these, while others are all the while carefully storing them away.   In ordinary times the reckless man may appear to be doing as well as, or even better than, the other.   But any man can be a pilot in a calm.   We may feel that all is well when the tide makes with us and the wind is fair ; but such times are of little value as a test of a man's real reserve power.   One might look into the genial face of the captain of that Cunarder on which he has taken passage as, when the weather is fine and everything running smoothly, he stands pleasantly chatting with his friends, and fancy it no great thing to run an ocean steamer, after all.   " But presently a great storm strikes the ship, and all night long, shuddering and panting through the wild waters, every beam and timber of the goodly vessel seems strained to the utmost by the fierce onslaught of wind and wave.   Peering deckward by the dim light of the approach-

ing dawn, he discerns the faithful fellow at his post upon the
bridge, where he has been all night watching the gale with
steady eyes and proud to see how splendidly his gallant ship
behaves, bringing her about in the teeth of the tempest and
the trough of the sea, that she may thus escape the terrible
strain and avalanche of waters that might well dismay the
stoutest heart. Now he begins to know the man." All undaunted, alert and cheerful, at length he brings the goodly
vessel into her desired haven. And so when a man is
smitten with a sore disease, if he have reserves of power and
strength laid up, he will doubtless in the end pull through.
If it be otherwise, however, the chances are all against him.
Collyer declares that reserves mean to a man also achievement,—"the power to do the grandest thing possible to your
nature when you feel you must, or some precious thing will
be lost ;......to do well always, but best in the crisis on which
all things turn ; to stand the strain of a long fight, and still
find you have something left, and so never to know you are
beaten, because you never are beaten."

The success even of professional men depends in no slight
degree on their organic stamina and cultivated physical
strength. "A well-developed thorax is considered," says
Smiles, "almost as indispensable to the successful lawyer
or politician as a well-cultured intellect. The thorough aera-
tion of the blood by free exposure to a large breathing surface in the lungs is necessary to maintain that full vital
power on which the vigorous working of the brain in so
large a measure depends. The lawyer has to climb the
heights of his profession through close and heated courts,
and the political leader has to bear the fatigue and excitement of long and anxious debates in a crowded House ;
hence the lawyer in full practice, and the parliamentary
leader in full work, are called upon to display powers of
physical endurance and activity even more extraordinary
than those of the intellect—such powers as have been ex-

hibited in so remarkable a degree by Brougham, Lyndhurst, and Campbell, by Peel, Graham, and Palmerston," and by our own Webster in the Senate—all full-chested men. The greatness of our great men is quite as much a bodily affair as a mental one. A Napoleon or a Wellington, who is to come off victorious at Austerlitz or Waterloo, must have immense resources in reserve; must be able to endure vast drafts upon his strength, to be harassed and perplexed in a thousand ways; must submit to great fatigue, be broken of rest at night and surprised by unexpected calamity by day, and yet be able to surmount and rise victorious over it all.

Let not, however, this fine power of endurance be confounded with mere physical strength. While great energy implies, indeed, a good body, it does not require great physical strength. Fine health and great nervous energy, or power to endure, may often exist without the latter endowment. Again and again it happened in our great Civil War that delicate-looking town-bred men would tire down the great strapping fellows from the farm, the young giants of the backwoods and prairies, outfight them and outlive them; and the fine reserves of the Harvard men, it has been observed, covered them with glory, while the shallow and brute force of " Billy " Wilson's regiment ended in disgrace. William M. Evarts is slender to frailness; but, as some one has said of him, he has a nervous system that enables him to endure a harder and longer mental strain than any other lawyer of the New York bar. It is curious to note how certain men have been found possessed of these exceptional powers of endurance, who to all appearance were deficient in this very thing; showing that the appearance of ill-health, while generally to be relied on, is not infallible. Many a man who to all appearance has inherited the most fragile of constitutions has been found possessed of such a wiry power of endurance as would indicate rather a constitution of iron or of brass. For years before he died, the venerable

Bishop Smith had the appearance of being in the last stage
of decline, and yet he lived to be nearly ninety.  Then, too,
there was Chief-Justice Taney, who lived to the age of
eighty-seven, and seemed all his life to be hanging on the
verge of the grave.  For a long time before Andrew Jackson appointed him Secretary of the Treasury, and got him
to remove the deposits from the United States Bank, he was
one of the leading lawyers of Maryland.  Luther Martin
and William Pinkney were for a time his chief competitors;
but they died, leaving him at the head of the bar.  At this
time, we are told, a man who had a Chancery suit which
had been a long time in the courts, and bade fair to become
a second Jarndyce v. Jarndyce, was looking for a new lawyer to take up his case.  He had employed both Martin and
Pinkney, and one after the other they had died on his hands,
leaving his case still unsettled.  He was recommended to
engage Taney, and with this in view he called upon him.
He entered the office, took a look at the emaciated form and
graveyard air of the great lawyer, and then, with an expression of disgust, he turned on his heel and went out.  "Give
that man my case!" he said to the first friend he met; "I
would as soon give it to a corpse.  He will die inside of two
months."  But Taney did not die, and he doubtless survived
the above prophet by a full generation.  One of the most
famous of these men who lived to a great age, in a characteristic letter to a friend of the present writer, once, with that
gentle facetiousness one sometimes finds in the most serious
and reverent souls, compared himself to Charles the Second,
who apologized to the noblemen about his bed for being such
an unconscionable while a-dying.

It goes without saying that "half a loaf is better than no
bread;" and if one must needs be a prisoner, let him garnish
the walls of his prison-house as best he may, and thank fortune that a kindly jailer spares him the lash and the thumb-
screw of torture.  But what a contrast, and how far inferior,

is such merely negative, passive enjoyment, to the robust, positive joy of bounding health! Surely no sensible man will affirm that a physical condition which compels the most studied caution and watchful anxiety is to be compared with that bounding exuberance of health and spirits which over-flows its banks and inundates all around it with its own immeasurable fulness of light and joy. Who would long hesitate in the choice between the apprehensive timidity of invalidism, which must perpetually trim and reef, and for ever scan both wind and tide lest it be caught and whelmed, and that thoughtless *abandon* of boundless health which sends its possessor, like Christopher North, bareheaded and free over his native hills, shouting for very joy from sheer exuberance of being?

One thing is certain. Aside from all considerations of mere enjoyment or comfort, if a man leave this factor out of his calculation in an age of such fierce rivalries and competitions as the present, he will discover that most of the great prizes and rewards for which men strive, and the tempting fruits of that legitimate toil and endeavour which excite men's noblest ambitions, are to him for ever denied. And let him not wonder, for the reason is obvious. The absolute prerequisite to perseverance, and consequently to any great success, is health. Of what use, then, were the mind, if its indispensable agent, the body, refuse or fail to carry out its plans? Take simply the hand, for instance. A little member surely, but so curiously wrought, so wonderful in its mechanism, as to call forth the world-famous essay of Sir Charles Bell. How manifold and necessary its functions! How marvellous its triumphs! "It wrought the statue of Memnon, and hung the brazen gates of Thebes. It fixed the mariner's trembling needle upon its axis, and first heaved back the tremendous bar of the printing-press. It opened the tubes for Galileo, until world after world swept largely before his vision; and it reefed the high-top-sail that rustled over Columbus in the morning breezes of the Bahamas. It has held the sword with which Freedom has fought her battles, and poised the axe of the dauntless woodman as he opened the paths of civilization, and turned the mystic leaves upon which Milton and Shakespeare inscribed their burning thoughts." What if that hand, nerveless and useless, refuse to obey the will of its owner?

Health in its fulness makes a man a king. Want has no terrors for such a man, and danger no dread. He courts it rather with exultant joy. Superb health breeds enterprise, for ever and always. Health, buoyant, confident, strides fearlessly abroad. It levels forests, it tunnels mountains, spans seemingly impossible chasms, and with untiring energy pushes its researches in all directions and ransacks the globe. Adding triumph to triumph, it lifts itself up in its proud consciousness of power, and cries out, "What is there that I cannot do?" Disease, on the other hand, despondent and faint-hearted, confined at home, sits cowering over the embers, filled with imaginary fears.

Courage, moreover, is the presage of success. To believe in one's self and one's own power is always half the battle. "Possunt quia posse videntur" is for ever true. Emerson declares that success itself is constitutional, and that it depends on a *plus* condition of mind and body, on power of work, on courage; and he cites the instance of Napoleon at Eylau, where, it seems, some thirty thousand of the men composing his army were thieves and burglars. "The men whom in peaceful communities we hold, if we can, with iron at their legs, in prisons, under the muskets of sentinels, this man dealt with hand to hand, dragged them to their duty, and won his victories by their bayonets." Again and again we find this shrewd thinker insisting upon the importance of this great factor.

Sir Andrew Clark once defined health as that state in which existence just of itself is a joy; and few of us will be inclined to disagree with him. Every one must have noticed what a vast difference there is in men in sheer recuperative force. One man falls from a scaffold at the height of three stories ; his injuries at first sight seem fatal, but he is out again in a week. Another suffers a slight injury, and is held a prisoner for months, if he does not succumb altogether.

Let it not be supposed, however, that mere physical force is of supreme value where there is nothing else. Like every good thing, physical culture may of course be overdone, and doubtless its importance is sometimes overestimated. It is not to be expected that one should so far forget himself as to allow the development of his muscle to crowd out every other worthy object from his life. It should never be the whole nor the chief object of one's life to make either an athlete merely or a savage of himself. When affairs reach such a pass as to lead a young Japanese student, in writing his impressions of America to friends at home, to describe our American colleges as "great boat-houses," as once happened, it might not inappropriately be asked whether, in certain quarters at least, the muscular phase of college life were not approaching a questionable ascendency. Every one knows that things most commendable are liable to abuse ; and yet—

> " I see no cause but men may pick their teeth,
> Though Brutus with a sword did kill himself."

After all is said, there is no denying the fact that practical success depends much more upon physical health than is generally imagined. "Suppose it were perfectly certain," says Huxley, "that the life and fortune of every one of us would one day or another depend upon his winning or losing a game of chess, don't you think that we should all consider it to be a primary duty to learn at least the names and moves of the pieces? Yet it is a very plain and ele-

mentary truth that the life, the fortune, the happiness of
every one of us, and more or less of those connected with
us, do depend on our knowing something of the rules of a
game infinitely more difficult and complicated than chess.
It is a game which has been played for untold ages......The
chess-board is the world, the pieces are the phenomena of
the universe, the rules of the game are what we call the
laws of nature. The player on the other side is hidden from
us. We know that his play is always fair, just, and patient;
but we know to our cost that he never overlooks a mistake,
or makes the smallest allowance for ignorance. To the man
who plays well the highest stakes are paid with that overflowing generosity with which the strong shows delight in
strength; and one who plays ill is checkmated without haste,
but without remorse." Let every young man remember
that while health once lost may be regained, it is also true
that it may not, even though one "seek it carefully with
tears."

The typical American allows himself too few holidays.
Living as he does under such continual pressure, with pulse
at fever heat six days at least out of seven, he should oftener
relax—should damp the furnace-fires for a while, and cool
off the boiler. What machinery could be expected to stand
such overheating and overworking without soon wearing
out? How seldom does he allow his recreation to quietly
filter through him, if one may so express it, and thus thoroughly to rest and recuperate him! How rarely does he say
to himself, "I enjoy this; I am happy *now!*" No! eagerly
reaching after some future good, he almost perpetually ignores
that which the present has thrown into his lap. "Is not the
life more than meat, and the body than raiment?" When
was more significant question ever put than that? Moreover, a man who by overwork cuts himself off in early life,
or in the midst of his career, not only loses sight of his own
best interests, but robs society of that which might prove

invaluable. All those mellowing influences of maturer years
which ripen and bring to rich perfection the splendid fruits
of toil and culture are thus lost. And who can compute the
loss? Some of the rarest achievements have been wrought
and many of our richest treasures conferred by men who
were past the meridian of life. A certain indefinable flavour
is often wanting in fruit ripened by the forcing process.
The kisses of the sun, the tender influences of dews and
showers, and all the genial persuasions of earth and sky,
cannot with impunity be dispensed with. In this country
nearly every active business or professional man is overworked. Now, a great steamer in mid-ocean, crippled and
disabled, with broken shaft, is not a pleasant sight to any
one. To be obliged to creep slowly homeward, and to *feel*
one's way into port, to say nothing of the increased perils of
such a state of things, is in striking contrast with the power
to stride resistlessly onward, setting wind and wave at defiance, and looking down upon the manifold perils of a stormy
Atlantic in triumphant scorn. And yet how often is this
very spectacle presented in the careers of professional and
business men! "We hear a great deal about the 'vile
body,'" says Spencer; "and many are encouraged by the
phrase to transgress the laws of health. But Nature quietly
suppresses those who treat thus disrespectfully one of her
highest products, and leaves the world to be peopled by the
descendants of those who are not so foolish." Was there
ever a more apt putting of the case than that?

It is certain that the deadliest foe to a man's longevity is
an unnatural and unreasonable excitement. Dickens brought
on his death by overwork and over-excitement. Mr. Dolby
tells us that the reading of the murder scene in "Oliver
Twist" by Dickens brought up the reader's pulse from the
normal seventy-two to one hundred and eighteen. On these
occasions he would have to be supported to his retiring-room,
and laid on a sofa for fully ten minutes before he could

speak a rational or consecutive sentence. Yet this reading he gave frequently. Can one help feeling that a course like this is little short of suicidal? Macaulay, too, was perpetually overworked by his History; and, as his biographer well remarks, there is no overwork like that which has grown to be dearer to a man than life itself. Trevelyan, writing of him at this period, tells us that he no longer had the nerve required to face the social efforts and to undergo the minute and unceasing observation to which he was, or fancied himself, exposed when on a visit to the city which he represented. Insatiable of labour, he regarded the near approach and still more the distant prospect of worry with an exaggerated disquietude which in his case was a premonitory symptom of the disease which was to kill him. Melancholy and suggestive passages abound in his journal. "In the midst of my triumphs I am but poorly." "I am out of sorts, and cannot write; why, I cannot tell." "I wrote some of my history—not amiss, but I am not in the stream yet. I feel quite oppressed by the weight of the task......I sometimes lose months, I do not know how, accusing myself daily, and yet really incapable of vigorous exertion. I seem under a spell of laziness. Then I warm, and can go on working twelve hours at a stretch. How I toiled a year ago!" Ah, who doubts that in that sentence lay the secret of all his trouble, which even he himself did not yet seem fully to apprehend, as the very next sentence betrays—"And why cannot I toil so now?"

No one can doubt the assertion that when a man gives health for money he makes the poorest investment of his life, nor that when he gives money for health he makes, from every worldly point of view, the best. Some one has justly observed that it is, as a rule, the small man who never gets a moment, and who can never find a pair of hands as good as his own. "The man who cannot leave his business, or thinks he cannot, shows that he lacks the highest grade of business capacity. Money avails nothing to a worn-out man, but to a man slowly wearing out it avails everything when properly used. Time and money will buy health."

In this connection it is interesting to note at what period of a man's career one may reasonably look for the best work. There is doubtless a certain point when it is full high tide, when men are at their best, when they are enabled to labour most assiduously, and when they may reasonably expect the best results from their work. Dr. Beard declares that from an analysis of the lives of a thousand representative men in all the great branches of the human family, he made the discovery that the golden decade was between forty and fifty, the brazen between thirty and forty, the iron between fifty and sixty. The superiority of youth and middle life over old age in original work appears all the greater when we consider the fact that all the positions of honour and prestige—professorships and public stations—are in the hands of the old. "Reputation, like money and position, is mainly confined to the old. Men are not widely known until long after they have done the work that gave them their fame. Portraits of great men are delusions, statues are false. They are taken when men have become famous, which, in the average, is at least twenty-five years after they did the work which gave them their fame. Original work requires enthusiasm. If all the original work done by men under forty-five were annihilated, barbarism would be the result. Men are at their best at that time when enthusiasm and experience are almost evenly balanced. That period, on the average, is from thirty-eight to forty. After this the law is that experience increases, but enthusiasm decreases. Of course there are exceptions, but this is the rule."

What then shall a man do? For one thing, he must learn to live more slowly. If you ask a comprehensive motto, let us say, "Less work and more repose." And by repose we

mean rest of every kind. To begin with, we would insist
upon more sleep. On this we lay great stress. Who doubts
that this generation is wearing itself out for lack of sleep?
One of our most gifted writers has declared that were he to
adopt a pet idea, as so many people do, and fondle it to the
exclusion of all others, it would be that the great want
which mankind labours under at this present period is—
sleep. "The world," he urges, "should recline its vast head
on the first convenient pillow and take a prolonged nap."
Is he not more than half right? Lack of sleep is a great
waster of vitality. There was poor Ward, in London, worn
out and dying before his time for want of sleep, his frail
constitution weakened yet more by late hours night after
night. Perhaps few learn to prize it at its true value until
taught by sad experience of its loss. The victim of insomnia
knows its worth. "Why is there no sleep to be sold?"
exclaims the French financier with a sigh. "Sleep was not
in the market at any price." If one would test its "commercial" value, let him compare, in any matter which requires nerve, one who has slept all night with one who has
not, and he will not be long in doubt, rest assured. "I
honour health," says Emerson, "as the first muse, and sleep
as the condition of health." Brain-workers require the best
of food and abundant sleep. As a rule, the larger the brain
the more sleep needed. Webster went to bed at nine o'clock
and rose at five. General Grant used to say during his
campaigns, "I can do nothing without nine hours' sleep."
Mr. Pitt was a sound sleeper, and slept night after night
in the House of Commons, while his colleagues watched the
debates and roused him when it was necessary that he should
speak. M. Guizot, Minister of France under Louis Philippe,
was a good sleeper. A late writer observes that his facility
for going to sleep after great excitement and mental exertion
was prodigious, and it was fortunate for him that he was so
constituted. After the most boisterous and tumultuous

sitting at the Chambers, he would go home, throw himself
down upon a couch, and sink immediately into a profound
sleep, from which he was undisturbed until midnight, when
proofs of the *Moniteur* were brought to him for inspection.
Once when the French army was manœuvring in Spain,
Wellington, who was watching them, became very tired.
Pointing out one of their corps to a staff-officer, he told him
that it was marching in a certain direction, and would be
seen by-and-by at such a point. "When it is seen there,
call me," he added, and wrapping himself in his cloak, slept
soundly until called and told that the French had reached
that point.

"I would keep better hours if I were a boy again," declared
Fields, the well-known publisher,—"that is, I would go to
bed earlier than most boys do. Nothing gives more mental
and bodily vigour than sound rest when properly applied.
Sleep is our great replenisher, and if we neglect to take it
regularly in childhood, all the worse for us when we grow
up. If we sit up late, we decay, and sooner or later we
contract a disease called insomnia. Late hours are shadows
from the grave." If one can, it is well to catch an interval,
say of half an hour, during the day. He will soon find it
amply repays him. Even the strongest man cannot work
strenuously day after day without occasionally becoming
jaded; but, as Blackie well remarks, "a tired man is many
removes from a tired-out one, and there is a great deal in
knowing whether your work is overdoing you or simply
tiring you." Moreover, every brain-worker should frequently
give himself a complete holiday, and scrupulously forget for
the time being, if possible, that there ever were such things
as books in the world. Then, too, a man ought early to
learn not to attempt too much,—in other words, not to allow
his ambition to override his better judgment. How many
men fail right here! I think it is Paxton Hood who somewhere says he believes a good prayer for many an overworked

man would be, "Lord, help me to take fewer things into my
hands, and to do them well."

No one has better expressed the idea, probably, than
Hamerton in his "Intellectual Life." "Let your rest," he
says, "be perfect in its season, like the rest of waters that
are still. If you will have a model for your living, take
neither the stars, for they fly without ceasing, nor the ocean
that ebbs and flows, nor the river that cannot stay; but
rather let your life be like that of the summer air, which has
times of noble energy and times of perfect peace. It fills
the sails of ships upon the sea, and the miller thanks it on
the breezy uplands; it works generously for the health and
wealth of all men, yet it claims its hours of rest. 'I have
pushed the fleet, I have turned the mill, I have refreshed
the city; and now, though the captain may walk impatiently
on the quarter-deck, and the miller swear, and the city stink,
I will stir no more until it pleaseth me.'"

The real intrinsic worth to a man of these periods of
absolute rest cannot easily be computed. And yet one will
find, here and there, certain "matter-of-fact" sort of men,
as they are pleased to count themselves, but who really are
nothing more than what Charles Astor Bristed most aptly
terms "the-just-see-before-your-nose-and-no-farther" sort, who
have an idea that all time not spent in doing something
tangible is lost; and Bristed gives an old but clever illustration for their benefit as follows: "A country manager saw
that the trumpets of his orchestra were not taking part in
an overture which the other musicians were executing. He
rushed upon them and inveighed against their idleness.
'But,' said one of the assailed, 'we have fifteen bars *rest*
here.' 'Rest!' retorted the other; 'I don't pay you ten
shillings a night for *resting:* blow away!' How the *rest*
of the trumpets should be essential to the harmony of the
piece was beyond his comprehension." There are certain
people who seem to think that nothing is doing unless a

great stir be made. To such we commend the words of Mrs. Browning :—

> " Think you 'mid all the mighty sum
> Of things for ever speaking,
> That nothing of itself will come,
> But we must still be seeking?"

The sap silently feeding the limbs of yonder oak may, at any one moment, seem insignificant, but it is forming timbers for a ship of the line.

If a man be wise, he will learn to husband his strength and give to each act only what is due. Some men waste their strength on trifles. Some use far more exertion than is really needed, even for their hardest work. It is with them much as if one should take a sledge-hammer to brush a fly off a man's face. This avoidance of waste amounts really to a fine art. Talma declared that the artist who tires himself is no genius ; and Legouvé, in his work on elocution, maintains that the breath has to play an immense part in that art, and its rules are the only inviolable ones. " An actor," he says, " launched on a stormy passage, carried away by passion, may forget the laws of punctuation, confound commas and periods, and hasten headlong to the conclusion of his phrase ; but he must always be master of his breath, even when he seems to lose it. An accomplished actor is never out of breath, except in appearance, and for effect." He gives this curious example of the science of economy applied to the breath. "Take a lighted candle," he says ; " stand in front of it, and sing *a*. The light will scarcely flicker ; but instead of a single tone, sing the scale, and you will see the candle quiver at every note. The singer Delle Sedie runs up and down the scale before a flame, and it never wavers. This is because he allows only the exact amount of breath to escape which is requisite to force the sound straight forward, and the air, being thus occupied in the emission of the note, loses its quality of wind,

and is reduced to its quality of sound. You or I, on the
contrary, waste a great deal of breath, and send the sound
right and left, as well as forward." From this elocutionary
rule he makes this fine deduction : In every act of life,
spend no more than the exact amount of energy required.
Every mental emotion is a jewel. Let us hoard it up for
fitting use. How many people waste, in impatient and petty
strife, the treasure of anger, so sacred when it becomes
'righteous wrath!'" Among his rules for the preservation
of health, Dr. Richardson of London insists upon the avoidance of anger, hatred, grief, and fear. "The strongest," he
declares, "cannot afford to indulge in them."

In this connection let us mention one factor not often
touched upon, but surely one of the most helpful adjuncts to
a man's largest success—namely, a restful home-life. "I
once asked the late Hepworth Dixon," writes a well-known
authoress, "with whom I happened to be talking on
this subject, what he thought was the reason why some
women held their husbands' hearts securely and for ever,
while others were but the brief tenants of a few months or
years. 'What,' I asked, 'is the quality in a woman that
her husband loves the longest?' 'That she should be a
pillow,' answered Mr. Dixon ; and then, meeting the inquiry
in my eyes, he went on, 'Yes, that is what a man needs in
his wife—something to rest his heart on. He has excitement and opposition enough in the world. He wants to feel
that there is one place where he is sure of sympathy, a place
that will give him ease as a pillow gives it to a tired head.
Do you think a man will be tempted to turn from a
woman whose eyes are his flattering mirror,—who heals
where others wound?' And surely," adds this gifted lady,
"he was right." The wife should do what the wife of
Mohammed did for him,—believe in him when other people
do not.

May not this sense of helpfulness and refreshment for his

work, which no one so keenly recognizes as the literary worker, explain also the striking public acknowledgments of indebtedness to their wives which world-famous men have sometimes made ? Will it not account for the touching dedications of famous volumes which one occasionally finds, —as if their authors would insist that she to whom the volume doubtless owed so much should share in the honours it received ? Now this may seem, at a casual glance, a secondary place, perhaps, for a woman to hold ; but no queen ever held so supreme a sway, nor so secure a throne, as she in her husband's heart. What can the doubtful honours and responsibilities, the unnatural burdens and festering atmosphere of public life, offer in comparison with the serener air of this enviable kingdom ? The thought of one sitting at home to welcome with restful and apprecia-tive tokens, has nerved many a man to knightly and heroic daring in the daily struggle with a hard-fisted world.

Perhaps one of the most curious features of this subject of health is the wonderful influence of will-power in warding off disease. It seems at times almost miraculous. The well-known instance of Bonaparte's visit to those sick of the plague is only one of many which might be cited. Such, in fact, is the reflex influence of the mind upon the body that even preoccupation will sometimes effectually ward off disease. A thoughtful physician once assured the author that if an express agent were to visit New Orleans in the yellow-fever season having forty thousand dollars, say, in his care, he would be in little danger of the fever so long as he kept possession of the money. Let him once deliver that into other hands, however, and the sooner he left the city the better. David Dudley Field declares that one reason for his being so well is that his mind has always been occupied. "I am never idle," he says ; "in fact, I have no time to be ill." "No, we don't get sick," said an actor just in after four months on the road, "because we can't get sick. Patti and a few other stars can afford that luxury, but to the majority of us it is denied. It is a case of *must* with us ; and although there have been times when, had I been at home, or a private man, I could have taken to my bed with as good a right to be sick as any one ever had, I have not done so, and have worn off the attack through sheer necessity. It's no fiction that will-power is the best of tonics, and theatrical people understand that they must keep a good stock of it always on hand."

As regards the matter of eating and drinking, there can be little doubt that many serious errors have been committed right here. Abernethy used to declare that the two great killing powers in the world are *Stuff* and *Fret*, and Jefferson is credited with the remark that nobody ever repented of eating too little. Cheerfulness is always commended. "To be free-minded and cheerfully disposed at meal-time" was one of Bacon's well-known rules for "long lasting."

It is curious to note that while some public performers eat heartily before their appearances, others practise entire abstinence. This may be accounted for doubtless in great measure by the condition of the nervous system. Of such moment is this regarded by Scalchi, the famous singer, that on one occasion when her manager, without consulting her beforehand, insisted upon changing the part previously assigned her for her evening performance, she absolutely refused to sing, and the matter resulted in a lawsuit in which she came off victorious. The court held that as she had been allowed to eat heartily, without due notice being given her of the change desired in the programme, and that it being, moreover, impossible for her to sing that particular part under the circumstances, the manager had no right to demand it. The reason for Scalchi's refusal was that "a hearty meal abated the nervous activity by means of which she throws her soul into her voice." It was simply a case of "food against mood." On the other hand, we are told of a

very distinguished orator who always wanted a good dinner
of meat cooked rare, and that on one occasion, being congratulated on a masterly effort, he remarked, " It was only that
duck I had just devoured."

Above all things, let one avoid getting into "ruts" from
which he cannot turn out at any time if it seem desirable.
One should early learn the secret of "dropping things."
The habit is invaluable, and it should be acquired at any
cost.  Kingsley possessed this power in a remarkable degree.
"Luckily for me," he says, "I can stop from all work at
short notice, and turn head over heels in the sight of all
creation for a spell."  Let the man of business, the banker,
the professor, learn to turn the key upon his cares in hours of
leisure, and shove the bolt inexorably against them.  Gladstone has never allowed business of any kind to enter his
chamber door.  "In all my political life," he declares, " I
have never been kept awake five minutes by any debate in
Parliament."  Few people can realize the decision requisite
at times on the part of public men in this matter of simply
maintaining an attitude of self-defence.  The inroads of
friends, and that hydra-headed monster the public, make
great demands upon both the time and the patience of a
public man.  When Andrew Jackson was President, certain
friends from a distance, visiting Washington, resolved to see
him.  Jackson happened to be unusually busy, and had been
worried and annoyed for hours by the incessant demands
made upon him, and when the cards were handed in he sent
back word that he must be excused.  Presuming upon old
acquaintance, the request was renewed.  He again sent back
word that he really could not see them.  Still persisting in
their attempt, Jackson presently appeared in person.  To
use a mild expression, the President was far from serene.
"My friends," he exclaimed, "I presume you think it a
mighty fine thing to live in this White House.  I assure
you, however, that I have found it a perfect *hell!*"  Even

on his death-bed he was tortured by office-seekers. "I am dying," said he, "as fast as I can, and they all know it; but they keep swarming about me in crowds, seeking for office,— intriguing for office." Poor Johnson, too, while President, was harassed beyond measure. It remained for Grant, with that fine decision and indomitable will of his, to show the dear public that a man's rights could and should be respected. None more faithful than he to all, until the hour came when the public duties of the day must cease. After that his time was his own, and his determination to have his needed rest was inexorable. And he was right. Alas, the ills endured by long-suffering men who lack decision !

Another great factor which all have insisted on is exercise. Indeed, all observation attests that the healthiest persons are those most fully employed. Rusting out, let it be remembered, is, after all, a more rapid process than wearing out. Look at David Dudley Field, for instance. What has made him so hale and hearty in his old age ? These are his own words : "My recipe for self-preservation is exercise ! I am a very temperate man, and have always been so. I have taken care of myself, and as I have a good constitution, I suppose that is the reason I am so well."

After all is said, in spite of one's best efforts and utmost care, unforeseen circumstances, an unnoticed draught from an open window, or some equally trivial circumstance, will now and then throw one upon the invalid list for a time. This is the common lot. Illness is a great leveller. When Cassius would show "great Cæsar" on a level with himself, he cries :—

> "He had a fever when he was in Spain,
> And when the fit was on him, I did mark
> How he did shake : 'tis true, this god did shake !"

As some one has truly observed, pedants write of kings, heroes, and statesmen as never doing anything but upon the deepest principles of sound policy ; but those who see and observe kings, heroes, and statesmen, discover that they have headaches, indigestions, humours and passions, just like other people, every one of which, in its turn, determines their will in defiance of their reason. Even the strongest and most prudent are doubtless at times betrayed into indiscretions and overwork under the spur of a noble ambition which has taken possession of the soul. Painfully, and through travail of soul, man comes to know at length his limitations. A writer in *All the Year Round* has finely voiced what many have doubtless felt. Asking himself what he should choose, whether fame, or love, or life, if some great angel spake and bade him choose " from treasure infinite," and finding in each of these somewhat to mar his great ideal, he says :—

> " I would choose Work, and never-failing power—
> To work without weak hindrance by the way,
> Without recurrence of the weary hour
> When tired tyrant nature holds its sway
> Over the busy brain and toiling hand.
> Ah! if an angel came to me to-night
> Speaking in language of the unknown land,
> So would I choose from treasure infinite.
> But well I know the blessed gift I crave,
> The tireless strength for never-ending task,
> Is not for this life. But beyond the grave,
> It may be I shall find the thing I ask ;
> For I believe there is a better land,
> Where will, and work, and strength go hand in hand."

# VII

# Enthusiasm.

People smile at the "enthusiasm of youth,"—that enthusiasm which they themselves secretly look back at with a sigh, perhaps unconscious that it is partly their own fault that they ever lost it.—KINGSLEY.

The labour we delight in physics pain.—SHAKESPEARE.

WHO has not seen men splendidly equipped in every particular, with fine endowments, much learning, and many advantages, yet who, notwithstanding all these, seem to accomplish nothing in the world? And why is it, we ask? Failure is evident; but from what cause? Is it not that they are too often lacking in the single trait of enthusiasm, which alone can fuse and make available one's other great qualities? The machinery is perfect, the boiler sound, but there is no fire, and hence no steam. They have no enthusiasm themselves, hence no power to kindle it in others. Life seemingly, so far as they are concerned, is a pitiful failure, barren of results. An intelligent lady remarked to the writer concerning one of her sons, that he had excellent natural abilities, a fine teacher, and all the elements apparently necessary to success; "but," she continued, "he has no enthusiasm, and will never exert himself enough to do that which he might, if he would, easily accomplish." Is not this true of many a one? One cannot help wishing at times for some potent influence to break, even rudely if need be, the strange spell, and arouse these natures of which so much might reasonably be expected.

What could be more beautiful and inspiring than the noble enthusiasm of youth? With its lofty aspirations, its "burnings to be great," youth fondly thinks its ingenuousness and trust will always last. It hears intimations ever and anon that it will be otherwise, but resolves that whatever may have been the experience of others, its own case shall be the exception. Its sensibilities shall not be blunted by the hardness of men nor the coldness of the world. It has not yet come to realize "all that mysteriously fatal pressure which the years exert to reduce every ideal aim to the commonplace standard." As this appears, however, to be well-nigh inevitable, it would certainly seem no more than fair that all right-minded persons should bear in mind that injunction of Julius Hare, never to check the enthusiasm of youth, because we need a good stock of it as a sort of reserve force on which to draw as we go on in life. "We naturally lose illusions as we get older, like teeth," said Sydney Smith, "but there is no Cartwright to fit a new set into our understandings. I have, alas! only one illusion left," he continued, "and that is the Archbishop of Canterbury."

Let it be understood that we are not advocating what is familiarly known as "gush," to use the vulgar term. That is one extreme. What we do urge is that mysterious something, call it what one may, which brings about great results,—that something which you will always find to have been a factor in the careers of all successful men,—that something which successfully laid an Atlantic cable after thirteen years of defeat; that sent Stephenson's locomotive on its triumphant way in spite of carping critics, and all else that might hinder its advance; that sent "Fulton's Folly" out upon the waters of the Hudson to demonstrate to all coming time the wisdom of its inventor; that swung the Brooklyn Bridge over the East River; that reared St. Peter's, and wrought the "Transfiguration" and the "Paradise Lost." Indifference never wrote great works, nor thought out striking inventions, " nor reared the solemn architecture that awes the soul, nor breathed sublime music, nor painted glorious pictures, nor undertook heroic philan-thropies. All these grandeurs are born of enthusiasm." And enthusiasm is not fanaticism. Some one has said it is *the expiration of an inspiration.* It is this inspiration that holds one, as has been already intimated, with unflagging attention to his work.

While, then, we repudiate mere gushing sentimentalism as unworthy of any man, there is another and far greater danger which menaces young men in this highly artificial and pretentious age ; and that is the affectation of indiffer-ence to all things, which is the opposite extreme. Fore-warned is forearmed, we are told. And it is well for one to remember that this lack of general sensibility which is becoming so prominent a characteristic of this age of affec-tations is the sworn foe to all simplicity of character. We warn any young man, therefore, whose aim is to make his way in the world and win real success, to give this sort of thing a very wide berth. The persons who labour under this disorder pretend to have lost their freshness of interest in everything. For them, as they would have it believed, there is no surprise and no enthusiasm. Does any one imagine such the most enviable of mortals ? The French *blasé* would seem most appropriately to describe their condition, or their assumed condition. Such a state, however, seems to us anything but tempting. It is like that genteel respect-ability of " our sovereign lord the king," who

> " Never says a foolish thing,
> Nor ever does a wise one."

Surveyed in some of its aspects, society seems one grand masquerade.

How seldom do we come to know each other as we really are ! Men pass and repass, day after day, and still are strangers. Women meet and converse, and part again, and still there are impassable gulfs never to be spanned. A thousand misunderstandings arise that never ought to arise. Uncounted alienations exist that a word, a look might have prevented. Differences, slight at first as the trembling of a summer's leaf, have by reason of these misunderstandings grown and magnified until ugly chasms yawn, over which the blessed angel of reconciliation may not pass.

There is, says a vigorous writer, a maxim underlying the whole pagan philosophy, ancient and modern,—*Nil admirari* (" Admire nothing!"). It is simply the spirit of the sneerer, as Horace says again, *Cum risu miror* ("I never admire, but I sneer"). Wonder at nothing! Never be excited to tones or thoughts of rapture or of reverence! That sentiment is worthy of a pagan,—worthy only of such a sad, irreverent age as this of ours. Rather let it be with you exactly the reverse. "Keep the pores of your spirit perpetually open to receive the health, the strength, and the excitement of all things : they are all shadows cast by invisible presences. Have high models. Neither men, nor gods, nor columns have allowed indifferent poets to exist. And we may expect that the soul without enthusiasm will be but a sorry and a poor thing. I must not be indifferent : here is the foundation of success." In strikingly similar vein are the trenchant words of John Stuart Blackie. "There is a class of young men in the present age," he says, "on whose face one imagines that he sees written, *Nil admirari*. This is not at all a lovable class of the 'youth-head' of our land, and, unless the tone of not wondering which characterizes their manner be a sort of juvenile affectation destined soon to pass away, rather a hopeless class. Wonder, as Plato has it, is a truly philosophic passion ; the more we have of it, accompanying the reverent heart, of course, with a clear, open eye, so much the better.

That it should be specially abundant in the opening scenes
of life is in the healthy course of nature; and to be deficient
in it argues either insensibility, or that indifference, selfishness, and conceit which are sometimes found combined with
a shallow sort of cleverness that with superficial observers
readily passes for true talent......We are small creatures,
the biggest of us, and our only chance of becoming great in
a sort is by participation in the greatness of the universe......
The chief end of man, according to the Stoics, was, 'Spectare
imitare mundum!'—a fine thought, and finely expressed.
But how shall a man see when he has no admiring faculty
which shall lead him to see? and how shall he imitate what
he does not know? All true appreciation is the result of
keen insight and noble passion; but the habit of despising
things and persons and holding them cheap blinds the one
factor which belongs to the complete result, and strangles the
other......He who wonders not largely and habitually in the
midst of this magnificent universe does not prove that the
world has nothing great in it worthy of wonder, but only
that his own sympathies are narrow and his capacities
small."

The worst thing a young man can do is to begin criticising. Such a maxim as the one mentioned may be excusable
in a worn-out old cynic, but is intolerable in the mouth of a
hopeful young man. "There is no good to be looked for
from a youth who, having done no substantial work of his
own, sets up a business of finding fault with other people's
work, and calls this practice of finding fault criticism. The
first lesson that a young man has to learn is not to find
fault, but to perceive beauties. All criticism worthy of the
name is the ripe fruit of combined intellectual insight and
long experience. Only an old soldier can tell how battles
ought to be fought." These are strong words, but they
are true ones; and the sooner a young man learns to
discriminate between the true and false in etiquette and

philosophy, the sooner and the more surely will he find himself approaching the success for which he yearns. Take for instance that so-called philosophy so widely prevalent in certain quarters,—that it is vulgar to be demonstrative. If an old friend greets you on the street, after no matter how long an absence, you are by no means to betray in any manner the joyous emotions that instantly throb within you for utterance : this would be a most flagrant violation of the code. On the contrary, you are to receive him with the utmost decorum and the most frigid politeness,—nothing further. Stifle your exuberant joy ; give the lie to your real self,—to be demonstrative is vulgar. Of all the fashionable follies of the day, what could be more absurd ? Could any code, indeed, be more false ? Self-possession, it has been said, is a strong quality ; but who believes in this kind ? People who school themselves to this are not apt to have the other and better kind. They are not apt to manifest self-possession on such occasions as really call for it,—occasions of difficulty, of danger, and of great trial. Touch their self-love, make any unusual demand upon them for self-denial, and their assumed and superficial self-possession vanishes in an instant.

Self-possession,—what do we mean by it ? The bull-frog has an unusual amount of that quality, of a certain kind. In his coldness and isolation he croaks a great deal, is noisy and complacent, and "eminently self-possessed." So, in certain quarters, that coldness and reserve which never allows itself to be startled into spontaneity of expression is greatly lauded. But is it desirable ? To affect an indifference one is far from feeling, and to diffuse an atmosphere like that of an iceberg whose chilling influence can be felt fifty miles away,—is it really worth while ? It is very true, as Holmes says, that we must not claim too much for sentiment. It does not, of course, go a great way in deciding questions of arithmetic, or algebra, or geometry. "Two and two will undoubtedly make four, irrespective of the emotions or other idiosyncrasies of the calculator ; and the three angles of a triangle insist on being equal to two right angles in the face of the most impassioned rhetoric or the most inspired verse. There is a great deal of false sentiment in the world, as there is of bad logic and erroneous doctrine ; but it is very much less disagreeable to hear a young poet overdo his emotions, or even deceive himself about them, than to hear a caustic epithet-flinger repeating such words as *sentimentality*, and the like, for the purpose of ridiculing him into silence. An over-dressed woman is not so pleasing as she might be, but at any rate she is better than the oil-of-vitriol squirter whose pro-fession it is to teach young ladies to avoid vanity by spoiling their showy silks and satins."

The more one sees of the world, the more one is convinced that simplicity is no less the inevitable accompaniment of true genius than it is of true greatness. A wise observer has said that true greatness never struts on stilts nor plays the king upon the stage. Conscious of its elevation above the rest of mankind, and knowing in what that elevation consists, it is happy to take its part in the common amuse-ments and business of life. It is not afraid of being under-valued for its humility. Chief-Justice Marshall was a fine illustration of this. In his hours of relaxation he was full of fun, and as natural as a child. He entered into the spirit of athletic exercises with all the ardour of youth, and at sixty odd years of age was one of the best quoit-players in Virginia. During the summer of 1820, at a quoit club near Richmond were collected at least half-a-dozen great judges and several distinguished persons of different professions, in-cluding Jarvis, the portrait-painter. A match was made, and the Chief-Justice threw off his coat and fell to work with as much energy as he would have directed to the decision of a question of neutral rights, or the conflicting jurisdiction of the general and State governments. In the course of the game, and when the parties were nearly a tie, some dispute arose as to the quoit nearest the ring. The Chief-Justice was chosen umpire between the quoit belonging to Jarvis and that of Billy Haxall. The Judge bent down on one knee, and with a straw essayed the decision of this important question, on which the fate of the game in a great measure depended. After nicely measuring, and biting off the end of the straw, he said : "Gentlemen, you will perceive this quoit would have it, but the rule of the game is to measure from the visible iron. Now that clod of dirt hides almost half an inch ; but then he has a right to the nearest part of the ring, and here, you will perceive, is a splinter which belongs to, and is a part of, the ring, as much as Virginia is a part of the Union. This is giving Mr. Haxall a great advantage ; but notwithstanding, in my opinion, Jarvis has it by at least the sixteenth part of an inch, and so I decide, like a judge, in my own favour." As has been said, a man who is not afraid, whatever exaltation he may have reached, to let himself thus down to the level of his fellow-men, must have that innate consciousness of genius which is in itself sufficient evidence of its possession. "How ages thine heart,—towards youth ? If not, doubt thy fitness for thy work."

Real enthusiasm is infectious. And by this is not meant that quality referred to sometimes by the word in its cheapened sense. It is not a simple spasmodic ebullition, agitating only the surface of the soul. Enthusiasm, in the best sense of the word, is not "a shallow estuary where a sloop might run aground," but is rather the mighty deep, bearing on its bosom the navies of the world. This it is which has ever been the inspiration of great endeavour ; this the majestic throbbing in all heroic souls. This through days of darkness and discouragement has nerved great spirits for their struggles, until at length the brilliant success was won. These,

> "Through long days of labour,
> And nights devoid of ease,"

saw afar the coming triumph. How such men take hold of
other men! How they stand out in history! How the
blood tingles along the veins at mention of their names!
Yet nothing is more illusive when one would define or
analyze this power. The secret for ever baffles and eludes
us; yet the spell remains. Who can estimate the influence
that the simple name of Cæsar had upon the career of the
brilliant hero of Austerlitz? France to-day has not shaken
off the spell of the latter's mighty name. In the fair city on
the Seine the mystic "N" confronts you everywhere. Do
not the finer pulses quicken at mention of Raphael and
Michael Angelo? Is not the spirit stirred at the recital of
names which have become synonyms of power and great
achievement? It is always thus. Protogenes still worships
Apelles; Dante has Virgil ever in his thought, the tribute in
his heart:

> " Thou art my master, and my author thou,
> Thou art alone the one from whom I took
> The beautiful style that has done honour to me."

Great men exist that there may be greater men. How true
that is! " We go forth," says Emerson, " austere, dedicated,
believing in the iron links of Destiny, and will not turn on
our heel to save our lives; but a book or a bust, or only the
sound of a name, shoots a spark through the nerves, and we
suddenly believe in will. I cannot even hear of personal
vigour of any kind, great power of performance, without
fresh resolution. We are emulous of all that man can do.
Cecil's saying of Sir Walter Raleigh, 'I know that he can
toil terribly,' is an electric touch. We cannot read Plutarch
without a tingling of the blood."

Enthusiasm often becomes contagious. What more remarkable than its manifestations at times among vast bodies
of men? What marvellous power one sees in the unity of

purpose which sometimes possesses an army or a people! How significant is the French *"esprit de corps!"* We have no expression in English that adequately renders this phrase. "Sheridan riding through the Shenandoah Valley exhaled that something which made all the difference between victory and defeat. Breathed into the soldiers, it turned the tide of battle. Advantages were less than before. The odds were more against them. There was simply one new factor,—that utterance of Sheridan." But the something implied in that utterance was a revelation. It seized all ranks and all orders of men, swept through the valley like a whirlwind, made those under its influence irresistible, and won the day. Who has not seen, under similar influence, vast multitudes swelling and surging like the swelling of the sea, and well-nigh as uncontrollable? A simple song may suffice to create it. Take that *Marseillaise*, for instance. Among the despatches found not long since in the Palace of St. Cloud was one to the following effect: "The Privy Secretary of the Emperor to the Minister of Fine Arts in Paris: You may authorize the song [Marseillaise]. The Emperor has charged me to inform you of this. It will be well if you will previously give notice of it to the Prefect of Police." Comment is unnecessary.

As regards this influence of men upon each other, there are certain natures with which it is impossible for one to come in contact without feeling ennobled and lifted up into a higher region of objects and aims than that in which one is tempted habitually to dwell. Artists have often felt this power. The genius of Haydn, for instance, was first fired by Handel, we are told; and Haydn himself believed that he would never have written the "Creation," had he not heard Handel play. The great are always friends. Nothing could exceed the admiration of Beethoven for Cherubini, and he most generously recognized the genius of Schubert. Young Northcote pushing his way through the crowd that

he might get near enough to Reynolds to touch the skirt of
his coat, and the satisfaction it gave him, as he afterwards
confessed, reveal the "true touch of youthful enthusiasm."
"Better, much better," says Blackie, "than even the mirror
of greatness in the biographies of truly great men, is the living influence of such men when you have the happiness of
coming in contact with them. The best books are only a
clever machinery for stirring the nobler nature, and they act
indirectly and feebly; but a living great man coming across
your path carries with him an electric influence which you
cannot escape,—that is, of course, if you are capable of being
affected in a noble way; for the blind do not see, and the
dead do not feel......To have felt the thrill of a fervid humanity shoot through your veins at the touch of a Chalmers, a
MacLeod, or a Bunsen, is to a young man of a fine suscepti-
bility worth more than all the wisdom of the Greeks, all
the learning of the Germans, and all the sagacity of the
Scotch."

How in contrast to the influence of these gifted souls is
the influence of certain other men whom we all know!
They are superbly educated, finely trained, but there is in
them no light and no heat. They stand apart, cold, stately,
glittering, "faultily faultless," but solitary and alone. Youth
is not drawn towards them; in fact no one is. They themselves, possibly, are amazed to find it so; but the human
heart instinctively knows its teacher, and cannot be deceived.

Some people remind one of Sydney Smith's "Utilitarian,"
—the man "so hard that you might drive a broad-wheeled
waggon over him and it would produce no impression, and if
you were to bore holes in him with a gimlet, sawdust would
come out of him." The same author, in his classification of
mankind, calls certain of this sort the "lemon-squeezers of
society,"—people who act on you as a wet blanket; who
always see a cloud in the sunshine; predictors of evil, extin-
guishers of hope; who, where there are two sides, see only

the worst,—"people whose very look curdles the milk and sets your teeth on edge." The brilliant Canon of Westminster in "Julian Home" pays his respects to a certain class of university men who profess to admire nothing, hope for nothing, and love nothing; who think warmth of heart a folly and sentiment a crime. These men, he tells us, would not display an interest in anything more important than a boat race to save their lives; are very fond of the phrase, " All that sort of nonsense," to express everything that rises above the dead level of their own dead mediocrity in intelligence and life. "If you would not grovel in spirit, if you would not lose every tear that sparkles and every sigh that burns, if you would not ossify the very power of passion, if you would not turn your soul into a mass of shapeless lead, avoid those despicable cynics who never leave their discussion of the merits of beer, or the powers of stroke oars, unless it be to carp at acknowledged eminence and jeer at genuine emotion. How often in such company have I seen men relapse into stupid silence, because, if they ventured on any expression of lively interest, one of the throng, amid the scornful indifference of the rest, would give the only acknowledgment of his remark by taking the pipe out of his mouth to give vent to a low guttural laugh! Deliver us from the world without souls!"

Many doubtless are familiar with that interesting passage in John Stuart Mill's autobiography where he takes stock of the loss and gain in his own training, and decides that even his great debt of gratitude to his father for setting him as a youth in the intellectual position of maturity was almost cancelled by the rigid coat of reserve in which the severity of his education had enclosed all emotion and impulse. We so perpetually act and react upon each other that one never knows, in any accurate way, the influence he exerts. As the reading and re-reading of a single book will sometimes reveal powers of thought in a literary student, so the really great work of art of a master will some day perchance, after having been gazed at, admired, and passed, by amateurs of the more thoughtless crowd, fan into sudden flame the fire slumbering in an enthusiastic breast, and encourage some youth, obscure and all unknown, to exclaim, "I, too, am a painter!" That inspiration shall carry the young man through his initial studies, shall blend the colours on his palette, guide his pencil, and shine upon his canvas, until some future Titian on witnessing his productions shall be ready to exclaim, "Were I not Titian, I should wish to be Correggio!" When a mere child, Couture was taken by his father to the Museum of the Louvre, and the first picture he saw was the "Marriage in Cana," by Veronese. His father corrected him for exclaiming aloud that it was the "Marriage in Cana," pointing out to him that it could not be, because the figures were dressed in the costume of the Middle Ages instead of that of the age of Tiberius. The father soon learned from a bystander the mistake he had made, and that his son was right. "I do not know why," says Couture in his book, "but it appeared to me very beautiful." It was long afterwards that this boy was able to paint his famous "Romans of the Decadence," which gave him an immediate and wide renown; but its striking similarity in matter and treatment to the great work of Veronese makes it seem a late result of that outburst of boyish enthusiasm.

No great man, it is said, really does his work by imposing his maxims on his disciples. He evokes their life. Nor let any one imagine that he can impress upon others the thought which has not mastered him and taken possession of his own soul. No one need expect others to respond to that which awakens no kindred enthusiasm in his own breast. The thought must breathe, and the word must burn, before it shall find lodgment and kindle the fire in the heart of another.

> " What poets feel not when they make
>   A pleasure in creating,
>   The world in its turn will not take
>   Pleasure in contemplating."

So writes Matthew Arnold, and nothing could be more true. Of course one cannot expect that the tide will never ebb. The wind goes down, and one suddenly finds himself becalmed. The sails flap idly, and he is left tugging at the oar. The old enthusiasm has fled. One wonders where all the aspirations which but yesterday so thrilled him are gone. He goes grieving, and desolate, and sad. "The fresh morning yields to the hot, white light of the long, dull afternoon of life." How monotonous and commonplace everything appears! Life seems to have resolved itself into a succession of petty cares. The season of depression has succeeded that of exaltation. Success is full of promise, it has been said, till men get it; and then it is a last year's nest from which the bird has flown. Care smothers the rising aspiration. The hollow-eyed goddess, haggard and wrinkled and wan, clutches the arm and shrivels the sinews of endeavour. One is amazed as he realizes how dull and stupid and aimless it is possible to be.

> " We, too, have autumns, when our leaves
>   Drop loosely through the dampened air ;
>   And all our good seems bound in sheaves,
>   While we stand reaped and bare."

We are tired of the daily sameness of life. The tide has ebbed, and left behind only the flat and oozing sands. All men, even the most heroic and enthusiastic, have come to such periods. This feeling is voiced in Shakespeare's famous sonnet—

> "Tired with all these, for restful death I cry ;"

and in Shelley's plaintive words—

> " I could sit down like a tired child,
>   And weep away this life of care."

Dr. Maurice Busch, the Boswell of Bismarck, tells us: "The prince passes for a man of iron character—for a spirit confident in and certain of itself. I do not deny that he is so; but he, too, has his moments of weakness—periods of apparent or real dissatisfaction with his own performances and his destiny—lackadaisical, or, let us rather say, gloomy tempers which express themselves in a sort of universal wailing." It is a part of that "inexorable weariness" which, as Goethe declares, lies at the basis of our life. Now, what is one to do? Let him do the duty that lies nearest.

Closely allied to this condition, too, is a certain lethargy to which youth, perhaps, is peculiarly liable, though it is not confined to youth. Earnest and conscientious workers, men of great ability and industry and corresponding ambitions, often feel its power, and for the time must yield. Dr. Wilson has said, "It is the scholar's great affliction; it is bred with thought beneath the brow that never sweats." Another has graphically portrayed its influence: "The editor busy at his desk suddenly feels the fatal influence steal over him; his grasp on his subject weakens, the pen drops from his hand, his ideas move sluggishly, or seem to escape altogether; he is utterly *gravelled* for lack of matter. The lawyer, listening to his client's story, discovers that he is not following him; his mind refuses to seize and apply to it the principles of the law; his thoughts wander and grow hazy; he wonders whether he will be able to avoid yawning in his client's face; a sort of aversion to the whole matter possesses him, and he feels that the utmost he is capable of is to get rid of his importunate visitor without betraying himself. So with the college student, eagerly cramming for his examination. Just at the time when he should put in double work he is aware of an irresistible inclination to lean back in his chair, throw away his books, and let his thoughts idly wander on fruitless objects. The very power to make the effort to resist this seductive influence is wanting. The stirring music of the coming years which ordinarily stimulates him sounds distant and feeble. Rather the subtle strain of the lotus-eaters whispers in his soul,—

> ' Death is the end of life; ah, why
> Should life all labour be ? ' "

Then, again, a habit of introspection and minute analysis is fatal to enthusiasm. Did one ever attempt to analyze the perfume of a flower without losing that subtile, ethereal something which gave it its charm ? Does not one find by pressing it too closely, by seeking to inhale its fragrance too long, as if to wring from it a still deeper secret than it chooses to give, that its very perfume is turned to bitterness ? And who ever sought to analyze a gorgeous sunset that thrilled him with delight, that did not find its glow already palling on his senses, and the thrill dying out of his heart, although the glowing splendour still burned radiantly in the crimson west? These finer emotions were never meant for the crucible. So surely as we treat them thus, the ethereal, evanescent spell will inevitably leave us, and forlorn and sad, a pale and ashen sky, or some barren relic of a nameless joy, will alone remain. One may then regret, but of what avail ?

> " Something beautiful has vanished,
> And we sigh for it in vain.
> We may seek it in the air,
> On the earth, and everywhere,
> But it never comes again."

In these intervals of depression, when the rare, fine light which flooded the horizon has died away, again we ask, What is one to do? Surely we need not despair. The sunrise never failed us yet. In such an hour one must "fall back on the steadfast resolve of a happier time." Adhere to lines marked out and projects formed in the hours of illumination, when the vision was clear. The dawn will

come. Nothing is more striking than the contrast when the
outlook brightens. The transition is sometimes sudden;
without a premonition it may come. A book may do it.
The glowing page of some vigorous thinker has often stirred
the soul to its depths. We rise up refreshed and strong.
What is there that we cannot do? Ah, the regal hour has
come. Thoughts crowd one upon another. It is no effort
to plan and resolve. As Emerson himself says: "Read
Plutarch, and the world is a proud place peopled with men
of positive quality, with heroes and demigods standing around
us who will not let us sleep." And elsewhere he says that
all poets have confessed to rare moments when a light, a
freedom and power, came to them, lifting them to perform-
ances far better than they could reach at other times. At
such periods the intellect is so active that everything seems
to run to meet it. "In spring, when the snow melts, the
maple-trees flow with sugar, and you cannot get tubs fast
enough; but it is only for a few days." It has been said
that Nature is prodigal, but never a spendthrift. She husbands her resources, that she may be able to distribute. In
days of plenty one must learn to anticipate the days of
famine. "In these hours of affluent thought and emotion,
when celestial gales are blowing strong, waste not a moment,
for they will not always blow. Make good speed towards
port while you may."

Even a slight disturbance or interruption in the flow of
one's thought at such times may make a marked difference
in results. Rossini, while snugly ensconced under the
blankets, in the midst of the glow and fervour of composition, loses his manuscript under the bed. He is too warm
and comfortable to get out and recover it, so he attempts
to rewrite it. To his disgust he cannot remember what he
has already written, so goes to work and composes another.
On comparing them afterwards, the first is found to be much
the better of the two. Doubtless many an instance might

be cited to show how a seemingly trivial interruption has often been disastrous to one's work.

It is surprising, too, what an influence one's surroundings have upon his enthusiasm. But he cannot escape it. No philosophy in the world can make bare walls, ungainly furniture, and cheerless rooms other than depressing. It is curious to note the effect upon one's spirits of even disorderly arrangement in one's surroundings. But it is decidedly unfavourable. If one has never tested this, let him sit down and try to compose in an apartment where everything is in confusion. Then when the servant has put the room in order, let him note the contrast. There is a reflex influence, refreshing and helpful, which one recognizes at once. Certain trained workers may, it is true, be capable of such concentration of mind as virtually to ignore surroundings for the time being; and yet there is an occult, subtle influence pervading the very atmosphere which makes against one. The confusion around is pictured unconsciously upon the retina, and transfers itself to the thought, making confusion within.

George Bancroft, the historian, is a firm believer in the theory that the brain at work is sensibly affected by the external objects around, and in some degree takes its tone from them. He works in a long, narrow room, adorned profusely with historical paintings. From his seat he has a full view of his art treasures, and frequently gazes at them as if for inspiration. A French critic of English manners once stated that in London a row of houses had been built along the river side of the Strand, with the view of guarding the inhabitants from the danger annually recurring of joining hands and rushing down together to drown themselves in the Thames, and he assigned as the cause the dulness of the weather prevailing there in November. "Of his facts," says an English writer, "I will say nothing; but I hesitate to accept his reasoning. If the temptation does really exist, it is the effect, not of the much-maligned month of fogs, but of the despondency arising from surroundings." Let us note, in passing, that not alone are such depressing influences disastrous to enthusiasm—they are positively injurious to health.

It is well known that there were certain streets in London through which Dickens would never allow himself to pass. With him, however, it was the painful associations which the surroundings recalled of the hardships and ill-treatment of his youth. There is no denying that certain surroundings are death to all enthusiasm, while others inevitably fill one with finest inspiration. The presence of high art, whether it be painting or architecture or statuary, at once sets the pulses throbbing. It may be even extremely minute—a bit of church window, or a strain from one of the old masters— yet the spell is there. It is not hard to believe that certain works could never have been produced in some surroundings; the depressing influence would have been too great. Nor is it difficult to understand the feeling which prompted certain of the old composers to don their full court dress whenever they were about to apply themselves to the task of composition. Some have experienced the fervour and glow of literary composition most fully under the influence of fine music, while others are baffled unless all around is pervaded with quiet; some have enjoyed working surrounded by their friends, others have found themselves helpless save in the perfect solitude of the study. As already intimated, visitors or society in any form are fatal to Verdi's work, and extinguish all the ardour of his genius.

No one can look upon the countenances of the old masters and not be impressed with that rapt expression which one so often sees. The intense enthusiasm which pervaded the soul reveals itself in every lineament—

"Like proud crags, high up, that wear the morning ere it comes."

Longfellow once said, in a pleasant letter to one of his

friends : "To those who ask how I can write 'so many things that sound as if I were as happy as a boy,' please say that there is in this neighbourhood, or neighbouring town, a pear-tree planted by Governor Endicott two hundred years ago, and that it still bears fruit not to be distinguished from the young tree in flavour. I suppose the tree makes new wood every year, so that some part of it is always young. Perhaps that is the way with some men when they grow old; I hope it is so with me." Louise Chandler Moulton declares that it must have been his thorough enjoyment of all that he had to do that kept Longfellow's work from telling on him. He was so full of fire and enthusiasm that one was insensibly beguiled in his presence into that frankness of the heart and the imagination which is so much rarer than the more commonplace frankness of thought and opinion. The intensity of feeling and enthusiasm with which Salvini throws himself into the part he is representing is remarkable. "This was especially evident," says one in speaking of him, "on the occasion of his playing 'Saul.' After the performance I was invited to go behind the scenes to speak with him, and was surprised, as well as pained, to find him utterly exhausted. I could not help saying, 'How can you exert yourself thus to please so few people?' There were scarcely four hundred persons assembled to witness this sublime performance. He answered with honest simplicity, 'They have paid their money, and are entitled to the best I can do for them ; besides that, when I am on the stage, I forget the world and all that is in it, and live the character I represent.' "

This, then, is one of the great secrets of success. One must have enthusiasm for his work ; and whether it be Bierstadt at the easel, or Brooks in the pulpit, depend upon it, this factor will ever be found one of the prominent attributes of the soul. It is a sad day when our ideal is reached. "Always think you shall succeed," was the advice of Dr. Arnold, "but never think you have reached the goal."

# VIII.

## 𝔐anners.

"Manner is *something* with every one, and *everything* with some."

There are certain manners which are learned in good society, of that force, that, if a person have them, he or she must be considered, and is everywhere welcome, though without beauty, or wealth, or genius.—EMERSON.

Give a boy address and accomplishments, and you give him the mastery of palaces and fortunes where he goes. He has not the trouble of earning or owning them; they solicit him to enter and possess.—*Ibid.*

Civility costs nothing, and buys everything.—LADY MONTAGU.

THOSE who aim to be thoroughly and always masters of the situation should realize that no one factor contributes so largely to this mastery as a man's manners and address. It was said of Hercules that whatever thing he did, he conquered. The same is true of some men. Their manners have made them simply irresistible, and have enabled them to carry their point in face of prejudice, envy, hatred, and all sorts of opposition, and seemingly even in spite of themselves transformed their enemies into friends. "I have known men," says South, "grossly injured in their affairs, depart pleased, at least silent, only because they were injured in good language, ruined in caresses, and kissed while they were struck."

What must have been the fascination of manner of the first Napoleon, which could lead the very soldiers sent to take him prisoner to bear him back in triumph to a throne?

There is no denying the fact that a man's manners give an immediate and permanent impression. We may not be able in so many words to analyze or define it, or to explain why, but the fact remains. Of course there are some who will affect to deny this, just as certain people affect to scout and deny the influence of " clothes ;" but who can safely ignore it? We can never wholly rid ourselves of *first impressions.* Reasoning or arguing against them will not avail. In spite of ourselves, we are influenced, say what we may ; and that these first impressions are governed largely by "manners" and " clothes," it were folly to deny. " In civilized society," says Johnson, " external advantages make us more respected. A man with a good coat upon his back meets with a better reception than he who has a bad one. You may analyze this and say what there is in it ; but that will avail you nothing, for it is a part of a general system. Pound St. Paul's Church into atoms, and consider any single atom. It is, to be sure, good for nothing ; but put all these atoms together, and you have St. Paul's Church." Every one knows that the manner of doing things is often more important than the things themselves. It has been truly observed that the very same thing may become either pleasing or offensive by the manner of saying or doing it ; just as in works of sculpture, though the material be valuable, as being silver or gold, the workmanship is still more so.

La Bruyère asserts that a man's worth in this world is estimated according to his conduct, and few who are acquainted with the world will be prepared to deny it. " Good-breeding alone can prepossess people in your favour at first sight, more time being necessary to discover greater talents."

Now, the achievement of this most desirable of accomplishments is not so difficult, after all. Graceful manners soon become a " second nature," if one really sets himself in

earnest to acquire them. The frequenting of good society
will inevitably confer them, and that, too, almost unconsciously. One naturally and insensibly acquires "the air,
the address, and the turn" of those with whom he converses.
Let one but consider for a moment the origin of the codes
of etiquette which prevail in polite society, and he cannot
fail to see how naturally fine manners arose. The good
heart and good intention is the basis of it all. The desire to
save annoyance or trouble, or to give pleasure to another,
even at the cost of some denial or inconvenience to one's
self,—this is indeed the real essence of all the codes. "There
is always a best way of doing everything," says Emerson,
"if it be to boil an egg. Manners are the happy ways of
doing things; *each once a stroke of genius or of love*—now
repeated and hardened into usage. They form at last a rich
varnish with which the routine of life is washed, and its
details adorned. If they are superficial, so are the dewdrops
which give such a depth to the morning meadows."

Lord Chatham, in one of his letters to his nephew, defined
politeness as benevolence in little things; and Hillard
affirms that we degrade politeness by making it anything
less than a cardinal virtue. This benevolence may manifest
itself in a thousand ways. It is revealed in little delicate
attentions, and thoughtfulness for another's wants or
pleasures. In unobtrusive manner it seems to anticipate
all one's wishes or preferences. Then, too, its favours are
conferred so naturally as to seem wholly spontaneous and
without premeditation; yet one finds every want anticipated. Is it not this which has always given that nameless
charm to Southern hospitality, and rendered it proverbial?
One visiting the South for the first time cannot fail to
recognize this delightful atmosphere,—this "old school"
suggestiveness in the courtesy and attentions he receives; nor
will he be slow to appreciate the charm. Say what we may,
in whatever else its people may be wanting, for charming

manners and delightful hospitality the South has ever enjoyed an enviable distinction, and deservedly so.

When one considers in what an infinite number of little things human happiness consists ; that it is not made up of " startling events and great emotions," but of little attentions often renewed, kindly offices, cheerful looks and salutations, unexpected little favours, glad surprises, and the like,—he comes to realize that mastership in this direction is as really admirable as the bringing about at rare intervals of some great and striking event. The opportunities for doing great things are so rare, after all, that they seldom come to any of us. To neglect, then, the little things that are sure to make life seem " more fair and sweet," is a great mistake. And the art is not difficult, as we have said. It is indeed very simple. The kindly heart will inevitably show us the way. It is Napoleon at St. Helena, meeting the labouring man bending under his heavy burden, and with his usual courtesy stepping aside, and mildly saying to his companion, who seemed still inclined to keep the narrow path, " Respect the burden, madame, respect the burden ! " It is Garibaldi entering mighty London, and amid all the tokens of welcome of the English nation, stooping to kiss the labourer's child, and in that single act " folding to his heart the working-people of England." It is good George Herbert stopping to lift the muddy wheel of the peasant's cart out of the ugly rut, and saying in response to the rallying of his friends on his soiled appearance, and the performance of so menial an act, that it would " make music for him at midnight." It is Wellington making room for the poor man at the altar rail, and remarking that all were equal there. It is the dying Sir Ralph Abercromby returning Duncan Roy's blanket ; or the King of the Belgians sending the wreath of immortelles to the weeping mother, as he happened to witness from the palace window the funeral procession of an unknown child. It is these, and a thousand other self-denying heroisms in

little things, daily repeated, in palace and in cot, that serve
to illustrate what we mean.

It is well to remember that pleasure is reciprocal; no one
feels it who does not at the same time give it. To be
pleased, one must please; and what pleases you in others
will generally please them in you. Rest assured of one
thing: if one is careless and indifferent whether he pleases
or not, he never will please. Swift declares that Nature has
left every man a capacity of being agreeable, though not of
shining in company; and there are a hundred men sufficiently qualified for both, who by a very few faults that they
might correct in half an hour, are not so much as tolerable.
They remind one of the story told of King James, who when
asked by a nurse to make her son a gentleman, replied: "I
will make him a baronet, if you will, but no power on earth
could make him a gentleman."

It has been said that one may do everything, however
unpleasant it may be to those around him, if one only does
it in the right way; and the instance given to prove the
truth of this assertion is taken from humble life. A cat
walks daintily into a room on a cold winter's day, and with
a benign glance at the company, and a melodious purring
sound, she walks leisurely round, selects for herself the
warmest place in the room,—perhaps the only warm place,
right in front of the fire,—curls herself up, and goes serenely
to sleep, secure that no one will be so unreasonable as to
question her right to sleep wherever inclination prompts her
to sleep. No one calls it selfish, no one is annoyed, because
she has done it so prettily and gracefully. Indeed, every one
experiences an access of warmth and comfort in himself from
beholding pussy's blissful repose.

Now imagine the same thing done in a different way, and
by a less self-possessed individual: if it were done hurriedly,
or noisily, or clumsily, or diffidently even, or in any way
obtrusively, what a storm of indignation it would excite in

the bosoms of all beholders. How thoughtless, how inconsiderate, how selfish! No, it must be done as the cat does it, without a sound or a gesture to provoke criticism, or it must not be done at all.

Many a man, by certain seemingly trivial faults of manner, has given rise to such a dislike at first that all his merit could not get the better of it afterwards.

> "I do not love thee, Dr. Fell,
> The reason why I cannot tell ;
> But this I know, and know full well,
> I do *not* love thee, Dr. Fell."

This familiar old epigram of Martial, thus anglicized by Tom Brown, has doubtless given apt expression to the feelings of many a one. Some, perhaps, would be puzzled to tell how it is possible not to love anybody, and yet not to know the reason why. But who doubts its truth? Nothing, we may be sure, can ever excuse a man for neglecting the civilities due from man to man. When Clement the Fourteenth was made Pope, the ambassadors of the several States represented at his court waited on his Holiness with their congratulations. As they were introduced and severally bowed, he also bowed to return the compliment. On this the master of ceremonies told his Holiness that he should not have returned their salute. "Oh, I beg your pardon," said he ; "I have not been Pope long enough to forget good manners."

It is a comforting assurance to know that the *desire of pleasing* is at least half the art of doing it, and that the rest depends wholly upon the manner. And this one learns simply by attention, observation, and frequenting good company. "If you always live with those who are lame," says the old Latin adage, "you will yourself learn to limp." In order to know the ways of good society one must of course avail himself of every proper occasion to make himself familiar with it, and carefully note the manners of those

who are its acknowledged leaders. He will find that among
well-bred people, as Hume says, a mutual deference is affected,
contempt of others disguised, authority concealed, attention
given to each in his turn, and an easy stream of conversation
maintained, without vehemence, without interruption, without eagerness for victory, and without any airs of superiority.
Now and then one will meet with a person "so exactly
formed to please that he will gain upon every one that hears
or beholds him : this disposition is not merely the gift of
nature, but frequently the effect of much knowledge of the
world, and a command over the passions." This mingling
with men occasionally will save a man also from that disagreeable, egotistical bearing which one sometimes sees manifested, and which reminds one, for all the world, of the personage of whom Tourguéneff tells, who "had the air of his
own statue erected by national subscription."

Chesterfield relates with charming frankness his own experience upon his first introduction into fine society. "I
remember," he says, "when, with all the awkwardness and
rust of Cambridge about me, I was first introduced into
good company I was frightened out of my wits. I was
determined to be what I thought civil; I made fine low
bows, and placed myself below everybody......If I saw
people whisper, I was sure it was at me; and I thought
myself the sole object of either the ridicule or the censure
of the whole company, who, Heaven knows, did not trouble
their heads about me. In this way I suffered for some time
like a criminal at the bar, and should certainly have re-
nounced all polite company for ever, if I had not been so
convinced of the absolute necessity of forming my manners
upon those of the best companies, that I determined to persevere, and suffer anything or everything rather than not
compass that point. Insensibly it grew easier to me, and
I began not to bow so ridiculously low, and to answer questions without great hesitation or stammering. If, now and

then, some charitable people, seeing my embarrassment, and being *désœuvré* themselves, came and spoke to me, I considered them as angels sent to comfort me, and that gave me a little courage. I got more soon afterwards, and was intrepid enough to go up to a fine woman and tell her that I thought it a warm day. She answered me very civilly that she thought so too; upon which the conversation ceased on my part for some time, till she, good-naturedly resuming it, spoke to me thus: 'I see your embarrassment, and I am sure that the few words you said to me cost you a great deal; but do not be discouraged for that reason, and avoid good company. We see that you desire to please, and that is *the main point;* you want only the manner, and *you think that you want it still more than you do.* You must go through your novitiate before you can profess good-breeding; and if you will be my novice, I will present you to my acquaintance as such.'" Elsewhere he shrewdly observes: "Have as much gold as you please in one pocket, but take care always to keep change in the other, for you will much oftener have occasion for a shilling than for a guinea. Give me a man who has ready cash about him for present expenses—sixpences, shillings, half-crowns, and crowns, which circulate easily; but a man who has only an ingot of gold about him is much above common purposes, and his riches are not handy nor convenient. Happy the man who, with a certain fund of parts and knowledge, gets acquainted with the world early enough to make it his bubble at an age when most people are the bubbles of the world, for that is the common case of youth."

It has been said that a man who knows the world will not only make the most of everything he does know, but of many things he does not know, and will gain more credit by his adroit mode of hiding his ignorance than the pedant by his awkward attempt to exhibit his erudition.

Who has not seen men highly gifted, and possessed of

most admirable qualities, their minds stored with all kinds
of knowledge—in fact, perfect walking encyclopædias—
appear at the utmost disadvantage in a mixed company in
a drawing-room ?  Awkward and blundering, they become
objects of the utmost concern, not to say terror, to their
friends because of the uncertainty created regarding what
overt breach of etiquette they may be guilty of next.  And
all this simply because of neglect in their early training, or
the absence of that instinct of fine breeding which often sup-
plies its place.  "We see a world of pains taken," says Steele,
"and the best years of life spent in collecting a set of thoughts
in a college for the conduct of life, and, after all, the man so
qualified shall hesitate in his speech to a good suit of clothes,
and want common sense before an agreeable woman.  Hence
it is that wisdom, valour, justice, and learning cannot keep a
man in countenance that is possessed with these excellences
if he wants that inferior art of life and behaviour called
good-breeding."  In the same vein La Bruyère has called
attention to the fact that although a man may have virtues
and many great qualities, he may still be disagreeable ; and
he affirms that there is a certain fashion in manners which
is too often neglected as of no consequence, but which frequently becomes the basis of the world's favourable or unfavourable opinion of you.  And he further shows that a
little attention to this, by which a man may render his manners polished and engaging, will prevent others from entertaining prepossessions respecting one which may be greatly
to one's disadvantage.

One thing is absolutely indispensable, and that is *unfailing
good-nature ;* the avoidance at all hazards, and at whatever
cost, of anything and everything which might wound, however slightly, and the manifestation, instead, of simple, cordial frankness, unassuming, winning manners, and a sunny,
perennial, golden temper.  This never fails to please ; and
so essential is it that Addison has declared that there is no

society or conversation to be kept up in the world without good-nature, or something which must bear its appearance and supply its place. "For this reason," he says, "mankind have been forced to invent a kind of artificial humanity, which is what we express by the word 'good-breeding.'" How charmingly has Steele portrayed the influence of this admirable quality! "Varillas," he tells us, "has this to the highest perfection, and communicates it wherever he appears. The sad, the merry, the severe, the melancholy, show a new cheerfulness when he comes among them. At the same time no one can repeat anything that Varillas has ever said that deserves repetition; but the man has that innate goodness of temper that he is welcome to everybody, because every man thinks he is so to him. *He does not seem to contribute anything* to the mirth of the company; *and yet upon reflection you find it all happened by his being there.*" And he further declares that men would come into company with ten times the pleasure they do, if they were sure of hearing nothing that would shock them, as well as expected what would please.

Let one beware of too much effort to make himself agreeable, and shun all excess. There is an ease and repose that characterizes those "to the manner born" which reveals itself unmistakably to the observant eye. Good-breeding shows itself most where to an ordinary eye it appears least. "One may now know a man that never conversed in the world by his excess of good-breeding. A polite country esquire shall make you as many bows in half an hour as would serve a courtier for a week. There is infinitely more to do about place and precedency in a meeting of justices' wives than in an assembly of duchesses." The *golden mean*, of which one hears so often, must be the rule here as elsewhere, in order to attain the surest success. A fine authority on elocution has observed that to serious-minded men there is but one true fashion in reading—namely, to pronounce distinctly

enough to be understood, but not so much so as to be remarked. Molé, the actor, has declared: "Without the
*middle register*, no reputation." The same is true here.
Both extremes are to be shunned. Sufficiently cordial to
be genial, but not so demonstrative as to attract special
attention. "Do not think," dryly remarks Zimmermann,
"that your learning and genius, your wit or sprightliness,
are welcome everywhere. I was once told that my company
was disagreeable because I appeared so uncommonly happy."

If one would like to test this influence of manners, and
would convince himself as regards their value, let him some
fine morning take a walk along a busy thoroughfare, and at
certain intervals stop a man and ask him the time of day,
for instance, or the way to some public grounds. Let him
demand the information from a few in a blunt and dictato-
rial manner, and then approach the others with well-bred
courtesy, and our word for it, he will not be left long in
doubt as to its "commercial" value, to say the least. And
right here let it be remarked: never be ashamed or afraid
of asking questions, for if they lead to information, and
you accompany them with some excuse, you will never be
reckoned a rude or impertinent questioner. All these things
depend entirely upon the manner; and in that respect the
vulgar saying is true, that one man may better steal a horse
than another look over the hedge. Preface your question
with a remark something on this wise, for instance: "I am
afraid I am very troublesome with my questions, but no one
can inform me as well as you." After an "exordium con-
ciliatory" like that, to use a phrase of the rhetoricians, one
need have no fear.

We may set it down as a truism that one will, as a rule,
find himself repaid in his own coin. The secret of the polite
attentions of French servants is to be found in the courtesy
of the higher classes toward them. Italian servants also, as
is well known, are models of politeness. The wildest mis-

take made in their language by a foreigner when giving an order does not cause even the shadow of a smile to flit across the servant's face. The words "coachman" and "spoon" are much alike in Italian, as are also "cabbage" and "horse," "hair" and "hats." "I have seen," says a writer in the *Century*, "a servant when told to order 'the spoon to harness the horses,' receive his instructions as if spoons harnessing horses was a sight he had been accustomed to from childhood. Tell your coachman to harness the cabbage, or your valet to hang up your hair, and they would bow and retire to carry out your absurd orders—which they perfectly understand, however—with most decorous solemnity. Though they never presume to disagree with their employers, yet these polite servants are very firm in carrying out their own ideas." The writer tells us of once having a man-cook whose aversion to cats was as great as his mistress's fondness for them. Yet in her presence he always spoke of cats as most charming animals to have about the house. But no cat could be kept in the house longer than a week. It always mysteriously disappeared; had been run over, or had strayed away, or been killed by a dog, and the cook was thrown thereby into the depths of grief. Here, surely, was diplomacy worthy a minister of state.

And why should not graceful little courtesies, both of language and of manner, be more common among us? One is not apt, as a rule, to be surfeited with happiness of such innocent sort in this prosy, working-day world of ours. Why is it not just as well to use the decorous phrases as the rude, the dainty as the severe and bald? Poetry is as cheap as prose. It was said of Villemain, that when he spoke to a lady, he seemed to be presenting her a bouquet. It lies much in one's own power whether the atmosphere which he shall create about him be ideal or otherwise. And who doubts that a man's surroundings, also, are not without a certain influence? As the editor of "The Thrift Book"

shrewdly remarks : " A neatly-spread table will probably
induce even the surly labourer to say, ' Please pass the
bread,' instead of ' Chuck over the loaf.' "

The expression, " manners of the old school," is familiar
to us all, and doubtless most of us have an idea more or
less distinct of what is implied in that phrase. Instantly
the picture arises in our minds of manners which must have
been very charming. Traces of them, as well as very
striking illustrations, at rare intervals still reveal to us that
this charm has not wholly passed away. " Sir Charles
Grandison," remarks a well-known writer, " would seem to
the youth of to-day an elaborate and very tedious man ; but
those youth might learn of him many a valuable lesson of
dignity and self-respect. It is, however, rather our conception of the old manners than the actual historical illustration
of them that we have in mind when we speak of the old
school. Indeed, in its common use in such phrases," he
continues, " the word ' old ' expresses an ideal view. Old
times are not merely the times of our youth, or of another
century ; they are times that never were, or rather they
are ' real times touched by the imagination with a celestial
glamour.'......To describe a person as a gentleman or lady of
the old school, therefore, is to speak of him or her not as
resembling Sir Charles Grandison or the Duchess of Newcastle, but as showing a gentle soul and refined courtesy,
with a certain endearing fascination of address and an
essential nobility of nature. There must doubtless be a
dignity of bearing fully to satisfy the phrase, and just that
slight and charming shade of difference from the current
ways of to-day which we call quaintness. There must be
also, for complete satisfaction, superior intelligence and
cultivation ; indeed, there must be a harmonious blending
of many high qualities." Speaking of a venerable lady who
had recently died as in the loftiest sense a lady of the old
school, he says her manner was that of one " accustomed to

association upon equal terms with the most superior men and women, and no less accustomed to the most thoughtful sympathy and regard for those who are called inferior...... Present or absent, her benign influence was always and everywhere perceptible in her household, as, whether the service is proceeding or not, the odour of incense is the perpetual atmosphere of St. Peter's."

Who does not instinctively and gratefully recognize the influence of manners like these? There is a charm which awakens our reverence as well as our delight. Dining at Mr. Grenville's, Sydney Smith, as usual, arrived before the rest of the party. Some ladies were shortly after announced. As Mr. Grenville, with his graceful dignity and cheerfulness, went forward to receive them, Sydney Smith, looking after him, exclaimed, "There, that is the man from whom we all ought to learn how to grow old!" Of Lady Elizabeth Hastings it was said that to know her was a liberal education. It is not difficult for those who have ever been favoured with the companionship of such, even for a limited period, to understand most thoroughly what Steele meant by this declaration.

True grace is elastic. In oratory, for instance, a very brief utterance expressed in a certain manner may mean vastly more than the mere words themselves. Thus one's manner of utterance may be intensely significant, and capable of producing effects undreamed of by the casual observer unfamiliar with such things. The manner of Bossuet was such when he pronounced the words, "The princess is dying —*the princess is dead*," in his funeral oration for Henrietta, that he could no longer proceed, so impassioned were the sobs and groans of his audience. So also, when Massillon, in the funeral oration of Louis XIV., raised his arms to heaven, and after remaining silent for a moment, in subdued tones said, "God only is great!" the vast audience, breathless and awe-struck, started to their feet as with one impulse, and bowed reverently before the altar. Garrick said, "I would give a hundred guineas if I could say 'Oh!' as White-field does."

So in one's daily intercourse there are certain manners that simply of themselves have great significance. "Every one knows how a gesture will cling to the memory; the merest little way of turning the head or lifting the eyes,—such slight peculiarities of movement,—although they may be not in the least strange or eccentric, seem to have some gift for fastening themselves on the attention beyond any outline of features in repose." The "artless manners," for instance, of certain graceful young persons whom one meets from time to time are a poem in themselves. And who has not been impressed with what Parton terms "that mysterious, omnipotent something which we call 'a presence'"? What is it? we ask. We have all from time to time recognized the vast difference in men in this regard. We understand fully what the term seeks to convey, but can we define the intangible something itself? One can easily believe it to be, in great part, physical. A writer on oratory maintains that for a man to be eloquent he needs no small degree of physical health and force. Other things being equal, he will be the more eloquent, he says, who is in the better condition physically; and he quotes a well-known philosopher who declares: "'Tis a question of stomach and constitution. The second man is as good as the first—perhaps better—but has not stoutness of stomach as the first has, and so his wit seems over-fine or under-fine." Doubtless something like this would in part account for the difference which we are considering, but one hesitates to attribute it wholly to it. Indeed, do not facts often prove it otherwise? Does not the great and hidden secret lie far behind all else, in the soul, the *personality*, after all? An instance is fresh in the memory of the author which cannot but serve to confirm this latter view.

Many, possibly, have noted the curious fact that a public speaker under the inspiration of a great theme, and in the midst of an eloquent passage, often appears, for the time, physically larger than he really is. The author's attention was first called to this by a remark made in his presence to a speaker who certainly was not far from medium in size. "How much do you weigh?" inquired the hearer, a man of middle age and some experience. "Not far from a hundred and thirty." "I should certainly have thought," continued the other, with the impression of the eloquent passage, doubtless, still vividly before him, "that you weighed over two hundred!"

There is often that expressed in looks and gestures which carries with it a nameless and mysterious power. George Eliot tells us, for instance, of Romola at Florence, and of an impalpable, golden glory, and *the long shadow of herself* that was not to be escaped. "One sees such mysteriously superior personages among those who have long breathed the air of privilege."

There is no denying that certain manners have an influence like that of fine music or high art. They flash upon one at times, appealing instantly to all the deeper emotions of the soul, and make one believe all things possible. In their presence the spell and inspiration of high art are upon one, and they are to a man what beauty is to a woman, creating at once a prepossession in his favour, while the opposite qualities exercise as quick a prejudice against him. "There are people who come in ever like a child with a piece of good news." It was said of the late Lord Holland that he always came down to breakfast with the air of a man who had just met with some signal good-fortune.

One thing we may rely on : *Naturalness* has a never-failing charm. It is doubtless true, as Jeffrey declared, that men are very long afraid of being natural from the dread of being taken for ordinary. "We are not natural by nature, and it

takes one a long time to come to himself—that is, to drop
his mannerisms and come to his own true selfhood." It is
ever true art which leads us back to unperverted nature.
The one event, we are told, which never loses its romance, is
the encounter with superior persons on terms allowing the
happiest intercourse.  Ah, these indeed are the soul's rare
opportunities!  It has perchance for days gone groping, disheartened and sad, under frowning skies, chilled by untoward
surroundings, environed by sinister circumstances, desponding
and desolate.  Life has seemed barren, fruitless, and naked
as the leafless branches swayed by the winter's blast.  Suddenly, without premonition perhaps, some slight turn is
given to our affairs.  We find ourselves ushered into charming surroundings, and lo, all is transformed!  The soul
breathes again its native air, the ideal life is realized, the
wintry past forgotten, the breath of the tropics is on cheek
and brow, and—ah, what a blossoming there is!

There is a certain "hardness of character" as Sydney
Smith calls it, which proceeds not from malignity or care-
lessness, but from "a want of delicate perception of those
little things by which pleasure is conferred or pain excited."
Persons possessing this gallop over a thousand fine feelings,
and leave "in every step the mark of hoofs upon your heart."
The same author declares the conversation of a well-bred
man of fine sympathies to be a perpetual homage of polite
good-nature, leaving you in perfect good-humour with yourself, because you perceive how much and how successfully
you have been studied, while this other, although he has
violated nothing which can be called a *rule*, has displeased
and dispirited you, "from wanting that fine vision which
sees little things, and that delicate touch which handles
them."

As regards that desirable quality, *naturalness* of manner,
—to which reference has already been made,—nothing could
be of greater importance to a public man.  Garrick's career

is a fine illustration of its influence and power.   Henry Clay is also an illustrious example.   It is said that Clay never indulged in an expression that was not instantly recognized as nature itself.   Some of his intonations, we are told, were indescribable.   " His mightiest feelings," says Dr. Alexander, "were sometimes indicated and communicated by a long pause, aided by an eloquent aspect and some significant use of his finger."   These men were *natural:* how in contrast to the "starched and unnatural" manners of certain other men !

One of the most common and often a seemingly insurmountable barrier in the way of appearing natural and at ease is one's own self-consciousness.   Now, every one must have observed that the almost inevitable result of self-consciousness is awkwardness; and awkwardness, Emerson tells us, has no forgiveness in heaven or earth.   " I was once very shy," says Sydney Smith, " but it was not long before I made two very useful discoveries : first, that all mankind were not solely employed in observing me ; and next, that shamming was of no use—that the world was very clearsighted, and soon estimated a man at his just value.   This cured me."

It is well to remember always that the best manners are the *simplest,* as it is in general proof of high culture to say the greatest matters in the simplest way.   " It is God who hangs the greatest weights on the smallest wires," is the ancient maxim.   Thus, the best style in writing, according to Coleridge, is that which forces us to think of the subject without paying any attention to the particular phrases in which it is clothed.   Thomas Sully, the artist, relates that, when in England, the higher the rank the more kind and affable he found the people.   There, " all is clear water and plain sailing in the best circles."   In these " best circles" speech is " low and clear, with that delicious intonation which no schoolmaster can teach, and with a grace which is the *fine fleur* of education, yet cannot be acquired,—which is one of the long results of time, the inheritance of generations generously bred. These soft and gracious manners, which are simplicity itself, yet the outcome of so much unconscious cultivation, are the most beautiful things in society. They come to some, indeed, who have had no training at all, nor any ancestors behind them, by gift of nature, like any other kind of genius; but ordinarily they belong to those who by nature have the best right to them,—the descendants of well-bred people for generations."

When one takes into account the fact that the whole significance of what is called society—the whole aim and end for which people assemble together in social ways—is to confer mutual pleasure, and to augment one another's enjoyment, he can readily see how utterly out of place must be anything disagreeable, whether it be in word or deed. Whatever has a tendency to make your friend dissatisfied with himself or with you is to be avoided. And yet, even with the best intentions, many a one has come to grief: some unforeseen circumstance, some ill-timed remark, or some innocent expression has leaped from the lips which one suddenly discovers, to his dismay, to be of doubtful interpretation, and instantly he feels himself to have fallen into disgrace. The word is now master which but a moment before was slave.

In a little volume kept for the autographs of literary men, in answer to the question, "What are your favourite topics of conversation?" Charles Kingsley once wrote, "Whatever my companion happens to be talking about." Who of us could have done better than that?

There appeared not many years since, in one of our prominent magazines, a somewhat notable article from the pen of Charles Astor Bristed, on "Impoliteness as a National Institution." Among other things the writer said : "There can be no doubt that what Walter Scott called 'the manners or

want of manners peculiar to Americans' has created a large
European prejudice against us, has been effective to deter
some desirable varieties of emigration, and has promoted a
tendency to absenteeism among many of our wealthy citizens,
and many who are by no means of the most wealthy. Of
course one of the first questions which occurs to the thinker
is : How far has this opprobrium been really merited ?" The
writer then goes on to speak of the "overbearing insolence
of the Jack-in-office through all his varieties, from the hotel
boot-black to the railroad anything-you-like," and mentions
the experience of a foreign diplomatic friend of his at a
certain hotel in New England. "I do not doubt," he continues, "or deny that it is *possible* to live some time, and
move about largely in our country, and receive, on the whole,
very civil treatment. *It's a lottery, and that is just the
trouble.* It's the invalid and the Shanghai cock next door,
over again. 'He doesn't crow all the time,—perhaps he
doesn't crow very often ; but I never know when he *will*
crow, and am always afraid he is going to.' It is just this
fear and dread of encountering rudeness which causes even
those who know better to be tenacious upon ceremonious
points of etiquette."

Doubtless the strictures of this gifted and brilliant man
are somewhat too severe ; and yet one can but acknowledge
that in certain quarters there is just ground for complaint.
Lest one should be led to think, however, that Americans
monopolize the disagreeable manners of the globe, it may be
well to recall, as a sort of companion picture to this last,
Sydney Smith's arraignment of the manners of our English
cousins. "I believe," he says, "the English are the most
disagreeable people under the sun ; not so much because Mr.
John Bull disdains to talk, as that the respected individual
has nothing to say, and because he totally neglects manners.
Look at a French carter ; he takes off his hat to a neighbour
carter, and inquires after 'la santé de madame,' with a bow

that would not have disgraced Sir Charles Grandison; and I have often seen a French *soubrette* with a far better manner than an English duchess."

Of all the unmitigated evils which infest society, the class denominated "bores" must surely carry off the palm. And a "bore," you know, some one has wittily said, is the person who wishes to tell you all about himself, instead of letting you tell him all about yourself. However this may be, there are few of us who would not vote the bore an intolerable nuisance. In the author's possession is an unpublished letter of Oliver Wendell Holmes;—does Holmes ever write even a letter, think you, in which one does not find the well-known and inimitable touches of his humour or pathos ere its close? This letter was written in response to a request for "a lyric," made by the managers of a great fair, held at Washington soon after the war, for the benefit of disabled soldiers and sailors. After saying that he must ask them to accept two of his volumes instead of the poem, he continues: "To write a lyric is like having a fit; you can't have one when you wish you could (as, for instance, when your bore is in his third hour and having it all his own way), and you can't help having it when it comes of itself."

Instead of parading one's information or learning, one must always keep it in reserve :—

> "Men must be taught as if you taught them not,
> And things unknown proposed as things forgot."

Above all else, bear in mind that *self-possession*, as already intimated, is absolutely essential to good manners, and is really the foundation of all grace. Without this one is never sure of himself, and is at the mercy of every chance. If he fail here, one is sure to be trammelled and fettered, and can never appear at his best nor seem at ease. For the time being he is a slave to that which is alien to his true self; and the consciousness of this, ever present,—the feeling that one is not giving expression to what his innermost instincts approve as right and fitting,—only makes matters worse. One must train himself to conquer this at all hazards. To be master of the situation, one should "find himself at home wherever he is; should by his own security and good nature impart comfort to all beholders."

What could have been more charming than the manner of Disraeli in society? One who knew him tells us that he always talked to the guest next to him as he would to an old friend. That remark surely expresses volumes. The accomplishment once ours, we may regard ourselves as having taken all the degrees in fine breeding; all else is implied. At the same time, our informant tells us, he had few intimates; "nor did his apparent frankness unveil anything more than he chose to reveal."

One's manners in conversation must by no means be overlooked. In general company, beware of lengthy harangues. Talk often, but not long. "Did you ever hear me preach?" said Coleridge, addressing Lamb. "Never heard you do anything else," was the witty response of the genial essayist. If one tells stories, let it be seldom; and then they must be brief and to the point. Omit every circumstance not essential.

There is no person living who is not susceptible to the influence of fine manners. Some men, it has been truly said, are more captious than others; some are always wrong-headed; but every man living has such a share of vanity as to be hurt by marks of slight and contempt. "Every man does not pretend to be a poet, a mathematician, or a statesman; but every man pretends to common sense, and to fill his place in the world with common decency, and consequently does not easily forgive those negligences, inattentions, and slights which seem to call in question both these pretensions."

Of one thing we may be confident, and it cannot be learned too early: if one wishes to appear agreeable in society, he must consent to be taught many things which

he already knows. This is especially true if one is often
thrown into the society of elderly people. And, by the
way, let no one ever allow himself to fall into the indiscre-
tion of using the word "old" in speaking of any such within
hearing. This were to commit an unpardonable blunder.

There is, we must confess, sometimes a tendency manifest
even on the part of certain well-bred people to wear a
theme threadbare before dropping it and changing to something else. No fault could be more wearisome. The great
charm of conversation is the art of passing naturally and
easily from one subject to another when due attention has
been given to the topic in hand. Failure to do this is often
the occasion of great annoyance; for, as Voltaire has remarked, the secret of tiring is to say everything that can be
said on the subject.

Above all things, avoid "lugging in" a subject, and beware of a reputation for riding a hobby, or of "harping for
ever on one string;" otherwise you may expect to be shunned
rather than welcomed. A certain individual who supposed
his friends particularly fond of hearing about characters of
Scripture availed himself of every opportunity to bring
these in. "I affirm," said he on one of these occasions,
"that this Samson was the strongest man that ever lived
or ever will live." "It is not so," instantly remarked one
of the company who had heard enough of this sort of
thing, and determined to put an end to the tiresome
twaddle,—"it is not so. You are a stronger man than
Samson, yourself." "How can that be?" "Why, you have
just lugged him in by head and shoulders." The worst
thing about the infliction is the fact that one is usually so
helpless in the presence of such people and so completely at
their mercy. Few of us can muster the moral courage to
"sit down" on them, or "squelch" them, as in the instance
mentioned. The most one can do under ordinary circumstances is to "smile and endure it."

To some, the prospect of entertaining literary guests is sufficient cause for apprehension. Those who have been favoured with the rare privilege, however, have found them the most agreeable and easily entertained people in the world, we dare say. One has but to remember that the makers of books are not apt to be the ones most eager to "talk book." In fact, Parton somewhere declares that those who produce literature seldom care very much for the literature of other men and times. In any event one thing is certain : The great fact that "one touch of nature makes the whole world kin" is always on one's side, and there is ever a common ground on which all can meet; for has not eminent authority declared that the way to a man's heart is through a certain portion of the epigastric region ? If there be attention here, minor matters may be safely disregarded. Thackeray's "Now, don't let's say a word," made so winningly and confidentially to the friend next to him, as they seated themselves before the smoking viands at a sumptuous banquet, conveyed a world of significance.

The gift of good sense is, after all, the foundation of all true politeness. Without this it is idle to think of success. One must know when to violate that code of conventional forms which common consent has established, and when not ; for it has been well observed that it is equally a mark of weakness to be a slave to these forms, as to despise them. Let one have the penetration and tact to adapt his conversation and manner to circumstances and individuals. If for no other reason than the fact that these little items of courtesy have often made the fortunes of their possessors, it were well worth a little extra effort to secure them.

Why is it that in presence of certain people one feels so ill at ease, under such a sense of oppression or tension, while with certain others one experiences such a sense of restfulness, something so grateful and refreshing, that their very presence is like a tonic ? Is not the secret to be found in this influence of manner of which we have spoken?

But aside from the mere question of pleasure and delight which they confer, and far beyond it, let us not forget that fine manners are really our safeguard, and that they constitute the great bulwark by which society is protected and preserved, just as the famous dikes of Holland protect its people from encroachment and destruction by the all-devouring sea. Though it may not appear at a glance, there is always a reason for the observances which society requires, and a philosophy behind them. And as regards the minor matters of deportment, one does not, for instance, eat with the knife,—that is, put the blade of the knife into the mouth, —not only because " the sight of the heaped-up morsel lifted on high disgusts the beholder, and allows opportunity for the exhibition of a voracity revolting to the delicate and sensitive," but because it is also dangerous; and worse still —as a recent authority has finely put it—such use of one's knife indicates that one's immediate ancestry, parents and grandparents, did the same thing, and were not in that grade of life where attention is given to the small matters of fine personal conduct, and one has consequently been deprived of good-breeding, and if deficient in that particular, is probably deficient in most other particulars of the sort. " Inspection will show that there is as much reason also for most of the lesser points of what is called polite behaviour, the observance of whose obligations is necessary, if for nothing else, in order to show that we are not sprung directly from barbarians."

If we were asked to mention any one principle as being well-nigh universal in its application, and as holding within itself the secret of pleasing under all circumstances, we should name the simple grace of *humility*. One must ever sink self if he would please and make others happy. There is a certain rare beauty in humility which imparts a nameless charm for all beholders. Let no one think that he shall please by merely showing off his own great abilities. "Learn to regard the souls around you as parts of some grand instrument. It is for each of us to know the keys and stops, that we may draw forth the harmonies that lie sleeping in the silent octaves." Each has the instinct of hero-worship ; and, strange as it may seem, instead of envy and hatred, there is "a loyal delight which even the most degraded and miserable of men take in every striking endowment or excellence of their more gifted fellows."

Of one thing rest assured : No one can escape the bondage of good manners. "Its fetters may be silken, but they are as strong as those that wheel the Earth along in her orbit. And while all must obey its laws, those laws furnish a currency with which if the beggar provide himself he is better off in all the markets of the world than the prince who is unprovided."

# IX

# "𝕎ait!"

We may not kindle when we will
  The fire that in the heart abides;
The spirit bloweth, and is still,
  In mystery the soul abides:
But tasks in hours of insight willed,
  In hours of gloom can be fulfilled.—ARNOLD.

And thus the empty-handed years went round;
Vacant, yet voiceful ever with prophetic sound.—LONGFELLOW.

' How much grows everywhere if we do but wait ! Not a difficulty but can transfigure itself into a triumph; not even a deformity but, if our own soul have imprinted worth on it, will grow dear to us.—CARLYLE.

THAT was a great night when, thrilled with the thought of his triumph, Edmund Kean rushed home to his trembling wife, and in a wild tumult of emotion cried out, "The pit rose at me ! Mary, you shall ride in your carriage yet, and Charles shall go to Eton !" How long he had toiled and suffered, poor fellow, and waited for that one great night when he at length had London at his feet ! There was no royal road to this triumph, nor is there a royal road to triumph in any art. The path which leads to the goal is long, steep, and narrow, and many grow weary and heart-sick by the way. Toil, patience, and unflinching persever-ance alone can win the day. The race is not to the swift, much less to the superficial and pretentious. To be mediocre, it has well been said, is within reach of many, but to be great can be accomplished by but few. "The number of unappreciated Juliets who, after having 'strutted their brief hour upon the stage,' have now subsided into the superintendency of the tea-urn and the buttered toast, is a sad commentary upon the fondness of young people essaying to mount Pegasus before they are out of their artistic swaddling-clothes."

One of the first and most important lessons for a young man is the learning how to *wait*. When will young men appreciate the wisdom contained in that old Latin motto, *Festina lente ?* In these days of scramble and rush, the man who really learns to "hasten slowly" will find himself vastly the gainer in the end. Scores of men are betrayed into failure through imprudence just here. They are always in haste, and always distanced. A distinguished traveller relates that while in Europe he started early one morning to climb a mountain. Stimulated by the bracing air and inspiring scenery, he pushed on briskly, instead of husbanding his strength for the uphill work before him. Soon after setting out he overtook a peasant on his way to the summit. The man was walking slowly, yet with a steady pace. Wondering, as he left the countryman behind, that the inspiration of the atmosphere and the surrounding scenery had not produced upon him the effect which he himself experienced, our enthusiastic tourist before long began to lag, and by noon he was glad to throw himself down in the shade of a wayside tree. As he realized how severely he had taxed his strength, and that his fatigue made him loath to leave his shady resting-place, he happened to cast his eyes down the valley. What was his surprise to behold the peasant of the morning swinging up the road with the same steady stride, as fresh as he was earlier in the day ! Presently passing the discomfited tourist, he disappeared in the distance, and left the traveller to his reflections on this new version of the fabled hare and tortoise.

The great danger which menaces young men in these days

is that of making quantity more important than quality.
Let it then not be forgotten that the best work is the work
that takes time; and nowadays more than ever before, perhaps, owing to the fierce competitions among men, the best
work is the work that is wanted.   In this country all delay
seems irksome.   It has been said that there are no apprentices; all from the start are journeymen—such as they are.
Those who would have passed for boys ten years since are
to-day at the head of business firms—such as they are.
Young men seem to scorn the serving of apprenticeships
such as their fathers served.   Their attitude and bearing
too often seems to say, "Go to, let us step out and make a
fortune."   One might infer from this that the making of a
fortune was the easiest thing in the world.   Such seem to
forget that ninety-five out of every hundred business men
fail.

Nothing is more to be deplored than this feverish haste,
this passion for "short cuts" in everything, which seems so
universally to prevail.   There are no longer any boys.   It is
but a step from childhood to the young man.   And these
young men, half-fledged, and in no wise prepared to fill them,
expect to step into positions of honour and trust and grave
responsibility.   Hence so many ill-starred careers.   Hence,
too, so often, the instances of certain young men, more
reckless than usual, finding accumulations too slow, and
quietly appropriating the funds of other men.   Let it ever
be remembered that forcing processes are injurious from first
to last.   Moreover, haste always betrays itself.   The house
constructed in haste and hurried to completion is apt to be
leaky and often in need of repairs.   In warping joints and
gaping crevices and shaky foundations the builder's haste is
always betrayed.   It is only the seasoned timber that never
gives.   So, too, the volume written in haste, and made "to
sell," is always short-lived and soon forgotten.   How many
in their feverish haste have thus marred their work, and

made a failure of what otherwise might have been permanent and enduring success! Let us remember that the richest and mellowest fruits are not the sudden result of a day's forced and unnatural growth; but in the luscious morsel which tempts the palate we can almost detect the breath of the zephyr, the gentle benediction of the dew, the caressing of the summer breeze, the kisses of the sun, and all the nameless influences which have nursed it into ripe perfection. So among men. The rarest products are never the result of haste, are never forced, but like the autumn fruitage are the outcome of a thousand mysterious influences which have brought them forth.

Longfellow long ago declared the great want of our national character to be "the dignity of repose." "We seem to live," he declared, "in the midst of a battle—there is such a din, such a hurrying to and fro. In the streets of a crowded city it is difficult to walk slowly. You feel the rushing of the crowd, and rush with it onward. In the press of our life it is difficult to be calm. In this stress of wind and tide all professions seem to drag their anchors, and are swept out into the main." Now, in the midst of all this stress and hurry, it is worth while for a young man to deliberately pause and take home to himself this truth— "The world is his who knows how to wait." Let him dare to believe it; for, rest assured, a conviction like this will prove invaluable to any man. "This idea of short cuts," remarks a certain writer,—"the notion that if a thing is to be done at all, then 'twere well 'twere done quickly,—admirable as it may be on the Exchange, is justly said to rub from life its delicacy and bloom when made the ruling maxim in all other relations and positions. A life with leisure hours in it for watching and examining all that we pass would seem a much more enviable and rational lot than a swift rushing from one goal to another, from one sort of fame or power or opulence to another and more remote."

As a rule, we are far too hasty and precipitate. We read the preface, and declare we know the whole book. Learn to wait. *Nondum* ("Not yet") was in early life the motto of Charles V.; and no less an authority than De Maistre has declared that the great secret of success is to know how to *wait*. Many a man has failed who might have succeeded had he but learned this lesson. True, it requires courage and self-denial; but what was ever attained worth the having without these? Patience, we are told, is the art of hoping.

> " How poor are they that have not patience !
> What wound did ever heal but by degrees?"

As Montesquieu well says, the success of the greater part of things depends upon knowing how long it takes to succeed.

"Don't be whining about not having a fair chance," says a vigorous writer. "Throw a sensible man out of a window, and he will fall on his feet and ask the nearest way to his work. A scant breakfast in the morning of life sharpens the appetite for a feast later in the day. Your present want will make future prosperity all the sweeter." The young man who means to reach the heights "by great men reached and kept" should understand that the broad and easy roads and short cuts, so popular in these modern days, do not lead to them. Those who have gained them were toiling upward in the night by the old-fashioned, rugged ways, while their companions slept. Men who rise in this way are not made dizzy by sudden elevation. The great moment comes at length, and they " walk up to fame as to a friend." The classic face of the first Napoleon, when he became master of Prussia as well as of all Germany, remained as cold and calm in those days of proud triumph as it had been in the days of adversity. His successes seemed to surprise him as little as his early misfortune had discouraged him. In Longfellow's "Falcon of Ser Federigo," in the "Tales of a Wayside Inn,"

we find this principle beautifully illustrated, and that last
line sums up the whole,—

"All things come round to him who will but wait."

Does not one sometimes look back wistfully to the good
old coaching days? How delightful they must have been !
A genial essayist has declared that he could be well content
to live upon the road, instead of getting on at the present
rate, and being impatient to arrive at some town, only,
perhaps, to be equally restless when arrived there. Not
that he was insensible to the pleasure of driving fast, stirring the blood as it does, and giving a sense of power ; but
everything seemed to be getting a little too hasty and
business-like, as though we were to be eternally getting on,
and never realizing anything but fidget and money—the
means instead of the end. Does it not fill one with positive dread to think of being hustled through Europe at the
rate realized by some of our modern travellers? Actually,
the very thought tires one. Well has a keen and observant
traveller cautioned such to "stay where you are happy ;"
and the caution may profitably be heeded. The age in
general has been rightly characterized as one of stimulus
and high pressure. Effect is everything ; results produced
at once—something to show, and something that may *tell*.
"The folio of patient years is replaced by the pamphlet that
stirs men's curiosity to-day, and to-morrow is forgotten."
Society wants "its new number of something to appear in-
cessantly. There is no rest nor repose, and one subject of
thought succeeds another faster than wave succeeds wave."
The crying need of our time is for more leisure, and for
more leisurely preparation for one's life-work, and, as a
result, better accomplishment. And let it be understood
that by leisure we do not mean idleness. The idler or the
"loafer," with "his idle hands always in his idle pockets,"
is only worthy of contempt. True leisure is the intermission

of labour—"the blink of idleness" in the life of a hard-
working man.

One's waiting years, indeed, should be fullest of work;
for then the toil is most needful, and will tell most effec-
tively in the line of success. And let it ever be remembered
that all knowledge will some time be of value. "They say,"
remarks Herbert, "it is an ill mason that refuseth any
stone;" and there is no knowledge but, in a skilful hand,
serves either positively as it is or else to illustrate some
other knowledge. The advantage of accurate knowledge,
though seemingly of no present value, is sometimes very
great. There is a notable instance in point. During one of
the earlier years of his professional life, as Harvey tells us,
a blacksmith called on Webster for advice respecting the
title to a small estate bequeathed to him by his father. The
terms of the will were peculiar, and the kind of estate trans-
mitted was doubtful. An attempt had been made to annul
the will. Mr. Webster examined the case, but was unable
to give a definite opinion upon the matter for want of
authorities. He looked through the law libraries of Mr.
Mason and other legal gentlemen for authorities, but in
vain. He ascertained what works he needed for consulta-
tion, and ordered them from Boston at an expense of fifty
dollars. He spent the leisure hours of some weeks in going
through them. He successfully argued the case when it
came on for trial, and it was decided in his favour. The
blacksmith was in ecstasies, for his little all had been at
stake. He called for his attorney's bill. Mr. Webster,
knowing his poverty, charged him only fifteen dollars, intending to suffer the loss of money paid out and to lose the
time expended in securing the verdict. Years passed away
and the case was forgotten, but not the treasured knowledge
by which it was won. On one of his journeys to Washington, Mr. Webster spent a few days in New York City.
While he was there, Aaron Burr waited on him for advice

in a very important case then pending in the State Court.
He told him the facts on which it was founded. Mr. Webster saw in a moment that it was an exact counterpart to
the blacksmith's will case. On being asked if he could state
the law applicable to it, he at once replied that he could.
He proceeded to quote decisions bearing upon the case,
going back to the time of Charles II. As he went on with
his array of principles and authorities, all cited with the
precision and order of a table of contents, Mr. Burr arose in
astonishment and asked with some warmth, "Mr. Webster,
have you been consulted before in this case?"—"Most
certainly not," he replied. "I never heard of your case till
this evening."—"Very well," said Mr. Burr; "proceed."
Mr. Webster concluded the rehearsal of his authorities, and
received from Mr. Burr the warmest praise of his profound
knowledge of the law, and a fee large enough to remunerate
him for all the time and trouble spent on the blacksmith's
case.

Be not too easily discouraged. It has been well said that
we know what we are, but know not what we may be; and
it is much less what we do than what we think which fits
us for the future. "Some men get early disgusted," says
Sydney Smith, "from some excesses which they have committed, and mistakes into which they have been betrayed,
at the beginning of life. They abuse the whole art of navigation because they have stuck upon a shoal; whereas the
business is to refit, careen, and set out a second time. The
navigation is very difficult: few of us get through it at first
without some rubs and losses—which the world is always
ready enough to forgive where they are honestly confessed
and diligently repaired."

The things of a man for which we visit him, says Emerson, were done in the dark and the cold. The hero is the
man who "forgets himself into immortality." The truly
heroic deed is always performed without a thought of the

blare of trumpets or the roll of drums. Fame enters in no wise into the calculation. In a fine article in the "Century," General Badeau, in commenting upon the hero of Appomattox, as he appeared at Galena in 1860, while as yet "un-important and unknown," uses these significant words: "No restless ambition disturbed his spirit. No craving for fame made him dissatisfied with obscurity. Those nearest him never suspected that he possessed extraordinary ability. He himself never dreamed that he was destined for great place or power. Yet his vicissitudes had given him a wide and practical experience, and made him, unknown to himself, a representative American. He had learned patience when hope was long deferred, and endurance under heavy and repeated difficulties; he had displayed audacity in emergencies, as well as persistency of resolve and fertility of resource. If one means failed, he tried another. He was not discouraged by ill fortune, nor discontented with little things. Above all, he never quailed and never despaired. The leather-merchant of Galena was not without preparation even for that great future which awaited him all unknown. There were many traits in him like those of Moltke. Both lived simply, and almost unknown to their countrymen, for many years. Moltke, it is true, remained in his profession, and was more fortunate, as the world goes; but until the great opportunity came, he also was comparatively obscure."

Fitz-Hugh Ludlow has pictured that mood of misanthropy which perhaps comes upon us all at times, in his striking poem, "Too Late:"—

> " When we want, we have for our pains
>     The promise that if we but wait
> Till the want has burned out of our brains,
>     Every means shall be present to sate ;
> While we send for the napkin, the soup gets cold ;
> While the bonnet is trimming, the face grows old ;
> When we've matched our buttons, the pattern is sold ;
>     And everything comes too late—too late !"

Thackeray once, somewhat facetiously perhaps, gave utterance to the same sentiment. "When I was a boy," said he, "I wanted some toffy. It was a shilling; I hadn't one. When I was a man I had a shilling, but I didn't want any toffy." A certain truth seems to reside in such sentiments as these, it must be confessed; but they are only partially true, after all. That is only one glimpse of the picture, and the darker one at that. Moreover, such sentiments are apt to be morbid, and the less one gives heed to them the better. There are too many exceptions on the bright side for one to believe long in shadows. Life is like one of Rembrandt's pictures—the shadow only serves to reveal in finer contrast the true outline and bright reality, after all. Hours of depression will come; but wait. It is always darkest, we are told, just before day; a brighter turn of affairs may come at any moment. If burdens are heavy and energies seem sorely taxed, be patient. Remember those striking words of Mendelssohn, "For me, too, the hour of rest will come; do the next thing." "There is always a black spot in our sunshine," exclaims Carlyle; "it is the shadow of ourselves!" Even in one's happiest hours there will come at times that curious moment's speck—that indefinable something—just enough "to dash our triumph and invade our joy." But these depressions, these hours of gloom, let us remember, are well-nigh universal; the stoutest-hearted are not exempt. The moth seems for ever striving to eat the garment, the shadow to devour the light. There are hours of darkness when we go grieving. Will God not enable us to fill out the ragged incompleteness of our lives, which so haunts us evermore? Is he so strong, and will he not remove the bars of sinister circumstance that environ us? Ah, if he only would! Then a sudden light breaks in upon the soul. The whole landscape of life seems lighted up. We see clearly the path which we should take—the high duties for which we should brace ourselves. Faint not, then, nor falter.

" Through efforts long in vain, prophetic need
    Begets the deed :
Nerve then thy soul with direst need to cope;
    Life's brightest hope
Lies latent in Fate's deadliest lair—
    Never despair ! "

The world is looking for men, and the success of all business enterprises depends on the character of those who manage them. "The trend of thought to-day is towards the accumulation of great fortunes. This has its influence upon the young, and in our great haste to be rich we have lowered the standard of business integrity. To be shrewd and sharp, even if not transparently honest, seems to be a favourite idea with some ; but a proper respect for the rights and feelings of others is sure to count largely in one's favour in the long run." The real object of all training and of all education should be to develop the best type of manhood. It is well to remember that, "while nothing but the fairy's wand can realize the capricious desire of the moment, as regards the objects of laudable wishes, deeply breathed, and for many a night and day ever present to the mind," these are placed by Providence more within our reach than is commonly supposed. "Generally speaking," says Sydney Smith, "the life of all truly great men has been a life of intense and incessant labour. They have commonly passed the first half of life in the gross darkness of indigent humility, overlooked, mistaken, contemned by weaker men, thinking while others slept, reading while others rioted, feeling something within them that told them they should not always be kept down among the dregs of the world ; and then, when their time was come, and some little accident has given them their first occasion, they have burst out into the light and glory of public life rich with the spoils of time and mighty in all the labours and struggles of the mind. Then do the multitude cry out, ' A miracle of genius !' Yes, he is a miracle of genius because he is a miracle of labour;

because instead of trusting to the resources of his own single mind he has ransacked a thousand minds ; because he makes use of the accumulated wisdom of ages, and takes as his point of departure the very last line and boundary to which science has advanced ; because it has ever been the object of his life to assist every intellectual gift of nature, however munificent and however splendid, with every resource that art could suggest and every attention diligence could bestow."

This inextinguishable courage is what men need. We are told of a young New York inventor who, about twenty years ago, spent every dollar he was worth in an experiment, which, if successful, would introduce his invention to public notice and insure his fortune, and, what he valued more, his usefulness. The next morning the daily papers heaped unsparing ridicule upon him. Hope for the future seemed vain. He looked around the shabby room where his wife, a delicate little woman, was preparing breakfast. He was without a penny. He seemed like a fool in his own eyes ; all these years of hard work were wasted. He went into his chamber, sat down, and buried his face in his hands. At length, with a fiery heat flashing through his body, he stood erect. " It *shall* succeed ! " he said, shutting his teeth. His wife was crying over the papers when he went back. " They are very cruel," she said. " They don't understand."—" I'll make them understand," he replied cheerfully.—" It was a fight for six years," he said afterwards. " Poverty, sickness, and contempt followed me. I had nothing left but the dogged determination that it should succeed." It did succeed. The invention was a great and useful one. The inventor is now a prosperous and happy man. " Be sure you are right," he says to younger men ; " then never give up."

During the long years in which he had to make his way against the majority in the House of Commons, Disraeli never seemed disheartened by his repeated defeats, nor did he ever relax the vigilance with which he watched his

adversary.   He never indulged himself, though he was
naturally indolent, and often in poor health, by staying
away from Parliament, even when business was slack;
never missed an opportunity for exposing a blunder of his
adversaries or commanding the good service of one of his
own followers.   "Here is a wonderful career," remarks an
eminent authority who knew him well, "even more wonderful to those who live in the midst of English politics and
society than it can appear to observers who live in other
countries.   A man with few external advantages, not even
that of education at a university, where useful friendships
are formed, with grave positive disadvantages in his Jewish
extraction and the vagaries of his first years of public life,
presses forward, step by step, through slights and disappointments which retard but never dishearten; assumes, as of
right, the leadership of a party,—the aristocratic party, the
party peculiarly suspicious of new men and poor men; wins
a reputation for sagacity which makes his early follies forgotten; becomes in old age the favourite of a court and the
master of a great country,—one of the three or four arbiters
of Europe."

Nothing was more striking about El Mahdi than his pertinacity and his power of holding his followers in spite of
defeat.   During the four years after he first raised the
standard of revolt he suffered nine or ten serious defeats,
with barely an equal number of successes.   After every defeat he returned to the attack stronger than before.   Three
times he was repulsed with heavy losses while besieging
El Obeid, but he finally captured it.   Hicks Pasha inflicted
a terrible defeat upon him, but he subsequently destroyed
Hicks Pasha and his entire army.   Clearly the Mahdi was
not a foe to be despised.

A young man should learn to bide his time.   "The horse
that frets is the horse that sweats," is an old saying of horse-
men; and it is just as true of men as of horses.   Good men,

it has been justly observed, by a natural gravitation come to the front, and accident, or want of accident, only temporarily retards or repels them. Therefore when a man looks forward to his chances in life, his great business is to prepare himself for those chances. Moreover, as every one knows, too early flattery, unless one have strength of character sufficient to resist it, has been more disastrous by far, in certain instances, than cold neglect and indifference. It behooves one to guard against this danger most assiduously. The infant Roscius, who set all England ablaze with what it was pleased to term his genius when a child, dwindled down into very meagre proportions as a man. What one most needs is a resolution not to be content with one's self or with one's present attainments or performance ; to scorn ephemeral for lasting fame ; to turn a deaf ear to the unwise flattery of the present, and look to the permanent honour of the future. This alone can bridge one safely over the dangerous current of popular fancy.

See how Balzac, in his lonely garret, toiled and waited. Neither poverty, debt, nor hunger could discourage or intimidate. That inner consciousness of the possession of great powers sustained him. All undaunted by privations, hindrances, or discouragements, he could *wait*. Did not the ample fortune and splendid residences of his later years attest the wisdom of his course, and prove his waiting had not been in vain ? Those familiar lines of the " Psalm of Life " have great meaning. Their influence may be a potent one if we are wise. Let them enter the soul, then, not only as the transient music of school-days, but as an inspiration for the sterner conflict of maturer years, and a clarion note for the battle of life :—

> " Let us, then, be up and doing,
> With a heart for any fate ;
> Still achieving, still pursuing,
> Learn to labour and to *wait*."

The late Secretary Seward advised a young man who consulted him regarding the study of law, to learn, first of all, some certain means of subsistence by the labour of his hands. The great prizes, as a rule, in the legal profession come only after toil and patient waiting. Smiles gives us a notable illustration in the case of Henry Bickersteth of the value of this patient waiting, and at the same time the laying under tribute whatever may present itself, until the way shall open. " Bickersteth was the son of a surgeon in Westmoreland, and was himself educated to that profession. As a student at Edinburgh he distinguished himself by the steadiness with which he worked and the application which he devoted to the science of medicine. Returned to Kirkby Lonsdale, he took an active part in his father's practice ; but he had no liking for the profession, and grew discontented with the obscurity of a country town. He went on, never-theless, diligently improving himself, and engaged in specula-tions in the higher branches of physiology. In conformity with his own wish, his father consented to send him to Cambridge. Close application to his studies threw him out of health, however, and he accepted the appointment of travelling physician to Lord Oxford. While abroad he mastered Italian and acquired a great admiration for Italian literature, but no greater liking for medicine than before. On the contrary, he determined to abandon it ; but returning to Cambridge, he took his degree, and that he worked hard may be inferred from the fact that he was senior wrangler of his year. Disappointed in his desire to enter the army, he turned to the bar, and entered a student of the Inner Temple. He worked as hard at law as he had done at medicine. Writing to his father, he said, 'Everybody says to me, " You are certain of success in the end, only persevere ; " and though I don't well understand how this is to happen, I try to believe it as much as I can, and I shall not fail to do everything in my power.' At twenty-eight he was called to the bar, and had every step in life yet to make. His means were straitened, and he lived upon the contributions of his friends. For years he studied and waited; still no business came. He stinted himself in recreation, in clothes, and even in the necessaries of life, struggling on indefatigably through all. Writing home, he confesses that he hardly knows how he shall be able to struggle on till he has had fair time and opportunity to establish himself. After three years waiting thus, without success, he wrote to his friends that rather than be a burden upon them longer, he was willing to give the matter up and return to Cambridge, where he was sure of support and some profit. The friends at home sent him another small remittance, and he went on. Business gradually came in. Acquitting himself creditably in small matters, he was intrusted with cases of greater importance. He never missed an opportunity, nor allowed a legitimate chance of improvement to escape him. His unflinching industry soon began to tell on his fortunes. A few more years, and he was not only enabled to do without assistance from home, but he was in a position to pay back with interest the debts which he had incurred. The clouds had dispersed, and the after career of Henry Bickersteth was one of honour, emolument, and of distinguished fame. He ended his career as Master of the Rolls, sitting in the House of Peers as Baron Langdale." Surely one may easily forget, "in the vision of the Chancellorship, the lonely evenings in the chambers at the Temple, the weary back benches in court, the heartsickening waiting, year after year, which are in the background of the picture;" for it is undeniably true that

> " There are points from which we can command our life,
> When the soul sweeps the future like a glass,
> And coming things, full-freighted with our fate,
> Jut out dark on the offing of the mind."

More than all this : while a young man is waiting, if he

be true to himself, he is forming character; and character in itself is one of the most singular of all our human qualities. There is a peculiar and subtile force belonging to it which we can perceive, and yet are unable to describe. Character is something entirely apart from its surroundings. "It is not the mere guinea's stamp, or the royal purple and crown, or the accident of birthright, or the whim of a capricious and admiring public. But it is the man—what he has made of himself." Character, as some one has said, like Achilles in disguise at the court of Lycomedes, does not disclose itself till the trumpet blast is sounded, and there comes the rush for arms. The slow growth of a great character is one of its special necessities. As a vigorous writer has said, this strange might in men is not, and by its very nature cannot be, the work of an hour. What great growth in this world bursts into maturity by the first breath of spring? "The weed has its abrupt strength, but its death is just as abrupt, while its life is purposeless. But the oak grows very tardily, and seems to be as useless as the pebbles through which the first germ shoots above ground towards the sun and its own destiny; nevertheless its life is a long one, and the centuries play harmlessly over its branches, and beat helplessly against its thick-barked trunk—its anchorage is broad and deep beneath the surface. The young man hastens towards a reputation; he gives ample proof of ability and success; but only later in life does he find out that the world will admit him into its favour only after years of steady wrestling with obstacles, and slow stages of personal growth. But this ultimate judgment of men is the safe one: it comes after hard effort; but when it does come, it will be the calm, deliberate declaration of the right." Life in all its departments is of one piece and one texture, and its difficulties bring trial, discipline, and mastery.

> " But heard are the voices,
> Heard are the sages,

The worlds and the ages :
Choose well ; your choice is
Brief, and yet endless."

"He that believeth shall not make haste," is the striking utterance of Holy Writ; and, as old George Herbert tells us, the sure traveller, though he alight sometimes, still goeth on. Some one once remarked to Salvini, "You will make a grand Lear." "Yes," he replied; "I think I shall be able to make something out of the old king. I have been reading the tragedy for some time, but it will still take me two years to study it thoroughly." Twain, in his "Innocents Abroad," has portrayed in graphic manner the unfaltering belief of the third Napoleon in his own brilliant future as he walked his weary beat, a common policeman of London, dreaming all the while of "a coming night when he should tread the long-drawn corridors of the Tuileries."

This faith in one's self is, without doubt, an important factor in all great achievement. Enthusiasm, and even castle-building, has a legitimate place : the most enthusiastic dreams of youth have again and again been realized, if not at times exceeded, in the after life of the man. "If you have built castles in the air," says Thoreau, "your work need not be lost; that is where they should be. Now put foundations under them." It is curious to note how patiently men have waited, and how long a period has elapsed at times between their early project and the final accomplishment of their plans. "It is quite astonishing," says Grove in speaking of Beethoven, "to find the length of time during which some of the best-known instrumental melodies remained in his thoughts till they were finally used, or the crude, vague, commonplace shape in which they were first written down. The more they are elaborated, the more fresh and spontaneous they become."

"It is never too late to mend," says the homely adage. It seems to find verification in the accomplishments of certain men.   There is something refreshing, it has been observed, in the fact that Plutarch began the study of Latin when past seventy ; that Dryden commenced his translation of the Iliad when sixty-eight ; that Colbert, the famous French minister, returned to his Latin and law studies when sixty ; that Ogilby, the translator of Homer and Virgil, was past fifty before he knew the rudiments of Latin and Greek ; and that both Sir Henry Spelman and Benjamin Franklin were past fifty before they engaged in the study of science and philosophy.   Milton in his blindness, when past the age of fifty, sat down to complete his world-known epic ; and Scott at fifty-five took up his pen to redeem an enormous liability. "Yet I am learning," said Michael Angelo, when threescore years and ten were past, and he had long attained the highest triumph of the pencil.   John Kemble is said to have written out the part of Hamlet thirty times, and each time discovered something which had previously escaped him ; and during his last season he remarked, "Now that I am retiring, I am only beginning thoroughly to understand my art."   His gifted sister, Mrs. Siddons, after she had left the stage, was visited by a friend, who found her in her garden musing over a book.   "I am reading over Lady Macbeth," said the incomparable actress, "and I am amazed to discover some new points in the character which I never found out in acting it."

Let no young man be disheartened on account of being unappreciated at home, or because, forsooth, his relatives persist in underrating him.   The opinions of relatives as to a man's power Holmes declares to be very commonly of little value ; not so much because they sometimes overrate their own flesh and blood, as some may suppose, as because, on the contrary, they are quite as likely to underrate those whom they have grown into the habit of considering like themselves.   It is curious to note how prone most people are to set an undue value on things at a distance, and to underrate that which is near. And yet how true and how common it is! It seems to be almost universally the case that that with which human nature is unfamiliar is straightway magnified, and easily believed to possess great qualities, while *Vile habetur quod domi est*, as Seneca tersely puts it. Doubtless in certain families there is an absurd and unwarrantable conceit regarding the gifts and abilities of members of the household; but in certain others, as we know, the very reverse is true. One writer assures us of a family known to him, in which the boys during their early education had it ceaselessly drilled into them that they were the idlest, stupidest, and most ignorant boys in the world; but no sooner had these very boys gone to a great public school, than like rockets they went up forthwith to the top of their classes, and afterwards were pre-eminent in university honours. "It will not surprise people who know much of human nature to be told that through this brilliant career of school and college work the home belief in their idleness and ignorance continued unchanged, and that hardly at its end was the toil-worn senior wrangler regarded as other than an idle and useless blockhead." So, too, we are told of a successful author whose relatives never believed, till the reviews assured them of it, that his writings were anything but "contemptible and discreditable trash." The fact is, as Disraeli somewhere observes, "custom blunts the fineness of psychological study; those with whom we have lived long and early are apt to blend our essential and our accidental qualities in one bewildering association." George Eliot has said many things truly, but none more truly than when she declares, with her customary and rare discernment, that our daily, familiar life is but a hiding of ourselves from each other behind a screen of trivial words and deeds; and those who sit with us at the same hearth are often the farthest off from the deep human soul within us, full of unspoken evil and unacted good.

Edmund Burke in early life was not happy at home, we are told, there being none among the household on Arran Quay to sympathize with his dreams and aspirations. "He might think himself a genius," says one of his biographers; "but it was not to be expected that his own relations should yet think him one." Macknight, referring to his position and influence in Lord Rockingham's administration, remarks that it is, after all, a man's own relatives who generally look with the least confidence on his long wrestle with adversity, and are most astonished when the tide turns, and a great victory succeeds to what had seemed to them a mere hopeless toil. "To some of the Irish Nagles on the Blackwater," he says, "the news that Edmund had been taken into the confidence of the great Whig, Lord Rockingham, must have seemed as extraordinary as it did to Joseph's brethren that he should have become so great a man in hostile Egypt." Then, too, there was Jean Bodin, neglected and slighted in his own land, yet at the same time exulting in the welcome accorded to his books in the English universities, which printed as well as prized them. Surely no young man, though slighted at home, need despair on that account, or even despond : it is a road that has been often travelled, and by illustrious spirits too. Let one learn in patience to work and wait, and calmly bide his time. It is a long lane that has no turn.

Above all, whatever happens, avoid precipitation. Anything but rashness; it is not only unwise, but often positively calamitous. In one of the wars between France and England, two English frigates approached each other in the darkness, and each supposing the other to be an enemy, opened broadsides, when, after a most terrific encounter, as the darkness lifted and the dawn appeared, what was their consternation and amazement to discover that both were flying the English flag ! Filled with grief and regret, the cannonading ceased, and mournfully they saluted each other.

Equally disastrous have been many of the misunderstandings among men. Many a man has jeopardized if not ruined
his prospects in life by his rashness, and bartered away his
success for the sake of gratifying a momentary ebullition of
wrath or ill-feeling. If a man has inherited a quick temper,
which by the way is often found along with some of the
finest qualities, let him mount guard over himself, and wait,
holding himself in check until, in coolness and candour, he
can survey the whole field; and, rest assured, he will save
himself many an after regret. A man never gains but
always loses by heat. Moreover, many a misunderstanding
may be easily corrected if rash words have not entered as
unmanageable factors into the affair. To be silent even
when one is conscious of being in the right is heroic, and in
any event waiting can do no harm. "He that is slow to
anger is better than the mighty; and he that ruleth his
spirit, than he that taketh a city." Nothing was ever truer
than that. Jacox, in his entertaining manner, calls attention to the fact that Sir Thomas Fowell Buxton's secretary,
Mr. Nixon, on his own showing, could not refrain from
blurting out just what he felt at the moment, when differences arose between the two. This used to vex Sir Thomas,
who, however, would say nothing till the next day; and
then, when the secretary thought that the whole matter had
passed off, having perhaps received great kindness in the
meantime, the remonstrance would come out, "What a silly
fellow you were, Nixon, to put yourself in such a passion
yesterday! If I had spoken then, we should most probably
have parted. Make it a rule never to speak when you are
in a passion, but wait till the next day." We are further
assured that if at any time Sir Thomas did happen to transgress this rule himself, he was seriously vexed and grieved,
and could not rest till he had in some way made amends for
his want of self-restraint.

It is exceedingly interesting, and not without encouragement, to note in this connection how many world-famous ones, who have had to struggle with this infirmity of temper, have at length made an almost entire conquest of themselves in this regard. Rudolf of Hapsburg, for instance, we are assured, was by nature warm and choleric, but as he advanced in years he corrected this defect. Upon some of his friends expressing their wonder that since his elevation to the imperial dignity he had restrained the vehemence of his temper, the founder of the House of Austria replied, "I have often repented of being passionate, never of being mild and humane." Of the sweet-mannered and well-nigh imperturbable Frederick Borromeo, Manzoni tells us that the admirable placability for which he was famous was not natural to the devout prelate, but was the result of continual combat against a quick and hasty disposition. Lord Macaulay, as Jacox shows, turns to the advantage of his favourite Chancellor the assertion of his detractors, that the disposition of the great Somers was very far from being so gentle as the world believed; that he was really prone to the angry passions; and that sometimes, while his voice was soft and his words kind and courteous, his delicate frame was almost convulsed by suppressed emotion. "His brilliant advocate is fain to accept this reproach as the highest of all eulogies." Then, too, there was Sir Robert Peel. If we are to believe Sir Archibald Alison, Peel was by nature afflicted with a most violent temper. By degrees, however, he obtained the mastery of this infirmity, and this at length so effectually that he passed with the world at a distance as a man of a singularly cold and phlegmatic temperament.

Lady Holland has given us a passing glimpse, yet full of interest in this direction, of her distinguished father, the Rev. Sydney Smith. She prefaces her statement that her father was naturally choleric, by the reflection that although it is not the part of a daughter to reveal faults, yet a fault nobly repaired or repented of adds to the respect and interest which a character inspires. It seems that the famous clergyman, though by nature thus quick and hasty, always struggled against the failing, and "made many regulations to avoid exciting any such emotion. When he did give way, one could not but be filled with admiration to see him gradually subduing his chafed spirit, and to observe his dissatisfaction with himself till he had humbled himself and made his peace it mattered not with whom, groom or child. He could not bear the reproaches of his own heart." In the journal and letters, too, of Dr. Chalmers one often finds the good man taking himself to task for infirmities of temper, and striving with unflinching resolution to keep down every tendency to irritation. How one entry after another betrays the persistent struggle going on, as for instance : " Try to maintain a vigorous contest with this unfortunate peculiarity of my temper ;" "to school down every irritable feeling." How remorsefully he records such instances as getting "into a violent passion with Sandy," and the like. And again : " Erred in betraying my anger to my servant and wife." Surely the world knows not always, indeed seldom imagines, the struggles within or the heroic discipline which at length confers upon a man that greatest of all triumphs, the mastery of himself. Above all things, never allow yourself to despatch an angry letter. A hasty word may be overlooked or forgotten, but *litera scripta manet.* In this direction, then, if a man would be master of the situation, and is aiming at success, let him learn—to wait.

It is indeed true that hope may be deferred, making the heart sick ; but let one not forget that " when the desire cometh, it is a tree of life." Hawthorne declared that before he became famous, during those long years of waiting for recognition, he had supposed himself familiar with every emotion possible to the human heart ; but he frankly confessed that when fame came to him, and recognition, it was an experience wholly new. At the time the " Scarlet

Letter" was passing through the press, Whipple tells us that he was permitted to read the proof-sheets. The circumstances, he further says, under which the work was published were very depressing to its author. He had been dismissed from his position in the Custom House. Then, too, he had failed so often in obtaining any large popular recognition of his peculiar powers, that he believed the "Scarlet Letter" would share the fate of the "Twice Told Tales." It was therefore " well that two young men, himself and Fields the publisher, who were enthusiastic admirers of his genius, should break in upon his solitude that summer afternoon and rouse him from his despondency. Mrs. Hawthorne, the very impersonation of hope and cheer, joined heartily in the attempt to make the great romancer feel that he had produced a work which would not only make a deep and immediate impression on the public mind, but live as long as American literature existed." " His grand face and brow gradually lighted up," says Whipple, " as he caught a little of the contagion of our enthusiasm, and we left him somewhat cheered as to the prospects of his book."

Never allow yourself " for one repulse to forego the purpose you resolved to effect." The annals of literature are full of instances of those who, feeling the consciousness within that they had something to say which the world ought to hear, have persistently toiled and waited, in spite of the fact that editors and publishers had failed to recognize their right to be heard, until at length they compelled recognition. The company of literary prophets and martyrs who have passed through this ordeal is very great. There was Brinsley Sheridan, in Orchard Street, Portman Square, diligently working away, and producing essays, pamphlets, and farces, many of which never saw the light, while others fell flat, or failed to bring him any fame. Indeed, as some one asks, what great authors have not experienced the same disappointments? What men would ever be great if they allowed such checks to damp their energy, or were turned back by them from the course in which they feel that their power lies?

Nothing is more remarkable than the vicissitudes which have befallen certain world-famous authors and their equally famous books. It is well known that many have waited long for recognition, and mourned bitterly at the rejection of their manuscripts. Even Thackeray's " Vanity Fair " was refused by a dozen publishers when offered in manuscript. Yet when " Vanity Fair " once appeared, its reception was immediate, and success was won. Charlotte Bronté wore out her patience and her hope in offering "Jane Eyre," in many respects the greatest novel ever written ; and the author of " Eöthen " had a weary time of it, trudging from publisher to publisher to get it into print. Yet this, as well as " Jane Eyre," when published took the world by storm. Even Murray, we are told,—one of the princes among publishers,—failed to discover the merits of Motley's " Rise of the Dutch Republic." Carlyle, it is said, was mortified by Jeffrey's sending back to him articles as unfit for the *Edinburgh Review.* Even Macaulay suffered a similar rebuff, through the petty jealousy, as he thought, of Lord Brougham. Scott and Disraeli retained in their desks manuscripts which no publisher would accept until their names had become famous. One of the most popular novels of the present day went from one publisher to another, and was at last accepted by Carleton, who made it a great success. Irving tells us that Murray declined the " Sketch Book," which was published by Millar. The latter failed, however, and then Murray was glad to take the " Sketch Book " and all of Irving's subsequent productions. Now, let us ask, was the waiting of these men a vain thing?

It is always interesting to know what estimate men who have attained fame in intellectual pursuits put upon their own powers, and to compare this with the estimate of others

who have had good opportunities of observing them. In
early life, Webster, it seems, took a very modest view of his
abilities and his prospects of professional success. His ambition was never fully aroused till Governor Gore advised
him to refuse the clerkship. " In his letters to his friends
written before this, he often spoke timidly, and sometimes
disparagingly, of his legal attainments and prospects. He
once spoke of a young lawyer who had not had a brilliant
success, but whose degree of prosperity would amply satisfy
his own ambition. That he was conscious, however, of the
latent powers within him is seen by his writing for the
papers in college, and delivering a Fourth-of-July oration
during his college term. He never shrank, moreover, even
at that early age, from any responsibility that was laid upon
him ; and whatever he undertook he did well."

What, indeed, is more noticeable than this consciousness
of the possession of great powers in those destined to distinction? "We judge ourselves," says Longfellow, "by what
we feel capable of doing; others judge us by what we have
already done." The strong aspirant not only has the master
in his eye, but the place of a master as well. This has had
many an illustration. When young Angelo was in the
school of Ghirlandajo, he was one day busily employed,
when a stranger entered, and after carefully scrutinizing the
work of the scholars, at length approached him. It was the
great Lorenzo of the Garden of St. Mark. He spoke to the
youth, examined his work, and then turning to Domenico,
said, " By your leave, I select this youth for the Garden of
St. Mark. Will it accord with his views?"—" Ay," replied
Ghirlandajo significantly ; "do you think the eagle does
not ken his eyrie?" It is always thus. Like Pitt waiting
for the Cabinet, and refusing all else with lofty scorn until
his opportunity came, such seem to feel that they can bide
their time, and while " it is not in mortals to command
success," are apparently sustained by the lofty consciousness

that they deserve it. One sometimes marvels to note how often to such as these the prizes come.

In these men, however, one may perceive a marvellous pertinacity which seems well-nigh omnipotent. In illustration of this, take that well-known incident in the career of Brinsley Sheridan. As an incentive and an encouragement to young men it cannot be too often repeated. Sheridan's maiden speech in Parliament was delivered November 20, 1780. The House listened to him with marked attention, but his appearance did not entirely satisfy the expectations of his friends. Woodfall, the reporter, used to relate, as Goodrich tells us, that Sheridan came up to him in the gallery when the speech was ended, and asked him with much anxiety what he thought of his first attempt. "I am sorry to say," replied Woodfall, "that I don't think this is your line. You had better have stuck to your former pursuits." Sheridan rested his head on his hand for some minutes, and then exclaimed with vehemence, "It is *in me*, and it shall *come out of me!*" He now devoted himself with the utmost assiduity, quickened by a sense of shame, to the cultivation of his powers as a speaker, and on the 17th of February 1787 made that famous speech against Warren Hastings so astonishing for its eloquence that at the conclusion the whole assembly broke forth into expressions of tumultuous applause. A motion was made to adjourn, that the House might have time to recover their calmness. Twenty years after, Mr. Fox and Mr. Windham, two of the severest judges in England, spoke of this speech with undiminished admiration. The former declared it to be the best speech ever made in the House of Commons. The latter said that the speech deserved all its fame, and was, in spite of some faults of taste, the greatest that had been delivered within the memory of man. Brinsley Sheridan had *waited* to some purpose.

Thus many a one, wayworn and weary though he may

often have been, on the pathway to the great achievement
whose purpose thrilled his earliest opening life, has found
that the waiting paid.

> " Who ne'er his bread in sorrow ate,
>     Who ne'er the mournful midnight hours
> Weeping upon his bed has sate,
>     He knows you not, ye heavenly powers."

Richter suggests as an excellent antidote against moral
depression the calling up in our darkest moments the memory of our brightest.    At all events refuse to be unhappy.
Remember Charles Kingsley's favourite motto, "Be strong!"
Indeed,

> " So many great
> Illustrious spirits have conversed with woe,
> Have in her school been taught, as are enough
> To consecrate distress, and make ambition
> Even wish the frown beyond the smile of fortune."

# X

# Opportunity.

"Opportunity is the command of God."

There is a tide in the affairs of men,
Which, taken at the flood, leads on to fortune;

\*      \*      \*      \*      \*      \*

And we must take the current when it serves,
Or lose our ventures.—SHAKESPEARE.

"The mill can never grind with the water which has passed."

A SCULPTOR once showed a visitor his studio. It was almost full of gods. One was very curious: the face was concealed by being covered with hair, and there were wings to each foot. "What is its name?" said the spectator.—"Opportunity," was the reply.—"Why is its face hidden?"—"Because men seldom know him when he comes to them."—"Why has he wings on his feet?"—"Because he is soon gone, and once gone, cannot be overtaken." Let it never be forgotten that in reckoning on success one must take into account that all-important factor, opportunity, after all; for it is an undeniable fact that this forms at least the two sides of the ladder on which men mount. With all his power and genius, a man must remain unknown unless opportunity shall open the way for the display of his gifts. For, as Pliny says, "no man possesses a genius so commanding that he can attain eminence, unless a subject suited to his talents should present itself, and an opportunity occur for their development."

But many a man has made a failure of life by neglecting

or frittering away his opportunity when it was full upon him.
As one looks over the lives of men he has known, as the
melancholy spectacle of broken careers and wasted lives
comes before him, Whittier's words but too truly express
the dreary truth,—

> "Of all sad words of tongue or pen,
> The saddest are these: It might have been!"

Let a young man "lay the flattering unction to his soul"
that because he has, forsooth, achieved a diploma, the greater
part of the battle of life has been fought, and henceforth he
can take things easy, and from that hour he is destined to
make rapid strides on the road to failure.  Once let the
"dry-rot" enter, and what could be worse?  A graduate
has but learned the use of weapons, if indeed even this has
been fully learned.  The world's work lies all before him,
and its demands will call for the strenuous use of all his
powers.  "The time comes to the young surgeon," observes
Arnold, "when after long waiting, and patient study and
experiment, he is suddenly confronted with his first critical
operation.  The great surgeon is away.  Time is pressing.
Life and death hang in the balance.  Is he equal to the
emergency?  Can he fill the great surgeon's place, and do his
work?  If he can, he is the one of all others who is wanted.
His opportunity confronts him.  He and it are face to face.
Shall he confess his ignorance and inability, or step into fame
and fortune at once?  It is for him to say."

In a world of such incessant changes, opportunities for rising
are not so rare, after all.  Vacancies are constantly occurring
in positions of trust, honour, and profit.  There is room for
numberless promotions every year.  "The everlasting swinging of the scythe of death is clearing the ranks for eager
aspirants."  "There are moments," says Dean Alford,
"which are worth more than years.  We cannot help it.
There is no proportion between spaces of time in importance

nor in value. A stray, unthought-of five minutes may contain the event of a life. And this all-important moment,— who can tell when it will be upon us?" It really seems, as some one says, as if our fortunes met us in the dark. The single hours and acts that like rudders steer us into wide seas of triumph or misfortune, how significant they are! Some one has well said that there is no view of life so inspiring as that which contemplates it as a constant preparation for important, unforeseen emergencies. What a man already is, we are told, generally determines his use or neglect of a grand opportunity. In England, as every one knows, it is not very difficult for a man of high birth, influential position, and liberal culture, to obtain a seat in Parliament. Hundreds of such men never once get the ear of the House. They are coughed down or laughed down on their first attempt, and they never repeat it. Pitt's triumph on the occasion of that first speech of his in the House of Commons was no accident. It was the well-earned reward of many years of laborious and complete preparation. A legislative debate, a diplomatic crisis, a battle, or many an occasion far less conspicuous, may in a single hour task to the utmost and crown with imperishable glory the preparation of a lifetime. Trafalgar was Nelson's opportunity; and his exclamation, "Westminster Abbey, or the peerage!" on the eve of that memorable engagement, reveals the man. Rear-Admiral Hamilton, of the British Navy, in his volume, "Naval Operations during the Civil War in the United States," referring to the prompt action of Farragut in ordering the fleet to move on despite the torpedoes that had just sunk the "Tecumseh" in Mobile Bay, remarks: "It appears to me that a disastrous defeat was converted into victory by (in so unexpected a contingency) the quickness of eye and power of rapid decision Farragut possessed, which saw at a glance the only escape from the dilemma the fleet was placed in, and which can only be acquired by a thorough practical knowledge in the manage-

ment of fleets, and for want of which no amount of theoretical
knowledge, however desirable in many respects, can make up
in the moment of difficulty." This "quickness of eye," which
sees at a glance one's opportunity, marks a striking difference
in men. Some men seem neither to see nor know their opportunity when it comes. Everything appears to them to wear
the air of commonplace. They are like Wordsworth's Peter
Bell :—

> " A primrose by a river's brim
> A yellow primrose was to him,
> And it was nothing more."

A vastly entertaining chapter might be written showing
the curious ways in which one's opportunity comes to him.
Take that case of Gavarni, for instance. His real name was
Chevalier. He was the son of poor parents, and began life
as a mechanic. Finding that a successful artisan should
possess some knowledge of drawing, Chevalier went during
his hours of leisure to an evening school where free instruction was given to mechanics. The beginning of his work as
a caricaturist, we are told, was the result of a chance conversation on the insipidity of the faces in a fashion plate.
He drew a picture as he thought it ought to be, and sent
it to the publishers, signed "Gavarni,"—the name of a
little hamlet in the Pyrenees where he had picnicked pleasantly. The deed was done, the sketch despatched and
accepted, and Gavarni became so decidedly the fashion that
he gave up his work as a surveyor and devoted himself to his
pencil. Adah Isaacs Menken found her opportunity in
"Mazeppa;" and many a similar instance doubtless might be
cited.

> " 'Tis Fortune's trick to muffle up her gifts in dusky hulls,
> That when they throw their mantles off,
> Surprise may richness overdouble."

"Nature creates merit, and fortune brings it into play,"
was an observation of La Rochefoucauld; and one sees it

verified every day. In what men regard as mere chance
work there is often order and design. "What we call a
turning-point," says Arnold, "is simply an occasion which
sums up and brings to a result previous training. Accidental
circumstances are nothing except to men who have been
trained to take advantage of them." And he cites the
familiar instance of Erskine making himself famous when
the chance came to him of making a great forensic display,
justly adding that unless he had trained himself for the
chance, the chance would only have made him ridiculous.
A great occasion is worth to a man exactly what his ante-
cedents have enabled him to make of it. "Every man,
sooner or later, is called upon to pass, so to speak, his cross-
examination. This it is which will thoroughly test what is
in him. The daily duties of his profession, the possible great
opportunities, the judgment-days, the crises of our lives."
And it has been truly said that it is only as one fulfils the
duties and bears successfully the tests of everyday life that
he will be ready for the great requirements, the great opportunities, the supreme test-days that may come. It is undeniably true that greatness seems to come to some men as
by a kind of destiny. "Probably they lack none of the
native elements of character that are the prerequisites for
future achievement, and the opportunities for their development are not wanting. At some other times, not very remote
from their own, they might have lived and died in obscurity;
but it falls to their lot to be at the head of affairs at some
momentous period of a country's history, and to conduct a
nation through progressive revolutions in rapid series to a
greatness of which few but themselves ever dreamed as
among things possible, and in this same process to become
themselves the most conspicuous figures of their age." Yet
the fact remains that the great mass of events with which
men have to do are simply opportunities that may be used
or neglected. From time to time we are called to confront

great emergencies which are "neither resistless engines to crush us, nor machines which we have framed to work out our fortunes, but hinges of destiny turning either way, as we choose. When we least expect it, we come to a fork in the road : here lies the unfrequented way to the mountain peaks of distinction ; there, to the dead level of obscurity and the morass of failure. Some men have a way of always taking the mountain path." The way in which her opportunity came to Pauline Lucca is full of interest, and reminds one of a somewhat similar incident in the career of Charlotte Cushman. Her high musical gifts showed themselves early. When a mere child she sang in the choir of the Karlskirche, in 1856. One Sunday the principal soloist was missing, and the young chorus-singer, put forward to supply her place in the solo of a mass of Mozart's, revealed a beauty of voice and charm of style that startled all who heard it. She studied under Uschmann and Levy, and her parents being in straitened circumstances, she entered the chorus of the opera at Vienna, but left in 1859 to come out at Olmütz. Just before leaving, it fell to her to lead the bridesmaids' chorus in the "Freischütz," her performance creating a sensation that made Vienna eager to retain her ; but it was too late. On the 4th of September 1859 she made her *début* in Olmütz as Elvira in "Ernani," and became a favourite at once.

To glance from art to trade, it was in a very simple circumstance that the greatest button-manufacturer in the United States found his opportunity. He had purchased, it seems, some cloth for a coat, and his wife was to make it up. He bought among other trimmings some lasting buttons, and paid a certain price for them,—say seventy-five cents a dozen. His wife asked him what he paid for them, and he told her. "Why," said she, "that is a large price ; with button-moulds and a little lasting I could make these buttons for a quarter of that price. If you will take these back and get some button-moulds I will show you." He did so, and the buttons she made were to all appearance as good as those bought at the store. That led to the idea of his making buttons to sell. He began by employing a few girls, and carrying his buttons to the country stores and selling them. He found it a profitable enterprise. The business grew. He afterwards employed machinery, and made an immense fortune.

It is very interesting, as Arnold observes, to read of a great advocate awaiting patiently his chance. " It comes at last, and with the thought of wife and children tugging at his robe, and urging him for their sakes to do his best, the full, brilliant speech is made." Or it may be the famous argument of plain John Scott, afterwards Lord Eldon, in the leading case of Akroyd *v.* Smithson. An opportunity at length occurred which enabled John Scott to exhibit the large legal knowledge which he had so laboriously acquired. In a case in which he was employed he urged a legal point against the wishes both of the attorney and the client who employed him. The Master of the Rolls decided against him, but on an appeal to the House of Lords, Lord Thurlow reversed the decision on the very point that Scott had urged. On leaving the House that day an attorney tapped him on the shoulder and whispered the homely but heart-cheering words, " Young man, your bread and butter is cut for life." And indeed the young man had started "straight and fair for the Great Seal." Smiles tells us that Lord Mansfield used to say he knew no interval between *no business* and *three thousand pounds a year ;* and Scott, he adds, might have told the same story, for so rapid was his progress that in 1783, when only thirty-two, he was appointed King's Counsel, was at the head of the Northern Circuit, and sat in Parliament for the borough of Weobley.

Such incidents, as has been said, do not happen so very infrequently after all. The man and the hour approach. The man is equal to the occasion; but often, perhaps oftener, the man is unequal to it. What would have been the use of the chance coming to men who were unequal to the chance? There are lawyers who if such a chance came to them would simply have to sit down, and truly enough tell the presiding judge that they could not get on without their leader. One must have had long training before he can skilfully avail himself of any sort of emergency. It is undeniably true that one may so prepare for a crisis that when it comes it shall be determined beforehand in the foreseen direction. As the lumberman when about to hew a giant of the forest, though powerless to move it with unaided strength, may by his rope still guide and determine the direction of its fall and the position it shall occupy, so in a certain sense a man may, so to speak, go into training for a crisis ere it come. "It matters not," says Foss, "what sea a ship is to sail : its keel must be securely laid, its masts firmly set, its rigging of the toughest fibre, in order to sail any sea in safety. One hour's tussle with the tempest will test the fibre of its timbers which were toughened by a hundred years' wrestle with Norwegian blasts. The student whose special work in life is yet unchosen should be made to feel that in *some* work he will have need of the completest possible discipline of all his powers, and the largest attainable acquirements. Now is the time to get ready. When the storm bursts there will be no time to set the masts or hang the rudder. Opportunities are sure to come which we shall most earnestly wish to employ to the utmost. Our actual use of them, however, will depend not on what we wish, but on what we are."

While the whole country was resounding with the praises of his reply to Hayne, Mr. Webster seemed almost unmoved by them, and to be scarcely conscious of the great forensic victory he had achieved. In reply to a letter congratulating him, he wrote as follows on the 8th of March 1830: "I thank you for your friendly and flattering letter. Your commendation of my speech was measured less by its merits than by your bounty. If it has gratified my friends at home, I am rewarded for any little trouble it has cost me. The whole debate was a matter of accident. I had left the court pretty late in the day, and went into the Senate with my court papers under my arm, just to see what was passing. It so happened that Mr. Hayne rose in his first speech. I did not like it, and my friends liked it less. I never spoke in the presence of an audience so eager and so sympathetic."

However useless it may appear to you at the moment, seize upon all that is fairly within your reach ; for there is not a fact within the whole circle of human observation, " nor even a fugitive anecdote that you read in a newspaper or hear in conversation, that will not come into play some time or other ; and occasions will arise when they involuntarily present their dim shadows in the train of your thinking and reasoning as belonging to that train, and you will regret that you cannot recall them more distinctly." How strange is that law of the mind by which an idea, long overlooked and trodden under foot as a useless stone, suddenly sparkles out in a new light as a discovered diamond ! One thing is certain : unless one is thus prompt to seize and fix the fact or incident which interests him as he comes upon it in his reading, or to look up, from time to time, points suggested, he will have occasion again and again to regret it. Who cannot bear witness to this, as he has sat trying vainly to recall some fact or illustration which now looms before his recollection dim and nebulous and undefined, which he feels sure is just what he wants, but cannot get? The tendency of human nature is to inertia. One hates to be disturbed or interrupted. He will go on with his reading to-day, and make the note to-morrow. He discovers his mistake, and repents too late, when the illusive thought evades and defies his capture. The same is true of the fleeting impulse to clear up a doubtful point or to add to one's stock of information.

Wirt hits it exactly when he says, "Seize the moment of
excited curiosity on any subject to solve your doubts; for if
you let it pass, the desire may never return, and you may
remain in ignorance."

A well-known journalist recently advised all boys and
girls to begin at once keeping a scrap-book, in which they
should set down descriptions of any noteworthy place or
scene which comes in their way; also accounts of any remarkable person whom they meet, with their photograph,
and any personal details. "In thirty years," he says, "such
a book will be invaluable to the owner, especially if he be
a journalist or literary man." The most trifling details, it
has been observed, in such a book as Pepys' Diary, or the
Memoirs of Madame de Rémusat, are read now with keen
interest, as they make flesh and blood of historical characters
who otherwise would be but shadows to us.

It may seem trivial, but it is a suggestion of no less a
personage than the late Bishop of Oxford, that if in the
course of your writing a good thought or illustration comes
into your mind which will come in well in some other part
of your discourse, for instance, do not think you will certainly remember it; stop and write it down at once, and
when you come to that part where you need it, work it in.
"Some years ago, if not now," says a visitor, "the studio
of Story, at Rome, presented the following appearance—
around the walls were shelves filled with small clay models,
single figures and groups. The sculptor explained that
often as he worked some splendid subject for a marble
figure or group would suggest itself. There was little or
no use in trying to remember it; so he would at once turn
aside from the work in hand and put his idea into a model,
small indeed and hastily shaped, but he had all that he then
needed—namely, the conception. At any time it could be
worked up."

Lord Oxford's maid-servant relates that in the dreadful

winter of 1740 she was called from her bed four times in one night to supply him with paper lest he should lose a thought; and it is told of Bossuet, that if while he was in bed his sleep was delayed or interrupted, he used to avail himself of it to commit to paper any interesting thought which occurred to him. Eginhard, his secretary, tells us of Charlemagne that he had always pen, ink, and parchment beside his pillow, for the purpose of noting down any thoughts that might occur to him during the night; and lest upon waking he should find himself in darkness, a part of the wall within reach from the bed was prepared like the leaf of a tablet, with wax, on which he might indent his memoranda with a stylus. In like manner, we are told of that indefatigable pursuer of literature, Margaret, Duchess of Newcastle, that some of her young ladies always slept within call, ready to rise at any hour of the night and take down her thoughts, lest she should forget them before morning.

Many an immortal production, as every one knows, has emanated from prison and the dungeon. Not to mention the familiar instance of the famous allegory written in Bedford Jail, we find that one of the best poems which British poetry can boast between the death of Chaucer and the accession of Henry VIII. was penned by James I. while a captive in Windsor Castle. The same is true of some of the most pleasing of Lord Surrey's poems and Sir Walter Raleigh's "History of the World;" and the list might be greatly extended. Many, too, have been the works produced while their authors were in exile. It was in exile that Thucydides composed his "History of the Peloponnesian War," and Xenophon his Anabasis. That sleep should possess creative power is remarkable; and yet Burns tells us that he dreamed one of his poems, and that he wrote it down just as he dreamed it. Voltaire informed one of his friends that the whole of the second canto of the "Henriade"

was composed by him in his sleep. Coleridge always said
that he dreamed "Kubla Khan;" and if one may rely upon
internal evidence, it can hardly be doubted. Campbell declared that he was indebted to the same source for the best
line in "Lochiel's Warning." It seems he was visiting at
Minto, and one evening went to bed early, his thoughts full
of a new poem. About two in the morning he suddenly
awoke, repeating,—

"Events to come cast their shadows before."

Ringing the bell sharply, a servant obeyed the summons, to
find the summoner with one foot in bed and one on the
floor. "Are you ill, sir?" inquired he. "Ill!" cried
Campbell; "never better in my life. Leave me the candle,
and oblige me with a cup of tea." Seizing his pen, he
promptly set down the happy thought, changing "events to
come" into "coming events," and over the non-inebriating
cup completed the first draught of "Lochiel's Warning."

Hardly anything is more remarkable than those instances
in which the soul, as if by instinct, seems to recognize its
opportunity for relieving itself of a great burden, or of the
anguish which perchance has long been tugging at the heart.
How little the public realize, at times, when thrilled by the
sudden burst of eloquence or song, that some secret anguish
is voicing itself, or that the burdened soul, after long neglect
and seemingly hopeless struggle, has suddenly been lifted by
the spell of a great inspiration, born of the memory of past
defeat, into such marvellous achievement as compels the
long-delayed recognition and conquers its place! Many a
recognition, doubtless, has come thus on the wings of this
cry of the soul. How many, think you, comprehended fully
all that went to make up Rachel's "Hélas"? In the
"Marble Faun," Hawthorne makes Miriam, the broken-
hearted singer in the midnight song that went up from the
Roman Coliseum, put into the melody the pent-up shriek

that her anguish had almost given vent to a moment before. "That volume of melodious voice was one of the tokens of a great trouble. The thunderous anthem gave her an opportunity to relieve her heart by a great cry."

It is also one of the characteristics of greatness to hide itself, and take refuge in commonplaces until its opportunity comes. Moreover, this opportunity which the soul sometimes finds for the utterance of its great secrets when surrounded by the multitude gives occasion for revelations often very beautiful. "I have known shy, reserved men," says Phillips Brooks, "who, standing in their pulpits, have drawn back before a thousand eyes veils that were sacredly closed when only one friend's eyes could see. You might talk with them a hundred times, and you would not learn so much of what they were as if you once heard them preach. It was partly the impersonality of the great congregation. Humanity, without the offence of individuality, stood there before them. It was no violation of their loyalty to themselves to tell their secret to mankind. It was a man who silenced them. But also, besides this, it was, I think, that the sight of many waiting faces set free in them a new, clear knowledge of what their truth or secret was, unsnarled it from the petty circumstances into which it had been entangled, called it first into clear consciousness, and then tempted it into utterance with an authority which they did not recognize in an individual curiosity demanding the details of their life. Our race, represented in a great assembly, has more authority and more beguilement for many of us than the single man, however near he be. And he who is silent before the interviewer pours out the very depths of his soul to the great multitude."

The same is doubtless more or less true in literature. How unmistakably behind the thin veil of "Copperfield," for instance, one discerns the personality of Dickens as he by a thousand delicate touches reveals to us the story of his life! And can any one doubt that the gentle soul of Irving is embalmed within his serene and sunny pages? In Goodrich's account of Webster's defence of his Alma Mater, he tells us that after closing his masterly argument, Mr. Webster stood for some moments before the court, while every eye was fixed intently upon him. At length, addressing the Chief-Justice, after a brief reference to the far-reaching influence of an adverse decision as affecting every college in the land, he continued : " It is, sir, as I have said, a small college, and yet there are those who love it—" Here the feelings which he had thus far succeeded in keeping down broke forth. His lips quivered ; his firm cheeks trembled with emotion; his eyes were filled with tears; his voice choked, and he seemed struggling to the utmost simply to gain that mastery over himself which might save him from an unmanly burst of feeling. " I will not attempt to give you," says Goodrich, "the few broken words of tenderness in which he went on to speak of his attachment to the college. *The whole seemed to be mingled throughout with recollections of father, mother, brother, and all the privations and trials through which he had made his way into life.* Every one saw that it was wholly unpremeditated—a pressure on his heart which sought relief in tears. Having recovered his composure, after a few intense, concluding words, he sat down. There was a death-like stillness throughout the room for some moments. Every one seemed to be slowly recovering himself, and coming gradually back to his ordinary range of thought and feeling."

In closing this chapter, too great stress cannot possibly be laid upon the importance of being ready when one's opportunity comes. There was just one fleeting moment on which hung the fate of England's early king, imprisoned in his dungeon, while the faithful Blondel, harp in hand, awaited his response without. Had it passed unfruitful, the fate of the king had been sealed. Some one has well said that

lost opportunities are so many funerals. The golden opportunity

> " Is never offered twice ; seize then the hour
> When fortune smiles, and duty points the way :
> Nor shrink aside to 'scape the spectre fear ;
> Nor pause, though pleasure beckon from her bower ;
> But bravely bear thee onward to the goal."

When once the chase is " in " and hounds are loosed, when
once you realize that the great moment is full upon you—
that one vital hour, the lord of time, on which all other
hours have waited—let nothing divert you from your aim
until your point is gained. Carry it by storm, even if it
task you sorely and demand the acquired strength of years.
If it take all there is of you, carry it. There will be
enough of the uneventful, enough of monotony and commonplace coming after, to afford ample leisure for rest and
recuperation when the crisis shall have been safely passed.

> " A thousand years a poor man watched
> Before the gate of Paradise ;
> But while one little nap he snatched,
> It oped and shut. Ah! was he wise ?"

Above all things, let there be preparation. "Get thy
spindle and distaff ready, and God will send thee flax."
Thus one waits calmly, as one refreshed with slumber and
awake betimes awaits the sure approach of day. No thought
is so inspiring to a man as to feel that possibly just before
him, in the dim and unforeseen to-morrow, lies his great
opportunity awaiting him. Nothing could be more sublime.
Did you ever note the coming of the dawn? From the time
when first " the casement grows a glimmering square " to the
full tide of the morning's glory, the gradual approach of light
is wondrously beautiful. Up from the eastern horizon steals
at first a faint glimmer; sudden breezes stir the rustling
leaves; clouds and the night-rack go scudding, like fugitives,

athwart the sky; the birds are astir; and ere you have
noted the thousand indefinable influences which come to you,
already broad streaks of light are growing apace in the
heavens.   The gradually glowing east is seized with sudden
tremulousness, and you feel instinctively that something is
impending; the trees sway more perceptibly in the breeze;
flashes of red shoot up towards the zenith; and now, above
the dark rim bounding the horizon, the grand old sun uplifts
himself, rears upward on his mighty shoulders the ponderous,
dreary burden of the dark, kisses the hills into sudden glory,
—and *day is born!*   So, if you are ready and waiting, out
from the darkness and gloom of adverse circumstances shall
come the dawn of opportunity and the day's risen splendour
of triumph and success.

# XI.

## Genius.

"It is no task for suns to shine."

From my youth upward
My spirit walked not with the souls of men,
Nor looked upon the earth with human eyes ;
The thirst of their ambition was not mine,
The aim of their existence was not mine ;
My joys, my griefs, my passions and my powers,
Made me a stranger.—BYRON.

Genius is greater than man :
Genius does what it *must ;* talent does what it *can.*
OWEN MEREDITH.

IN reviewing the life and works of Edgar A. Poe, Lowell says of him : " He had that indescribable something which men have agreed to call genius. No man could ever tell us precisely what it is, and yet there is none who is not inevitably aware of its presence and its power. Let talent writhe and contort itself as it may, it has no such magnetism. Larger of bone and sinew it may be, but the wings are wanting. Talent sticks fast to earth, and its most perfect works have still one foot of clay. Genius claims kindred with the very workings of nature herself, so that a sunset shall seem like a quotation from Dante or Milton, and if Shakespeare be read in the very presence of the sea itself, his verses shall but seem nobler for the sublime criticism of ocean. Talent may make friends for itself, but only genius can give to its creations the divine power of winning love and veneration......

To the eye of genius the veil of the spiritual world is ever
rent asunder, that it may perceive the ministers of good and
evil who throng continually around it. No man of mere
talent ever flung his inkstand at the devil."

It is curious to note the attempts of men to define this
subtile faculty. One has caught a certain fugitive phase of
it and spoken of that; another has given his impression from
another point of view; but few, if any, seem to have defined
it fully. The artist catches the evanescent hue of emerald
from the crested wave as it breaks upon the strand, and with
rare skill fixes the sudden gleam for ever on his canvas; but
let one attempt to capture this, and reveal its secret, and it
eludes him. The Greeks, as we know, gave it the name of
*demon,* from their word signifying a spirit or immaterial
being of an intermediate nature between the divine and the
human. This being, they thought, hovered over them and
suggested their finest thoughts. Socrates believed this.

But let us note a few of these definitions. Sir Joshua
Reynolds declared it to be "a power of producing excellences which are out of the reach of the rules of art,—a
power which no precepts can teach and which no industry
can acquire." This is doubtless true. Something is "breathed
into a man at his birth—a divine fire, a gift of God." This
makes great things possible to him which may be for ever
denied to his brother in the next cradle. It is undeniably
a gift, and usually where most manifest to the beholder,
there is a most delightful unconsciousness on the part of its
possessor. Like beauty and childhood, it is unconscious of
self. "When a child enchants us by his innocent smile,"
some one has said, "he does not know that it is innocent;
but does this detract from its charm?" In illustration of
what we have said, could anything be more delightful and
ingenuous than the remark made so naïvely by Jenny Lind
when at the zenith of her fame to one of her friends: "Isn't
it beautiful that I can sing so?" "Some one once showed

Corneille certain obscure verses of his own composition," says Legouvé, "asking for an explanation. 'When I wrote them,' was his artless reply, 'I understood them perfectly, but now they are as vague to me as to you. You see that there are certain things in the works of the masters insoluble even by themselves. In the fire of creation they instinctively use expressions which they do not realize, but which are none the less true.'"

But the gift granted, fuel must be furnished; and what more remarkable than the prodigious industry of our greatest men? One element, at least, seems absolutely essential—namely, *growth*. "A man of genius," says Gilfillan, "is always a man of limitless growth, with a soul smitten with a passion for growth, and open to every influence which promotes it; one who grows always like a tree, by day and by night, in calm and in storm, through opposition and through applause, in difficulty and in despair. With the dying Schiller he can say, 'Many things are becoming plain and clear to me now.'"

But to return to definitions. De Quincey declares genius to be mind steeped and saturated in the genial nature. Others have declared it to be impassioned truth, thought become phosphorescent; while some have even defined it as simply great patience. Perseverance is genius, several have declared, whose position would seem to entitle them to a hearing. But this would appear to be manifestly inadequate, to say the least. This capacity for taking infinite pains, and of unwearying patience until its end is gained, seems indeed ever present where genius is found, but it is by no means the thing itself. Perhaps Owen Meredith hits nearest the mark, or at least as near as any broad generalization could be expected to come, in the striking line: "Genius does what it *must*; talent does what it *can*." In its real essence it is doubtless "the unsearchable and subtile result of a combination of rare faculties with rare temperament." Where this

combination is finest we have a Shakespeare or a Longfellow,
a Rachel or a Gerster.

One thing is certain : no law is competent to explain the
miracle of the rise and action of these gifted souls.  Moses
is the divine lawgiver for all coming time.  He appears
among an enslaved and half-savage people.  Praxiteles is
still unsurpassed, Raphael still the inimitable, and Shakespeare remains for ever the universal, the "happy poet by no
critics vexed."  But whenever the great soul appears, men
know it.  Envy or hate may obscure it for a season with
clouds of detraction ; it matters little.  A man of real power
is, like Homer's laughter of the gods, "inextinguishable."
Moreover, the great always recognize one another.  Genius
has the fine and subtile power of reading between the lines.
It is the single stroke of Apelles upon the panel of Protogenes.
It is Napoleon at the tomb of the great Frederick, rebuking
the fulsome flattery of his courtier, and saying, "I wish I
had known Frederick the Great.  I think we should have
understood each other !"  The revelation comes.  The chords
of its inmost soul begin to vibrate.  Its infinite heart
responds—

> "Responds,—as if with unseen wings
>   An angel touched its quivering strings ;
>   And whispers, in its song,
> 'Where hast thou stayed so long ?'"

Of course we are familiar with its counterfeit,—"the con-
tortion of the Sibyl without the inspiration."  But men are
not deceived.  Young England with its turned-down collars
and dishevelled hair is in reality as far removed from its
great idol as ever.  Samson's strength is not acquired by
simply cutting off the locks of his head, nor the secret of
genius discovered by gazing on its clothes.  As well might
one hope to appropriate the fine qualities and accomplishments of a man after the manner of certain South Sea
Islanders,—by eating him.  "We can examine," says a

recent writer, "the meat upon which our Cæsar fed, the stupidities he had to explode, the malaria into which he drove his ozone; but when we have done all this, what have we got? We have got a plexus of causes which operated on a thousand other minds as well as his, and we have missed the invisible chemistry which created in him and in him alone the personal endowment that enabled him to do his work. Explain and analyze as we will, there is always in the greatest men an unexplained residuum of personal power. We do not say that it must for ever be inexplicable. We only say that it is thus far unexplained, and is pretty likely to remain so until the fundamental riddle of psychology is solved. We may then anatomize our Hercules as much as we choose; we may examine the marshy *habitat* of his monsters, and survey the forest from which he got his club; but we need not forget, in doing that, that there is, after all, between Hercules and Cacus a difference worth accenting, and that the only way of accenting it to any purpose is by means of the old-fashioned ' Bravo, Hercules!'"

The unexpected way in which this strange gift reveals itself at times is not a little remarkable. It turns up in most unlooked-for quarters. Like the cereus from its homely stalk, it appears amid most untoward surroundings; but the common air is at once surcharged with fragrance. Amid the plain prose of everyday life there it stands, "a joy for ever." Take the case of Gerster, for instance, her fame and fortune made in one night,—the night of her first appearance in opera. Hitherto an unknown Hungarian, she jumped from obscurity to popularity and wealth in less than a week. Like Erskine's famous leap in that one great speech of his before Lord Mansfield, it was at once seen that a great star had appeared. The immortal fire had been slumbering in silent depths, awaiting only the breath of great occasion to fan it into flame. Charlotte Cushman's experience was very similar. She somewhere tells us of the

astonishment of the audience, as well as of the performers,
when she first made her wonderful *entrée* as Meg Merrilees.
Miss Cushman was then simply a "utility" woman. "Guy
Mannering" was running, and the artist who acted the old
witch, and who did it in the ordinary stage manner, being
ill, Miss Cushman was called upon to take the part. It
suddenly flashed upon her that she might make a hit, so she
rushed on the stage and assumed the *pose* which is now so
well remembered in connection with her assumption of the
part. To her must be accredited the creation of this striking
picture. The marvellous performance, for downright power,
has never been surpassed.

Then, too, the apparent ease with which genius accom-
plishes its tasks, however difficult, is noteworthy. How
simple its products appear when seen as accomplished
results! What wonder that many are deceived by this,
and led to think the same achievement possible to all! Not
till the attempt is made is the mistake discerned. The
struggling aspiration of a thousand hearts is crystallized
into felicitous speech. A thousand had the thought; it
remained for genius to coin the waiting phrase and put its
stamp upon it. "I will frame a work of fiction upon
notorious fact," says Horace in his "Art of Poetry" as
quoted by Reade, "so that anybody shall think he can do
the same; shall labour and toil attempting the same, and
*fail*—such is the power of sequence and connection in
writing." There is ever a certain indefinable something
present in the works of genius which even the highest talent
cannot attain to, although the work of the latter may be far
more perfect as regards detail. In illustration of this, it
is related of a certain French sculptor who had erected an
equestrian statue to Peter the Great at St. Petersburg, that
once, while lecturing to a class of students, in criticising
works of art he called attention to the celebrated equestrian
statue of Marcus Aurelius at Rome. He pointed out a great

number of anatomical faults in the figure of the horse, all of which, as he called the class to note, were avoided in the horse which he had modelled. And yet, after noting all this, he frankly declared, "Notwithstanding, this poor beast is alive, while mine is dead !"

How readily, too, it transports itself at will from the cold hard facts of the present, from its frowning realities, to its own ideal world. Another sun rises on its dominions. Another moon with serene, unearthly splendour illumes its weird and silent nights. Scorned, it may be, and insulted in the market-place, it goes home and recounts its treasures, like Zaccheus, all undisturbed. What pranks it plays! Let its foes lie in wait all night and seek to slay it, and like Samson it will arise betimes and carry off in triumph the gates of Gaza upon its shoulders. Its horizon is boundless. Heaven and hell are open to it. A beggar's garment is transformed to a prince's robe. The abode of poverty is transfigured. The worn rug assumes the beauty of Brussels or Axminster. The thatched roof is glorified with a nameless charm. How it idealizes! In the rude and uncouth architecture of the quaint old village church it finds suggestion of the "long-drawn aisle and fretted vault," and in the wheezy organ still hears the lofty diapasons and wailing symphonies of grand cathedral tones. It weaves its woof of golden threads into the warp of homespun circumstance, and, lo ! there emerges a rare and costly fabric from its mystic loom. It thus possesses the fine power of transmuting common things to gold. It can seize upon suggestions from passing life and common events anywhere. Thorwaldsen was famous for this. He sees a young labourer for a moment in an unusual but natural posture. A new statue stands before his imagination. He hurries home, and presently his "Mercury as the Slayer of Argos" appears, long known as one of his finest works. Like others of his class, he had his seasons of unproductiveness. At such times he

was moody and dejected, and had no energy.  Except super-
vising the work of his assistants, he would be thus idle or
unproductive for weeks and months.  His two figures
" Night " and " Day," so universally admired, were the
work of a single day,—a day of gloom and dejection.  The
same was true of Irving.  For weeks he would not write a
word ; then, catching a sudden inspiration, he would turn
off page after page of most brilliant work.  It is interesting
to think of those periods when, after prolonged and monotonous ebbing, at length the tide comes in.  The eagle upon
the earth is but a dull and drowsy-looking bird, moving
about seemingly dejected and with drooping pinion ; but let
once the inspiration of his native heaven come over him, and,
lo ! on tireless wing he cleaves the sky.  This tendency to
seasons of indolence may well be regarded as one of the safe-
guards of genius.  Who can doubt that but for this the heat
of the furnace and fierceness of the flames might often en-
danger if not destroy the earthen vessel ?

What could be finer than its rare power of incarnating
itself, and wreaking its thought upon expression on the immortal canvas or in the imperishable stone ?  Da Vinci
spends four years upon that marvellous head of Mona Lisa
in the Louvre, and leaves a thought there for all coming
time ; the depth of expression in the face being at once the
wonder and despair of artists.  Roebling, the living martyr
to his own great enterprise, gazes from his invalid's pillow
upon the completed towers of that majestic bridge now
spanning the East River, and exclaims with the enthusiasm
of a child, " Ah ! that's just as I expected to see it ! "  The
dream of the great engineer is realized.  The lonely, recluse
genius of Hawthorne toils away untiringly at its self-imposed
tasks unrecognized for twenty years.  At length the fitting
recognition comes.

There are certain wiseacres who pride themselves on being
practical, matter-of-fact individuals.  In their estimation men

of genius are visionary and their projects "moonshine." Physical activity is considered by many very sincere people the chief end of man. Unquestionably there exists a very general impression that "the study lamp of the student shines on an idle dreamer,—a drone in the great hive." The favourite and ever-recurring challenge of these utilitarians seems to be, "Will it bake bread?" and that it will not, is sufficient condemnation in their eyes. As if the "Apollo," or the "Transfiguration," or the "Paradise Lost" were concerned with a wheaten loaf or questions of the pantry! Such, doubtless, have forgotten that it is written, "Man shall not live by bread alone."

Holland, indeed, has conclusively shown the fallacy of such ideas, and one of the profoundest of English philosophers has declared: "It would not be difficult by an unbroken chain of historic facts to demonstrate that the most important discoveries in science and improvements in the mechanic arts had their origin, not in the cabinets of statesmen, nor in the practical insight of men of business, but in the visions of recluse genius." This suggests, naturally, the associated thought of the pecuniary rewards of genius. In our day, at least, these are not unworthy of note. The profits of authors, for instance, is an interesting subject. Here, as elsewhere, we find genuine material always in demand. For the "Hanging of the Crane" Longfellow received four thousand dollars,—twenty dollars per line. Tennyson received, we are told, three guineas a line from the *Cornhill Magazine* for his "Tithonus," and nearly twice that for the "Revenge." The Harpers paid as copyright to Motley about sixty thousand dollars; to Jacob Abbott, about fifty thousand dollars; and to Professor Anthon, about one hundred thousand. In the "Life and Letters" of Macaulay we are told that twenty-six thousand five hundred copies of his History had been sold in ten weeks. Longman, his publisher, one day came to him, and said they were overflowing with money, and proposed to pay him £20,000 the following week. The cheque is still preserved as a curiosity among the archives of Messrs. Longman's firm. "I went into the city," says Macaulay, "to give instructions, and was warmly congratulated on being a great moneyed man. I said that I had some thoughts of going to the Chancellor of the Exchequer as a bidder for the next loan." Scott received £8,000 for "Woodstock," and George Eliot the same amount for "Middlemarch." For receipts from actual writing, indeed, it has been affirmed that no one has yet approached Scott, whose income for several years ranged from £10,000 to £15,000, mainly drawn from this source. He was paid £110,000 for eleven novels of three volumes each and nine volumes of "Tales of my Landlord." Lord Beaconsfield received £12,000 for his last novel, which it is believed represents the largest amount ever given in England for any single work of fiction. Beaconsfield's earlier novels, notwithstanding the success of the first, "Vivian Grey," had a very limited sale. He is said to have made by his pen, in all, £30,000. The "Curiosities of Literature" of the elder Disraeli must have produced a large sum of money. It forms a part of every good collection of English books, and has passed through many editions. Byron is said to have earned by his pen £23,000. Thiers and Lamartine received nearly £20,000 each for their respective histories. Lord Lytton made £80,000 by his novels, and Trollope in twenty years made £70,000. Dickens, it has been computed, ought to have been making £10,000 a year for the three years prior to the publication of "Nicholas Nickleby." He left £80,000, and a considerable slice of this came from books, but it was his "Readings" which made him affluent; and so too with Thackeray. Richardson, it is said, was the first Englishman who made a really good thing out of writing. Miss Braddon's receipts from writing are estimated as among the half-dozen highest of writers of fiction. It has been noted that many of those books which pay so well are the last which would occur to persons as being lucrative. Thus "Thornton's Family Prayers" has been a mine of money to an English family ; and Marcius Willson received a surprisingly large sum as copyright from the Harpers for his series of school readers. These figures certainly would seem quite sufficient as a hint and incentive to those about to enter upon literature as a profession. Turning to the stage, we find Edwin Booth in a single tour through the South realizing fifty-two thousand dollars, and Patti receiving five thousand dollars a night for her singing.

On the other hand, I suppose a record of the sorrows and misfortunes of the sons of genius would suffice to fill many a volume. We remember that Milton and Addison were secretaries, and that Byron was a peer ; it is hard also for us to conceive of Homer as a beggar, and to realize that Cervantes died of hunger, and that the "Vicar of Wakefield" was sold for a trifle to save its author from the grip of the law. And yet, after all, may it not well be questioned whether men have not oftener been indebted to the frowns than to the smiles of fortune ? True, a man need not be useless because he happens to be rich ; and yet had Shakespeare been a member of the British aristocracy, how much might the world have lost ! Scott's motto for life seems to have been, as he says in his journal, *Il faut d'argent* (" I must have money "). To come nearer home, take the testimony of one of the most famous of young American authors in a recent conversation concerning his motive for writing. He made no secret of it. "As I tell the publishers," he said, " the love of money is the root of all literature."

But beyond all this, high genius invests its possessor with a power which cannot be measured by pecuniary values. Angelo, incensed with the Pope, indignantly leaves Rome for Florence. Even the threat of excommunication cannot bring him back. Appeased by the proposal of his Holiness

to meet him half-way and escort him into his own dominions, he returns. Some of the courtiers having proposed
the punishment of such insolence with death—"I will," replies the wily pontiff, "if you will first find me another
Michael Angelo!" At the end of the Seven Years' War
D'Alembert went to visit the great Frederick at Potsdam,
and spoke of the glory he had acquired in the war. "The
king," writes D'Alembert, "answered, with the greatest
simplicity, that a large deduction should be made from the
glory due him, and that chance had much to do with it. 'I
would,' said Frederick, 'much rather have written "Athalie"
than be the hero of the Seven Years' War.'" No less striking is the well-known tribute of General Wolfe to the
"Elegy." Receiving a copy on the eve of the assault on
Quebec, he was so struck with its beauty that he declared
he would prefer being its author to being the victor in the
projected attack, in which he so gloriously lost his life. The
secret of it all may doubtless be discovered in the observation of Charles II. to a courtier as he picked up Titian's
mall-stick: "A king you can always have; a genius comes
but rarely."

It is curious to note, though, among those who have
achieved permanent fame, how small is the parcel which
this one or that is seen to be carrying with him down the
ages. A single effort, however, has often sufficed to im-
mortalize one. The "Marseillaise," for instance, was the
one effort of its author, Rouget de l'Isle. The "Elegy"
is about the only production which the masses, at least,
associate with Gray. Swift is remembered principally as
the author of "Gulliver's Travels," De Foe as the author
of "Robinson Crusoe." Southey's fame rests on his Lives
of Nelson and Wesley. Bunyan is generally known as the
author of the "Pilgrim's Progress" only. Steele lives
chiefly as the friend of Addison. Lady Ann Barnard never
wrote anything but "Auld Robin Gray;" but then that is

probably one of the most beautiful and pathetic songs ever written.

A chapter concerning the great, *en déshabillé*, showing how they relieved the strain and tension under which they have worked, and sought to unbend themselves, could hardly fail to be vastly entertaining. It has been justly observed that a bow need not always be strung—an acrobat is not always on the tight-rope. Those who have known the world best have told us that there is far less radical and intrinsic difference between one man and another than the uninitiated would suppose ; that there is, running through nature, an all-levelling principle, which permits no Titans except those which credulity would create. Oxenstiern was no cynic when he turned and said with a sigh to his son, " Ah, my child, you know not how little wisdom is required for governing the world." " I remember," says Bolingbroke, in one of his letters to Swift, "to have seen a procession at Aix-la-Chapelle wherein an image of Charlemagne is carried on the shoulders of a man who is hid by the long robe of the imperial saint. Follow him into the vestry, and you see the bearer slip from under the robe, and the gigantic figure dwindles into an image of the ordinary size, and is set by among the lumber." And such, in his opinion, are those who make history. Lord Waldegrave, in his memoirs, writes : " I must not lift up the veil, and shall only add that no man can have a clear conception how great personages pass their leisure hours who has not been a prince's governor or a king's favourite." It has been truly said that man is what he is, not by nature, but by effort ; and as it is by artificial means that water is raised above the level of the original fountain, so it is by artificial means that man raises himself above the level of ordinary humanity. " Nature has, it is true, her favourites, but she is more impartial than we give her credit for. The life of what we call a great man is a continual struggle ; and it matters little what character on the stage of

the world he is supporting, whether he be a poet or a statesman, a Napoleon or a Michael Angelo—it is equally arduous,
it is equally incessant." Swift, we are told, relieved his
tense and tragic moods by harnessing his servants with cords
and driving them up and down the stairs and through the
rooms of his deanery. Peter the Great sought to unbend
himself by being wheeled over the flower-beds and parterres
of his host's garden in a wheel-barrow, as poor Sir William
Temple found to his cost. Cardinal Mazarin is said to have
been fond of shutting himself up in a room and jumping over
the chairs, arranged in positions varying according to the
degrees of difficulty in clearing them. Of this weakness on
the part of his Excellency an amusing anecdote is told. On
one occasion, while engaged in these athletics, he forgot to
lock the door. A young courtier, inadvertently entering the
room, surprised the great man in his undignified pursuit.
It was an embarrassing position, for Mazarin was, he knew,
as haughty as he was eccentric. But the young man was
equal to the crisis. Assuming the intensest interest in the
proceeding, he exclaimed with well-feigned earnestness, "I
will bet your Eminence two gold pieces I can beat that
jump." He had struck the right chord, and in two minutes
he was measuring his leaping powers with the Prime Minister, whom he took care not to beat. He lost his two gold
pieces, but he gained, before long, a mitre. Samuel Clarke
was accustomed to seek relaxation in the same way ; and on
one occasion, seeing a pedantic fellow approaching, said to the
pupil who was sharing his amusements, "Now we must stop,
for a fool is coming in." Old Burton, the author of the
"Anatomy of Melancholy," the only book, we are told,
which got Dr. Johnson out of his bed two hours before he
intended to rise, found his chief recreation in going down to
Folly Bridge at Oxford and listening to the ribaldry of the
bargemen ; "which did cleare away his vapoures, and make
him laugh as he would die." Sir Robert Walpole "could

never enjoy a dinner without lively conversation going on around him. If the company were dull, he would send to the circus and order musicians and actors to come across and enliven them. At other times he would summon story-tellers and anecdote-mongers, or set two philosophers by the ears that he might listen to their argument. Goldsmith, Shelley, and Macaulay would idle away whole days in romping with children." Machiavelli and Burke delighted to forget politics by sharing the labours of their farm-servants; and even the stately Bolingbroke, as Pope tells us in one of his delightful letters, was not above shouldering a prong. How true it is that there is but a step between the sublime and the ridiculous! It has been well observed that the famous saying that no hero is a hero to his valet was, unhappily, not refuted by Goethe, when he asserted in his magnificent way that a hero is a hero, and a valet is a valet. " How Howard's servants and family must have smiled when they read Burke's magnificent panegyric on the great philanthropist! We wonder what Antonina thought of the Conqueror of the World, and the Duchess of Marlborough of the 'Scourge of France.' The one, if we are to believe Procopius, was an abject slave of his contemptible consort; the other, it is well known, never durst wag a finger in opposition to his wife." But the contrast between a great man as he appears to the world and as he appears in private life was never more strikingly illustrated than in the case of the younger Pitt. Lady Hester Stanhope tells us that when he was at Walmer he used to go to a farm where hay and corn were kept for the horses. He had a room fitted up there with a table and two or three chairs. " Oh, what slices of bread and butter I have seen him eat there, and hunches of bread and cheese big enough for a ploughman! He used to say that whenever he could retire from public life he would have a good English woman-cook. To see him at table with vulgar sea captains and ignorant militia colonels

with two or three servants in attendance,—he who had been
accustomed to a servant behind each chair, to all that was
great and distinguished in Europe,—one might suppose disgust would have worked some change in him ; but it was
always the same."

"We must take men, however," observes a clever essayist,
"even the greatest, as we find them. When the late Lord
Westbury remarked of one of his contemporaries that he had
not a single redeeming vice, he made an observation which
was far less cynical than it would at first sight appear to be.
To expect a human creature to be all genius, all intellect, all
virtue, all dignity, would be as absurd as to expect that
midnight should be all stars. Curiosity about the minor
incidents in the lives of great men is to a certain extent
legitimate, and even profitable. To find the great on a level
with ourselves may gratify our vanity, but it sometimes may
lead to very erroneous conclusions. We have often been
struck," he continues, "with the significance of an anecdote
which Mr. Hookham Frere once related to his nephew about
Canning : ' I remember one day going to consult Canning on
a matter of great importance to me, when he was staying at
Enfield. We walked into the woods to have a quiet talk,
and as we passed some ponds I was surprised to find that it
was a new light to him that tadpoles turned into frogs.
"Now, don't you," he added, "go and tell that story to the
next fool you meet."' Canning could and did rule a great
and civilized nation ; but people are apt to fancy that ' a
man who does not know the natural history of frogs must be
an imbecile in the treatment of men.'"

There is one trait which every truly great genius seems
to possess, and that is a certain playful, almost childlike
simplicity of character. It was true of Chalmers ; and we
all know how genial and sunny a companion was good Nor-
man Macleod, the beloved and honoured chaplain of the
Queen. As has been finely said of Shakespeare, "the spirit

that could conjure up a Hamlet and a Lear would have broken had it not possessed, as well, the humour which could produce a Falstaff and the ' Merry Wives of Windsor.' " If it be true, as doubtless it is, that there exists a widely prevailing tendency to hero-worship among men, one occasionally meets with instances which reveal the fact that some, at least, are exempt. At the Radstock station on the North Somerset Railway two rustics met. Said one, " Hast been to Vroom to-day ? "—" Ay," replied the other.— " Didst hire Gladstone speak ? "—" Noa," rejoined the second. " Ee be no moar than any other man ; why should I go to year ee speak ? What be ee moar than thee or I ? " It reminds one of the remark of one of his countrymen concerning Shakespeare. " Eh, man," said the worthy bailie, " he maun hae been a wonderfu' man, that Shackspear. There war things cam' into his heid that wad never hae coom into mine ava." " Even Wordsworth," said Charles Lamb, " one day told me he considered Shakespeare greatly overrated. ' There is an immensity of trick in all that Shakespeare wrote,' he said, ' and the people are taken by it. Now if I had a mind, I could write exactly like Shakespeare.' So you see," proceeded Lamb quietly, " it was only the mind that was wanting."

The absent-mindedness of genius is proverbial. A decidedly entertaining volume might no doubt be written recounting the laughable illustrations of this alone. Who, indeed, can picture to himself without smiling Sydney Smith rapping at the door of his friend's house and suddenly discovering, with confusion, that he has actually forgotten his own name ? The drollest of all, however, it seems to us, belongs to Lessing. In his old age he was subject to extraordinary fits of abstraction. On his return home one evening, after he had knocked at his door, his servant looked out of the window to see who was there. Not recognizing his master in the dark, and mistaking him for a stranger, he called out, "The professor is not at home!"—"Oh, very well," replied Lessing.  "No matter; I'll call at another time."

However men may seek to define this rare, mysterious gift, one thing is certain—we never fail to recognize its presence.  Whenever great genius appears, castle gates at once fly open.  The patronage of kings and princes is assured.  From newsboy to royalty comes spontaneous and willing tribute.  In presence of its great achievements we inevitably feel within us the throbbings of a noble joy.  The subtile spell is upon us—a power which we instantly recognize and gratefully confess.  What wonder, then, its possessors should be both envied and adored?

# XII

# Masters of the Situation.

Men who have taken the giant world by the throat, and thrown him.
PHILIP JAMES BAILEY, *Festus.*

To be great, one must know how to profit by the whole of one's fortune.
LA ROCHEFOUCAULD.

There are no circumstances, however unfortunate, that clever people
do not extract some advantage from.—*Ib.*

"Something in fires depends upon the grate."

IT has been our aim in this volume to bring out in as strong
a light as possible some of those qualities which have proved
to be secrets of success and power in the careers of those
who have attained to fame and exalted station in the various
walks of life. We have seen how men have risen on these
sure stepping-stones to the highest places. We have found
them, thus equipped, organizing victory out of defeat, and
proving themselves, even amid circumstances most adverse,
masters of the situation.

Unquestionably some allowance should be made for the
difference in men in native power, since nothing is more
noticeable. "One man speaks, and his words are edicts.
Nations run to obey, as if to obey were the only joy they
coveted. Another speaks, and only makes us question
whether the gift of speech be on the whole a blessing."
That was a significant remark of an ancient general when
about to bring on a battle. His officers endeavoured to dis-

suade him from his purpose on account of the superior numbers of the foe. Impatiently turning upon them, he demanded, "For how many men do you count me?" It is indeed true that one man may sometimes count for thousands for or against. On the other hand, there are men whose very presence seems to foreshadow defeat from the start. As the discerning bishop said to the young ecclesiastic, "I do not forbid you to preach, but Nature does." Now nothing, as we have found, is more remarkable in successful men than their strong and pronounced individuality. Clearly all men are not masters; with some it is "as though they laid a finger on the keyboard of an organ, touching a note here and there. A flute voice answers, or a vox humana, perhaps even a vox angelica; but they do not *know* the instrument until the master musician sits down before it, and they hear the thunder of the diapason, the rush of mighty harmonies—the tender strains of melody." There is no denying that Nature herself has lavishly gifted certain men, and thus placing them on vantage-ground, has made achievement easier and success seemingly almost inevitable. All things appear to be in league with such as these. In their own province they are irresistible; you cannot come upon them unawares and keep them at disadvantage; their resources seem indeed almost infinite. Take Marlborough, for instance. Burton, in his "History of the Reign of Queen Anne," says of him: "Unlike most men of great firmness and self-reliance, Marlborough courted counsel and discussion; he could conduct it with absolute calmness and courtesy. On his own clear views of what was to be done it had no effect, but it gained him coadjutors; for he was, like Wolsey, fair-spoken and persuasive. His patience was inexhaustible. He was cautious, but his caution had its corrective in an unmatched promptitude of vision. He thus never committed a rash act or missed an opportunity for striking an effective blow. His fertility in resources made him less amenable to disappointment when his favourite scheme was thwarted than men of smaller resources, whose mind contains but one scheme at a time, and that being forbidden, are destitute of other resource, and helpless. To him, if one way were closed, there was ever another opening. He felt secure in himself; be the conditions that were to be wrought with what they might, he would bring out of them results which no other man could effect."

Of course the interest with which we regard such men is natural and inevitable. We admire them, and we cannot help it; it is as natural for us as breathing. Yet we must not forget that such instances are rare, and that we always concede to such that indefinable gift which we call genius. But, after all, have we not found the most effective genius to be the genius of hard work? Have we not seen, moreover, that even those whose great achievements seem spontaneous have been indebted for their seemingly easy triumphs to an intensity of toil and previous preparation of which their admirers little dreamed? We marvel, for instance, at the skill which enables a great artist to take a little colour that lies inert upon his palette—a little gray and brown and white—and presently to so "transfigure it into a living presence" that our hearts throb faster only to look upon it, and there come upon the soul all those influences which one feels beneath the shadow of the Jungfrau or the Matterhorn, or amid the awful solitudes of Mont Blanc. But behind that apparent ease and skill are the years of struggle and effort and application which have conferred the envied power. The same is true elsewhere. Say what we may, we have found that, after all, the greatest difference in men consists in the cultivation or non-cultivation of those qualities which we have had under consideration; in other words, in the improvement or neglect of those faculties and endowments which are for the most part the common inheri-

tance of all. If one aspires to distinction, he must be willing
to pay the price; there is no other way. Nothing is denied
to well-directed energy. "The barriers are not erected
which can say to aspiring talents and industry, 'Thus far
and no farther.'"

We have discovered that numerous factors have entered
into all distinguished success, one of which has been an
unmistakable promptness—the faculty of seizing at once
upon every circumstance which "makes" in one's favour.
The great herd of mankind, the *fruges consumere nati*,
pass their lives, as Wirt has said, in listless inattention and
indifference as to what is going on around them, "being
perfectly content to satisfy the mere cravings of nature,
while those who are destined to distinction have a lynx-eyed
vigilance that nothing can escape. You see nothing of the
Paul Pry in them; yet they know all that is passing, and
keep a perfect reckoning not only of every interesting passage, but of all the characters of the age who have any
concern in them." A certain well-known writer some years
since published a series of articles entitled, "Thoughts as
they occur, by one who keeps his eyes and ears open." In
that very title we find one secret of their author's great fame
and success. On the other hand, thousands go through life
perpetually looking, but never seeing anything; having ears,
it is true, but never really hearing anything—at least to
their advantage.

This *alertness* has enabled its possessors again and again to
cover even defeat with the semblance of victory,—indeed to
organize victory out of defeat. Cæsar, for instance, at his
landing stumbles on the sands. Instantly he covers his
mischance and hides the evil omen from his followers by
grasping the very sand which threw him, and holding it
aloft, with heroic utterance turns his threatened defeat into
a shout of triumph. It was the same spirit—a spirit which
brooks no defeat—which voiced itself in the utterance of the

savage when he exclaimed, "Indian no lost; wigwam lost!"
One cannot hide the fact that at times there will occur, even
to the most gifted and successful, certain unlooked-for combinations which test most severely the finest qualities of even
an adept, and which require a sort of desperation to extricate
one's self cleverly. Yet a man of first-rate powers will
usually find a "happy issue" out of even these. Who has
not had days come to him that have led him to believe
most fully in what some one has felicitously called "the total
depravity of inanimate things"? In these very crises, however, lookers-on come to realize that, as the Greeks used to
say, one *finished* man is worth a thousand ill-disciplined and
grovelling ones. In order to be master of the situation at
all times, one must needs be, in fact, as Chesterfield puts it
in one of his letters, *omnis homo.*

"If we sometimes deceive ourselves," says Marshal Mar-
mont, "in judging by facts, we should deceive ourselves
much more in directing ourselves solely by personal knowledge of individuals. Fortune may once or twice overwhelm
with her favours a man who is not worthy of them ; she may
betray the finest combinations of genius, and humble a noble
character; but when the struggle is prolonged, when events
are multiplied, the man of true talents infallibly conquers
her favours."

In order to attain this full command of one's powers, we
have seen, moreover, that sound physical health is indispensable. One's reserves must be carefully looked after
and his resources in this direction must be always at command. Some men have such a fund of vitality that from
sheer magnetic, physical force they seem resistless and everything bows before them. Thus, doubtless, there are families
that have "clutched success and kept it through generations
from the simple fact of a splendid physical organization
handed down from one generation to another." Holland,
indeed, maintains that the remarkable influence of such men

as Hall and Taylor is due in large measure to this fact of fine physical endowment.

Then there is the influence of *habit*, which enters so largely as a factor into all real and permanent success that it cannot safely be ignored ; while, mingling itself with all one's efforts, there must be that deep enthusiasm, that *passion* for one's work, whatever it be, that makes toil easy and holds one unflinchingly to his task.

Thus equipped, one may serenely bide his time, as oppor tunities, sooner or later, are sure to present themselves for the fullest display of all his powers. Even if failure over-take one occasionally, he need not be disheartened. Real success in life does not consist, of course, in never failing,—in never making a blunder or mistake. Many men who have succeeded have first failed, and some of them more than once before achieving their success. The real wisdom con-sists in not making the same blunder a second time. The negroes of Central Africa have a saying that the man is a fool whose sheep run away twice. There is no little philos-ophy underlying this. What could be finer than that saying of Macaulay's concerning Alexander the Great, "Often de-feated in battle, yet always successful in war "?

A curious society still exists in Paris composed of dra-matic authors, who meet once a month and dine together. Their number has no fixed limit, only every member to be eligible must have been *hissed.* An eminent dramatist is selected as chairman, and holds the post for three months. His election generally follows close upon a splendid failure. Some of the world-famous ones have enjoyed this honour. Dumas, jun., Zola, and Offenbach have all filled the chair and presided at the monthly dinner. These dinners are given on the last Friday of the month, and are said to be extraor-dinarily hilarious.

Few sights are more impressive than that of the incoming tide. How surge after surge plunges in as if to stay ! But no; the very next instant sees it disappear. Apparently nothing has been gained. But stay. Behind all this surface fluctuation, this seeming defeat, has been the awful, resistless purpose of the unconquerable sea,—and now it is full high tide. So with successful men. Behind all else, scorning disaster and defeat, has been the single eye, the steady purpose of an unconquerable soul. If you are a close observer, you will almost always detect in the countenances of these men traces of the struggle through which they have passed; for success, wherever real and lasting, is *wrought out* by mighty endeavour. *The sculptor's chisel always leaves its lines of power upon the statue's front.*

Let it not be forgotten that the demand for the qualities we have been considering is a steady one in the markets of the world, and will not cease. Never was there an age which offered greater incentives or grander inspirations to young men than the present. The great places of trust and power and responsibility are waiting for you. In a few brief years they will be in your hands. It is for you to prepare yourselves for them. Resolve to make yourselves masters of the situation. Study *great* models; mercilessly avoid and ignore inferior ones. It was said of Sir Peter Lely that he would never allow himself to look upon an inferior painting, believing that unconsciously his brush caught a taint by even such contact. The age wants *men*. "There is but one thing which God has given us the right to claim when we are sent into the world, and that is, *character*. We may not ask for riches and popularity, but we can build up a character of faithfulness, goodness, and honesty. We may send out the claim, and the world will not deny the claim. For other things, which are gifts, we may be thankful, but this alone may we demand."

Never for a moment allow yourself to believe that there is any necessary antagonism between success and downright integrity of character,—uprightness of heart and life. The long array of Christian jurists and statesmen and merchant-princes which might be cited would seem to give to an error like this a sufficient refutation. Amid the prevailing irreverence and scepticisms and frivolities of the day, seek ever to cherish and cultivate a reverent spirit. Remember that the proudest earthly triumphs are, at best, but transient and fleeting. "The fashion of this world passeth away," and even the paths of glory "lead but to the grave;" whereas "godliness is profitable unto all things, having promise of the life that now is, and of that which is to come."

> "We live in deeds, not years; in thoughts, not breaths;
> In feelings, not in figures on a dial.
> We should count time by heart-throbs. He most lives
> Who thinks most, feels the noblest, acts the best."

# The Master's Touch.

In the still air the music lies unheard;
  In the rough marble beauty hides unseen:
To wake the music and the beauty, needs
  The master's touch, the sculptor's chisel keen.

Great Master, touch us with Thy skilful hand,
  Let not the music that is in us die;
Great Sculptor, hew and polish us, nor let,
  Hidden and lost, Thy form within us lie.

Spare not the stroke, do with us as Thou wilt;
  Let there be nought unfinished, broken, marred;
Complete Thy purpose, that we may become
  Thy perfect image, O our God and Lord!

BONAR.

# Index.

# "Living to Purpose" Series.

**General Grant's Life.** (From the Tannery to the White House.) Story of the Life of Ulysses S. Grant: his Boyhood, Youth, Manhood, Public and Private Life and Services. By WILLIAM M. THAYER, Author of "From Log Cabin to White House," etc. With Portrait, Vignette, etc. Reprinted complete from the American Edition. 400 pages. Crown 8vo, cloth extra, gilt side and edges. Price 3s. 6d. *Cheaper Edition*, 2s. 6d.

**Success in Life.** A Book for Young Men. With Plates. Post 8vo, cloth extra. Price 3s.

*The great principles of action which, under God, secure "success in life"—perseverance, industry, integrity, economy, etc.—illustrated by many examples.*

**Living to Purpose;** or, Making the Best of Life. By JOSEPH JOHNSON. Post 8vo, cloth extra. Price 2s. 6d.

*An earnest, practical book; shows how some of the greatest and most gifted men of the past have lived, and links counsels to their examples.*

**Kind Words Awaken Kind Echoes.** Six Engravings. Post 8vo, cloth extra. Price 2s. 6d.

*"The law of kindness," and its happy effects in overcoming prejudice, softening enmity, making home happy, rescuing the perishing, elevating the degraded, etc., illustrated by a variety of authentic narratives and incidents.*

**Living in Earnest.** Lessons and Incidents from the Lives of the Great and Good. By JOSEPH JOHNSON. Post 8vo, cloth extra. Price 2s. 6d.

*True "life in earnest" described in its various forms, with counsels as to study, health, amusement, etc.*

**Earnest Women.** Their Efforts, Struggles, and Triumphs. By JOSEPH JOHNSON, Author of "Self-Effort," "Living in Earnest," etc. Small crown 8vo, cloth extra. Price 2s. 6d.

*In this volume are narrated the results which have been achieved by women in various spheres of life; with examples of their loving and serving disposition amidst scenes of sickness and suffering.*

**No Cross no Crown.** A Tale of the Scottish Reformation. By the Author of "The Spanish Brothers." Post 8vo, cloth extra. Price 2s. 6d.

*A tale, more of facts than fiction, of the plague in Dundee, 1544, and the life and times of George Wishart.*

**Records of Noble Lives.** By W. H. DAVENPORT ADAMS. Post 8vo, cloth extra. Price 2s. 6d.

*A most suitable volume for a prize or a present. Its object is to inspire, by graphic biographical notices of great and good men.*

**Seeking a Country;** or, The Home of the Pilgrims. By the Rev. E. N. HOARE, M.A., Rector of Acrise, Kent; Author of "Heroism in Humble Life," "Roe Carson's Enemy," etc. Post 8vo, cloth extra. Price 2s. 6d.

*An historical tale, founded on the first voyage of the "Mayflower," and early experiences of the Pilgrim Fathers. With a portrait of Captain Miles Standish, and many other interesting illustrations.*

**Stories of the Lives of Noble Women.** By W. H. DAVENPORT ADAMS. Post 8vo, cloth extra. Price 2s. 6d.

*A book that every girl should read. It contains a series of biographical sketches of illustrious women who, by their domestic or public virtues, have won for themselves a name in history.*

T. NELSON AND SONS, LONDON, EDINBURGH, AND NEW YORK.

# Self-Effort Series.

**"Above Rubies;"** or, Memoirs of Christian Gentlewomen. By Miss BRIGHTWELL. Post 8vo, cloth extra. Price 3s. 6d.

*Examples of the "virtuous woman" in various times and countries—Queen Louisa of Prussia, the wife of Luther, Mrs. Susannah Wesley, Mde. Necker, etc.*

**Aiming Higher;** or, Perseverance and Faithfulness Triumphant. By the Rev. T. P. WILSON, Vicar of Pavenham, Author of "True to His Colours," etc. Post 8vo, cloth extra. Price 3s. 6d.

*An interesting tale of true prosperity and the blessings of Providence following the faithful discharge of duty.*

**Doing Good;** or, The Christian in Walks of Usefulness. Illustrated by Examples. By the Rev. R. STEEL, D.D. Post 8vo, cloth extra. Price 3s. 6d.

*A series of short biographical sketches of Christians remarkable for various kinds of usefulness, for example and encouragement to others.*

**The Early Choice.** A Book for Daughters. By the late Rev. W. K. TWEEDIE, D.D. Post 8vo, cloth extra. Price 3s. 6d.

*The duties, influence, responsibilities, trials and joys, etc., of women. Religion the only true source of happiness and safety. Illustrated by many examples.*

**Earnest Men:** Their Life and Work. By the late Rev. W. K. TWEEDIE, D.D. Post 8vo, cloth extra. Price 3s. 6d.

*Contains biographical sketches of eminent patriots, heroes for the truth, philanthropists, and men of science.*

**The Young Huguenots;** or, The Soldiers of the Cross. A Story of the Seventeenth Century. By EDITH L. FLOYER. With Six Illustrations. Post 8vo, cloth extra. Price 3s. 6d.

**Heroes of the Desert.** The Story of the Lives of Moffat and Livingstone. By the Author of "Mary Powell." New and Enlarged Edition, with numerous Illustrations and two Portraits. Post 8vo, cloth extra. Price 3s. 6d.

*In this handsome new edition of the two deeply interesting biographies, that of Dr. Moffat is completed; a sketch being given of the principal incidents in the last twenty years of his life.*

**Lives Made Sublime by Faith and Works.** By the Rev. R. STEEL, D.D., Author of "Doing Good," etc. Post 8vo, cloth extra. Price 3s. 6d.

*A volume of short biographical sketches of Christian men, eminent and useful in various walks of life,—as Hugh Miller, Sir Henry Havelock, Robert Flockhart, etc.*

**Noble Women of Our Time.** By JOSEPH JOHNSON, Author of "Living in Earnest," etc. With Accounts of the Work of Misses De Broën, Whately, Carpenter, F. R. Havergal, Macpherson, Sister Dora, etc. Post 8vo, cloth extra. Price 3s. 6d.

*A handsome volume, containing short biographies of many Christian women, whose lives have been devoted to missionary and philanthropic work in our own and other countries,—Sister Dora, Mrs. Tait, Frances Havergal, etc.*

**Self-Effort;** or, The True Method of Attaining Success in Life. By JOSEPH JOHNSON, Author of "Living in Earnest," etc. Post 8vo, cloth extra. Price 3s. 6d.

*This book of example and encouragement has been written to induce earnestness in life, the illustrations being drawn from recent books of biography.*

T. NELSON AND SONS, LONDON, EDINBURGH, AND NEW YORK.

# Stories of Home and School Life.

**Stepping Heavenward.** A Tale of Home Life. By the Author of "The Flower of the Family," etc. Post 8vo, cloth extra. 2s. 6d.

*A tale of girlhood and early married life, with discipline and trials, all resulting in good at last. Every girl should read this remarkably truthful and fascinating book.*

**Ever Heavenward;** or, A Mother's Influence. By the Author of "Stepping Heavenward," "The Flower of the Family," etc. Post 8vo, cloth extra. Price 2s. 6d.

*A tale of home life, with its ordinary joys and sorrows, under the guidance of its leading spirit,—a wise, loving, pious mother.*

**The Flower of the Family.** A Tale of Domestic Life. By the Author of "Stepping Heavenward," etc. Post 8vo, cloth extra. Price 2s. 6d.

*A tale of home life,—the central figure being an unselfish, devoted, pious eldest daughter.*

**Changed Scenes;** or, The Castle and the Cottage. By Lady Hope, Author of "Our Coffee House," "A Maiden's Work," "Sunny Footsteps," etc. Post 8vo, cloth extra. Price 2s. 6d.

*An interesting story for girls, of two English orphans and their guardian, in the course of which valuable moral and religious lessons are conveyed by some pleasing allegories.*

**Salome;** or, "Let Patience have her Perfect Work." By Mrs. Emma Marshall, Author of "Mrs. Haycock's Chronicles,"etc. Post 8vo, cloth extra. 2s. 6d.

*An interesting tale for young people. Trials form the true test of character; and one member of a family, by self-denying energy, may do much for all the others.*

**True to the Last;** or, My Boyhood's Hero. By Evelyn Everett-Green, Author of "Fighting the Good Fight," etc. Post 8vo, cloth extra. Price 2s. 6d.

*A story for boys; the scene in England. A fine manly Christian character is developed and perfected by trials in early life.*

**Fighting the Good Fight;** or, The Successful Influence of Well Doing. By Evelyn Everett-Green, Author of "True to the Last." Post 8vo, cloth extra. Price 2s. 6d.

*A vigorous story of an orphan boy who is adopted by his uncle, and tries to be a little soldier with the weapons of faith, love, and obedience. There are many points of interest in the story, and Cousin Corrie is a character full of pathos and beauty.*

**The Grey House on the Hill;** or, Trust in God and Do the Right. A Tale for the Young. By the Hon. Mrs. Greene. Post 8vo, cloth extra. Price 2s. 6d.

*A tender, touching story; one which cannot fail to interest all true-hearted boys and girls.*

**Jubilee Hall;** or, "There's no Place Like Home." A Story for the Young. By the Hon. Mrs. Greene, Author of "The Grey House on the Hill." Post 8vo, cloth extra. Price 2s. 6d.

*It recounts the holiday experiences of a party of children in a pleasant country-house.*

**Look at the Bright Side.** A Tale for the Young. By the Author of "Little Sunbeams." Post 8vo, cloth extra. Price 2s. 6d.

*A tale showing the fault and misfortune of a fearful, foreboding spirit, and the happiness of cheerful trust in God.*

T. NELSON AND SONS, LONDON, EDINBURGH, AND NEW YORK.

# Works on Nature and Natural History.

**Chips from the Earth's Crust;** or, Short Studies in Natural Science. By JOHN GIBSON, Natural History Department, Edinburgh Museum of Science and Art; Author of "Science Gleanings in Many Fields," etc. With 29 Illustrations. Post 8vo, cloth extra. Price 2s. 6d.

*"A popular account of the Earth's surface and formation, such as may interest and instruct boys of an inquiring habit of mind. It comprises chapters on earthquakes, meteors, tornadoes, and other phenomena."—SATURDAY REVIEW.*

## Science Gleanings in Many Fields.
By JOHN GIBSON, Natural History Department, Edinburgh Museum of Science and Art. With 18 Illustrations. Post 8vo, cloth extra. Price 2s. 6d.

*The reader will find "Science Gleanings" rich in information regarding such interesting topics as animal intelligence, animal mimicry, the weapons of animals, their partnerships, and their migrations. Much information is also given regarding food fishes and about animals with which, whether as friends or foes, man has more especially to do. Glimpses of the past life of the globe are obtained in the essays on the mammoth, the great auk, and other extinct animals.*

## Monsters of the Sea, Legendary and Authentic.
By JOHN GIBSON, Natural History Department, Edinburgh Museum of Science and Art, Author of "Science Gleanings in Many Fields," etc. With 16 Illustrations. Foolscap 8vo, cloth extra. Price 1s. 6d.

*"An instructive as well as interesting little book, giving an account, not only of genuine sea monsters and the huge snakes of Brazilian rivers, but also of real or fabled appearances of the great sea-serpent that has yet to be caught."—SCOTSMAN.*

**In the Polar Regions;** or, Nature and Natural History in the Frozen Zones. With Anecdotes and Stories of Adventure and Travel. 46 Illustrations. Post 8vo, cloth extra. Price 2s. 6d.

**In the Tropical Regions;** or, Nature and Natural History in the Torrid Zone. With Anecdotes and Stories of Adventure and Travel. 78 Illustrations. Post 8vo, cloth extra. 2s. 6d.

**In the Temperate Regions;** or, Nature and Natural History in the Temperate Zones. With Anecdotes and Stories of Adventure and Travel. 72 Illustrations. Post 8vo, cloth extra. 2s. 6d.

*"In the Polar," "In the Tropical," and "In the Temperate Regions," are three companion volumes, though each is complete in itself. The full title suggests the character of the books. They are replete with information on the animal and vegetable life of the countries described, and abound in illustrations in elucidation of the text. Good books either for school or home libraries.*

## Gaussen's World's Birthday.
Illustrated. Foolscap 8vo. 2s. 6d.

*Lectures delivered to an audience of young people, in Geneva, on the first chapter of Genesis. The discoveries of astronomical and geological science are simply explained, and harmonized with the statements of Scripture.*

## Nature's Wonders;
or, How God's Works Praise Him. By the Rev. RICHARD NEWTON, D.D. With 53 Engravings. Post 8vo. 2s. 6d.

*Addresses to young persons, on various subjects of science and natural history, to show "how God's works praise him." With illustrative anecdotes and engravings.*

T. NELSON AND SONS, LONDON, EDINBURGH, AND NEW YORK.

# Travel and Adventure.

**Jack Hooper.** His Adventures at Sea and in South Africa. By VERNEY LOVETT CAMERON, C.B., D.C.L., Commander Royal Navy; Author of "Across Africa," "Our Future Highway," etc. With 23 Full-page Illustrations. Crown 8vo, cloth extra, gilt edges. 5s.

*"Our author has the immense advantage over many writers of boys' stories that he describes what he has seen, and does not merely draw on his imagination and on books."—*SCOTSMAN.

**With Pack and Rifle in the Far South - West.** Adventures in New Mexico, Arizona, and Central America. By ACHILLES DAUNT, Author of "Frank Redcliffe," "In the Land of the Moose, the Bear, and the Beaver," "The Three Trappers," etc. With 30 Illustrations. Crown 8vo, cloth extra, gilt edges. 5s.

*A delightful book of travel and adventure, with much valuable information as to the geography and natural history of the wild American "Far West."*

**The Eastern Archipelago.** By the Author of "The Arctic World," "Recent Polar Voyages," etc. With 60 Engravings and a Map. Crown 8vo, cloth extra, gilt edges. Price 5s.

*A description of the scenery, animal and vegetable life, people, and physical wonders of the islands in the Eastern Seas.*

**Early English Voyagers;** or, The Adventures and Discoveries of Drake, Cavendish, and Dampier. Numerous Illustrations. Crown 8vo, cloth extra, gilt edges. 5s.

*The title of this work describes the contents. It is a handsome volume, which will be a valuable gift for young persons generally, and boys in particular. There are included many interesting illustrations and portraits of the three great voyagers.*

**Our Sea Coast Heroes;** or, Tales of Wreck and of Rescue by the Lifeboat and Rocket. By ACHILLES DAUNT, Author of "Frank Redcliffe," "With Pack and Rifle in the Far South-West," etc. With numerous Illustrations. Post 8vo, cloth extra. 2s. 6d.

**The Forest, the Jungle, and the Prairie;** or, Tales of Adventure and Enterprise in Pursuit of Wild Animals. With numerous Engravings. Post 8vo, cloth extra. Price 2s. 6d.

*A party of weather-bound schoolboys are here supposed to relate in turn the stories that form the book. They are full of romantic adventure and deeds of daring; but at the same time they are true, and cannot be read without imparting valuable information on natural history.*

**Scenes with the Hunter and the Trapper in Many Lands.** Stories of Adventures with Wild Animals. With Engravings. Post 8vo, cloth extra. Price 2s. 6d.

*A party of school-boys spend some of their half-holidays in relating to one another stories of adventure in search of wild animals. These stories, though often full of romantic and stirring incidents, are all true. They cannot fail to be attractive to young readers.*

**The Swiss Family Robinson;** or, Adventures of a Father and his Four Sons on a Desolate Island. Illustrated. Post 8vo, cloth extra. Price 2s. 6d.

*A cheap edition of this well-known work. As the title suggests, its character is somewhat similar to that of the famous "Robinson Crusoe." It combines, in a high degree, the two desirable qualities in a book,—instruction and amusement.*

**Sandford and Merton.** A Book for the Young. By THOMAS DAY. Illustrated. Post 8vo, cloth extra. Price 2s. 6d.

---

T. NELSON AND SONS, LONDON, EDINBURGH, AND NEW YORK.

# Stories of Noble Lives.

The Story of Audubon, The Naturalist. Royal 18mo, cloth extra. Price 1s.

The Story of Benvenuto Cellini, The Italian Goldsmith. Royal 18mo, cloth extra. Price 1s.

The Story of Galileo, The Astronomer of Pisa. Royal 18mo, cloth extra. Price 1s.

The Story of the Herschels—A Family of Astronomers. Royal 18mo, cloth extra. Price 1s.

The Story of John Howard, The Prison Reformer. Royal 18mo, cloth extra. Price 1s.

The Story of Palissy, The Potter. Royal 18mo, cloth extra. 1s.

The Story of Scoresby, The Arctic Navigator. Royal 18mo, cloth extra. Price 1s.

The Story of John Smeaton and the Eddystone Lighthouse. Royal 18mo, cloth extra. Price 1s.

*It is scarcely possible to provide the young with reading more beneficial and stimulating in character than that which is afforded by the lives of great and good men. The biographies of this series are pleasantly written, and contain a large store of useful information. The books are produced in a style rendering them particularly suitable for rewards or prizes.*

The Rocket; or, The Story of the Stephensons, Father and Son. By H. C. KNIGHT. Illustrated. Royal 18mo, cloth extra. 1s.

*"A capital little biography of a life all boys should be familiar with."—S. S. CHRONICLE.*

*"The edition before us contains an additional chapter, in which the author speaks of the recent Stephenson centenary, and the development of the great work originated by the man who was once a poor lad."—PRACTICAL TEACHER.*

The Search for Franklin. With Engravings from Designs by the Artist of the Expedition. Royal 18mo, cloth extra. Price 1s.

*"Our boys cannot do better than read this narrative. It will nerve them, we trust, to deeds of high moral daring."— SUNSHINE.*

No Gains Without Pains; or, The Story of Samuel Budgett, the Successful Merchant. By H. C. KNIGHT. Royal 18mo, cloth extra. Price 1s.

Jane Taylor : Her Life and Letters. (*One of the Authors of "Original Poems for Infant Minds."*) By H. C. KNIGHT, Author of "No Gains without Pains," "The Rocket," etc. Post 8vo. 1s.

*A most interesting biography, for young readers, of this talented and Christian authoress.*

Life and Travel in Tartary, Thibet, and China. Being a Narrative of the Abbé Huc's Travels in the Far East. By M. JONES. With Coloured Frontispiece and numerous Engravings. Royal 18mo. Price 1s.

*The information is varied and full of lively incidents, and much useful knowledge is compressed into its pages.*

Stories of Invention, told by Inventors and their Friends. By EDWARD E. HALE. With numerous Illustrations. Post 8vo, cloth extra. Price 2s. 6d.

*"We have seldom met with a book which has given us greater pleasure. It is full of incidents and anecdotes, which are selected and well told. There are no dull pages."—SWORD AND TROWEL.*

Triumphs of Invention and Discovery. By J. HAMILTON FYFE. Illustrated. Post 8vo. 2s. 6d.

*Rise and progress described of the art of printing, the electric telegraph, manufactures of cotton, silk, iron, etc.*

T. NELSON AND SONS, LONDON, EDINBURGH, AND NEW YORK.